Augustus John Cuthbert Hare

Days Near Rome

Vol. I.

Augustus John Cuthbert Hare

Days Near Rome
Vol. I.

ISBN/EAN: 9783744782388

Printed in Europe, USA, Canada, Australia, Japan

Cover: Foto ©ninafisch / pixelio.de

More available books at **www.hansebooks.com**

By AUGUSTUS J. C. HARE

AUTHOR OF "WALKS IN ROME," "MEMORIALS OF A QUIET LIFE," ETC.

With Illustrations

TWO VOLUMES.—I.

LONDON
DALDY, ISBISTER & CO.
56, LUDGATE HILL
1875

PREFACE.

IN submitting these volumes to the public, I would earnestly apologize to my readers for their imperfections. The ground, in many instances, had been almost untrodden; several of the places described are difficult of access, and have never before been visited by foreigners; and, in most cases, published descriptions either do not exist at all already, or are so inaccurate and untrustworthy as to be only misguiding. A great field for discovery still remains, even within a day's journey of Rome; and if, in opening the way to others, I lead them to enjoy half the pleasure I have received from my own researches, I shall be more than rewarded.

Some of the chapters of this book have already appeared, in a condensed form, as Magazine Articles in "Good Words."

The illustrations of buildings and scenery are

from my own sketches, taken on the spot; the figures I owe to the kindness of friends; for their transference to wood I am indebted to the skill of Mr. T. Sulman. The subjects chosen are purposely selected where verbal descriptions may fail to delineate the character of the places visited.

AUGUSTUS J. C. HARE.

Holmhurst, Sept., 1874.

CONTENTS.

	PAGE
INTRODUCTION	9

CHAPTER I.
OSTIA AND CASTEL FUSANO 39

CHAPTER II.
ALBANO AND LARICCIA . . 50

CHAPTER III.
MONTE CAVO, NEMI, AND CIVITA LAVINIA 81

CHAPTER IV.
FRASCATI, TUSCULUM, AND COLONNA . . 97

CHAPTER V.
GROTTA FERRATA AND MARINO 123

CHAPTER VI.
VEII 131

CHAPTER VII.
GALERA AND BRACCIANO 143

CHAPTER VIII.
GABII AND ZAGAROLO 154

CONTENTS.

CHAPTER IX.
CERVARA, LUNGHEZZA, AND COLLATIA . . . 162

CHAPTER X.
ANTEMNÆ AND FIDENÆ 167

CHAPTER XI.
MENTANA AND MONTE ROTONDO 177

CHAPTER XII.
TIVOLI 184

CHAPTER XIII.
LICENZA AND MONTE GENNARO 207

CHAPTER XIV.
VELLETRI 220

CHAPTER XV.
THE VOLSCIAN HILLS—CORI, NORMA, NINFA, AND SEGNI . . 226

CHAPTER XVI.
THE HERNICAN HILLS—FERENTINO, ALATRI, AND ANAGNI . 248

CHAPTER XVII.
PALESTRINA 268

CHAPTER XVIII.
GENAZZANO, PALIANO, AND OLEVANO . . . 282

CHAPTER XIX.
SUBIACO 294

INTRODUCTORY.

ONLY about one traveller in five hundred of those who cross the Alps ever sees Italy. Those who go to Milan, Venice, Florence, Rome, and Naples, and who stay at the hotels of New York, Washington, Brighton, Paris, or Londres, dining daily on a well-cooked English or French dinner, at hot *tables d'hôte* amid a vociferous throng of their own countrymen, attended by obsequious waiters who talk bad English ; visiting hackneyed sights, led in tow by haughty couriers or ignorant *ciceroni;* driving out to meets in the Campagna, making parties for illuminations in the Coliseum, or devouring chickens and champagne on the slopes at Veii :—these do not see Italy. They lead a pleasant life and pass very agreeable days ; but the life they are leading is not Italian, the land which they allow to be doled out for them, or dole out for themselves, is not Italy : and as regards the real, true, un-Anglicized, un-Americanized country, they might just as well, on their return home, have been attending an admirable series of panoramas and dioramas in Leicester Square.

In order, however, to enjoy the Eden of sights which couriers guard with their two-edged swords, a very different line of conduct, a very different phase of character, must be assumed by our countrymen, to those which they usually indulge in. It is no use to look for French cookery in the Abruzzi, or to hope to find tea and toast amid the sepulchral cities of Etruria, neither need any one expect to be treated with great deference, to be placed on a mental pedestal and regarded as a superior being, in these unconventional places. Travellers will certainly meet with nothing of the kind. They will learn that the only way to have what you like, is to like what you have; they will find that they are treated with just as much courtesy and deference as they are willing to bestow; that if they regard the natives as their equals, are genial, frank, modest, and unsuspicious, they will receive a boundless amount of small kindnesses in return, and that if they are only open-hearted, their being open-handed is a matter of comparative indifference. There is no greater mistake than that of supposing the Italian character to be extortionate and avaricious; except in the old kingdom of Naples, it is neither. In the beaten track, couriers have raised the prices, or travellers have done it for themselves, to an English and American standard, and the constant habit of bargaining recommended in guide-books, has led to extortionate demands, and thus become a necessity; but in *Italian* inns, any overcharge is exceedingly unusual, and is only suggested by suspicion. The more distant the place and the more difficult of attainment, the greater is usually the attention shown to strangers, and the warmer a disinterested welcome. Their wants are sometimes little understood, often a cause of great surprise and amusement, but every effort is made to supply them, and little is expected from those whom some misfortune alone, it is supposed, can have driven from the delights of the capital into such desolate places. But if travellers give themselves airs, if they are too exacting in their demands, heedless of passing salutations, especially of the Abruzzi peasant, who always meets you with, " May God accompany you—may your return be happy : " above all, if they always act in the inns as if they were being cheated, and chatter in the churches during mass as if they were at a London party, they must expect to be laughed at, despised, insulted, and occasionally robbed. " Non sono Cristiani, come noi altri," is the national comment upon strangers who do not know how to behave themselves, and they are sure to be treated with contempt for they deserve nothing better.

It is strange how wonderfully little the country around Rome has been investigated, even by those who are not usually daunted by little difficulties and discomforts. Such attention as has not been expended upon the interest of the capital, has been almost entirely devoted to the " Campagna " in its narrowest sense of the plain girdled in by the hills which may be seen from the walls of Rome, but into, and beyond those hills, travellers scarcely ever penetrate, and they generally have not an idea of the glories which lie concealed there. It is, therefore, as an invitation and a companion into these unknown regions that these volumes are intended.

"The country which is described by the name of the Roman Campagna, has a narrower or a wider circumference, in proportion as one regards its geographical limits. Taken in the narrower sense, the Campagna is that grand and desolate district, which spreads around the walls of Rome, and is enclosed by the Tiber and the Anio. Its circumference might be marked by a series of well-known points : Civita

Vecchia, Tolfa, Ronciglione, Soracte, Tivoli, Palestrina, Albano, and Ostia. But in its wider sense the Campagna extends almost to the former kingdom of Naples and its boundary is the Liris or Garigliano.

"The Campagna of Rome is nothing else than the land of Latium, which is separated from Tuscany by the Tiber. From the time of Constantine the Great the name of Latium has fallen into disuse, and that of Campania has been used in its place, and in the middle ages this name indicated a great part of the so-called 'Ducatus Romanus.'

"Since the middle ages this district has been divided into two parts, the Campagna, which comprises the inland district, and the Maritima, which extends along the sea-coast as far as Terracina. Nature herself has separated it by mountains and plains into distinct compartments. It is divided into three plains; first, the Campagna around the city, watered by the Tiber and the Anio, and hemmed in by the Alban and Sabine mountains, the hills above Ronciglione, and the sea-coast: secondly, the great plain in which the Pontine Marshes are situated, bounded on one side by the Alban and Volscian Hills and on the other by the sea; and lastly, the valley of the Sacco which runs between the Volscian and the Equian and Hernican Hills, and falls into the Liris near Isoletta below Ceprano."—*Gregorovius*.

The more distant excursions described in these volumes are perhaps the most interesting, but cannot generally be recommended for aged or delicate persons. There are, however, some even of these which may be undertaken without the slightest inconvenience or discomfort, and which form a delightful change from Rome in the Spring. The most advisable of these easy tours is that by the southern railway, making the excursions (separately) to Cori and Ninfa from Velletri, ascending the valley of the Liris from Rocca Secca to Sora, and, while there, visiting Arpino and its neighbourhood, and staying at the inn at S. Germano and thence seeing Aquino. Subiaco, Olevano, and Palestrina may be comfortably visited from Rome in a carriage. Orvieto is now easily accessible by railway. The neighbourhood of the Pontine Marshes always presents a certain amount of risk from fevers. The Abruzzi will only delight those who can enjoy the savagest moods of nature. In the Ciminian Hills, which, combined with Caprarola, afford in Spring perhaps the most delightful of the excursions from Rome, the accommodation is indifferent, though much may be seen in drives from Viterbo, a central situation, where a week may be passed most agreeably.

There is no town in the world whence such a *variety* of excursions may be made as from Rome. They are so entirely different from one another. The phase of the scenery, the architecture of the towns, the costume, the habits, the songs (and this means so much to Italian peasants), even the language, is changed, according to the direction you take on leaving the capital. And whether tourists confine themselves to the inner circle of sights usually known to strangers and roughly indicated in " Murray's Handbook," which is hemmed in by the hills which encircle the Campagna; or whether they are induced to penetrate into the glorious heights of the Volscian and Hernican Mountains, the deep recesses of the Sabina, or amid the lost cities of Etruria, they will find that the small disagreeables and the occasional difficulties, which must frequently be endured at the time, weigh as nothing in the balance against the store of beautiful mental pictures, of instructive recollections of people and character, and of heart-stirring associations, which will be laid up for the rest of life. And they will come to feel that it is just because there were *not* good roads, *not* easy carriages, *not* comfortable inns, that it was all so interesting, because thus, not only the places themselves remained the same, but the simple poetical character of the people was unspoilt.

The comparative stagnation of life under the Papal government did even more to preserve the mediæval character of the distant towns in the Papal States than of Rome itself. And in Rome now the ancient characteristics have entirely perished, having been swept away in three years in a manner which sounds incredible, and which would have seemed impossible beforehand. And, while acknowledging certain beneficial changes introduced by the present Government, it is not only the artist who will recognize that much of the interest, and as much as possible of the beauty, of the "Eternal City" has been destroyed. Not only has all trace of costume perished, together with the mediæval figures and splendid dresses which belonged to the Papal Court, and walked in the footsteps of crimson cardinals; but all the gorgeous religious ceremonies, all the processions, and benedictions, and sermons preached by the shrines of martyrs, have ceased to exist. Even the time-honoured *Pifferari* have been chased from Rome by the present Government as a public nuisance. The closing of so many convents and the robbery of the dowries of so many nuns (given on their entrance in the same sense in which a marriage portion is given), has not only been an act of crying injustice in itself, which even the strongest Protestant must feel, but while it has flooded the streets with starving, helpless, or infirm persons, who subsisted on the daily convent dole of coarse bread and soup, it has thrown thousands of helpless ladies, who believed themselves provided for during their lives (and by their own families), into a state of utter destitution, for the relief of which the miserable and irregularly paid pension of a few pence a day appointed by the Government sounds merely like a mockery. Many famous antiquarian memorials have disappeared, together with other well-known buildings, of which the interest was confined to Papal times. The Agger of Servius Tullius and the ruined Ponte Salara have been swept away. The incomparable view from the Ponte Rotto has been blocked out, the trees on the Aventine and the woods of Monte Mario have been cut down. The Villa Negroni-Massimo, the most beautiful of Roman gardens, with the grandest of old orange avenues, and glorious groves of cypresses amid which Horace was buried,—a villa whose terraces dated from the time when it belonged to Mæcenas, and which was replete with recollections of the romantic story of Vittoria Accorambuoni, of Donna Camilla Perretti, and of Alfieri, has been ruthlessly and utterly ploughed up, so that not a trace of it is left. Even this, however, is as nothing compared with the entire destruction of the beauty and charm of the grandest of the buildings which remain. The Baths of Caracalla, stripped of all their verdure and shrubs, and deprived alike of the tufted foliage amid which Shelley wrote, and of the flowery carpet which so greatly enhanced their lonely solemnity, are now a series of bare featureless walls standing in a gravelly waste, and possess no more attraction than the ruins of a London warehouse. The Coliseum, no longer "a garlanded ring," is bereaved of everything which made it so lovely and so picturesque, while botanists must for ever deplore the incomparable and strangely unique "Flora of the Coliseum," which Signor Rosa has caused to be carefully annihilated, even the roots of the shrubs having been extracted by the firemen, though, in pulling them out, more of the building has come down than five hundred years of time would have injured. In the Basilica of Constantine, the whole of the beautiful covering of shrubs, with which Nature had protected the vast arches, has been removed, and the rain, soaking into the unprotected upper surface, will soon bring them down. Nor has the work of the destroyer been confined to the Pagan antiquities; the early Christian porches of S. Prassede and S. Pudenziana, with their valuable terra-cotta ornaments, have been so smeared with paint and yellow-wash as to be irrecognisable; many smaller but precious Christian antiquities, such as the lion of the Santi Apostoli, have disappeared altogether. And in return for these destructions and abductions, Rome has been given . . what? Quantities of hideous false rock-work painted brown in all the public gardens; a Swiss cottage and a clock which goes by water forced in amid the statues and sarcophagi of the Pincio; and the having the passages of the Capitol painted all over with the most flaring scarlet and blue, so as utterly to destroy the repose and splendour of its ancient statues.

Should the present state of things continue much longer, and especially should Signor Rosa remain in power, the whole beauty of Rome will have disappeared, except that which the Princes guard in their villas, and that which the everlasting hills and the glowing Campagna can never fail to display. It is to the environs that poets must turn for their inspiration and artists for their pictures, and as the destroying hand advances, they must wander further away, for though the Villa Adriana, which was like a historical Idyll of Nature, has already fallen, and the amphitheatre of Sutri is threatened, Cori and Ninfa, Alatri and Anagni, Aquino, Subiaco, Narni, Soracte, and Caprarola must long remain unspoilt.

On the immediate neighbourhood of Rome much has

already been written. Sir William Gell's "Topography of Rome and its Vicinity" is a mine of antiquarian information. Some slight sketches of different points of interest, especially of the monasteries in the neighbourhood, may be found in the different works of Hemans. The author would especially express his constant debt of gratitude to "Cramer's Ancient Italy," and to many of the wonderfully accurate articles in "Smith's Dictionary of Greek and Roman Geography." Story's charming "Roba di Roma," and several admirable novels, especially "The Marble Faun" (foolishly called "Transformation" in England), "Barbara's History," and more especially George Sand's "Daniella," abound in charming word-pictures of the Campagna and the nearer places on the hills. But for more distant excursions, the English books of reference are easily exhausted, with one great exception,—" Dennis' Cities and Cemeteries of Etruria." In studying this delightful work, and even in the few extracts given in these volumes, the reader who knows Rome will seem to feel again the fresh breeze from the Sabine and Alban hills sweeping over the Campagna, laden with a scent of sweet basil and thyme, and he will enjoy again in their remembrance that glow of enthusiasm which the real scenes brought into them. The great volumes of Dennis are too large to be companions on the excursions themselves, but in preparation for them will be charming fireside companions for Roman winter evenings. German scholars will delight in the charming volumes of Gregorovius, and especially in his "Lateinische Sommer," than which no descriptive book is more pictorial or more interesting. The best and most accurate Hand-books of Italy which have yet been published are also in German—those of Dr. Th.

Gsell-fels, assisted by admirable maps, and though they are exceedingly unequal, as if the author had only visited in person a portion of the district he describes, in some places they are almost exhaustive. The small Hand-books of Bædeker are very convenient and practical, and are generally very carefully corrected.

It must necessarily be with the present work as with the many which have preceded it. Some who follow in the paths it indicates will think its descriptions exaggerated, others will find them not sufficiently glowing. For Rome, more than any other place, produces different impressions on different minds. The Campagna in its ruin and desolation will be described as "dismal and monotonous," or "solemn and beautiful," according to the feelings of those who traverse it. Some will only be impressed with the dirt, the poverty, the ruinousness of the mountain-towns; others with their picturesqueness and colour. It is necessary to real enjoyment of these mountain places to cast out all the black motes which too often obscure our vision. When this is done, what a store of sunny memories may be laid up.

> "Yea, from the very soil of silent Rome
> You shall grow wise; and walking, live again
> The lives of buried peoples, and become
> A child by right of that eternal home,
> Cradle and grave of empires, on whose walls
> The sun himself subdued to reverence falls."—*J. A. S.*

Rome is unlike other towns in having scarcely any suburbs; on nearly every side one is in the country almost directly.

"St. John describes Rome, in the Apocalypse, as sitting upon her seven hills in the wilderness. And a wilderness indeed it is. First, in every direction that leads into the Campagna, you pass the inhabited streets; then comes a belt of vineyards and villas, fading off into desolation as you proceed; then come the grand old walls, stretching away, with their richly-coloured brickwork and flanking towers. You pass out through a stately gate, through which legions have gone out and in fifteen hundred years ago, and you are in the Campagna. There it is before you, mile after mile, brownish green in the foreground, red in the middle distance, melting away into purple and blue in the farther distance, and bounded by a glorious bank of mountains, of colours not to be attempted by pen or pencil. Hardly a human habitation is visible, save where, on the Alban Hills to your right, the villages gleam out, sprinkling their gorgeous sides with spots of pearl. Ancient towers and tombs are cast at random about the waste. Flat it is not, but full of the most picturesque undulations, and even lines of low cliffs and winding streams. Endless are its varieties of beauty, in outline, in grouping, and above all, in colour. For miles and miles the ancient and modern aqueducts bridge it with their countless arches—haunts of all the lovely hues of the bow of heaven. Watch them in the yellow and orange of the morning and noonday sun; watch them mellowing off as the westering beam slopes on them, turning their gold to copper, then casting that copper into the glow of the furnace, then cooling it down into the dull iridescence of parting evening; watch them till the green grey of the fading light has subdued them into the sober mass of undistinguished plain and mountain; then wrap your cloak double round you, and stride away through the chilled streets and the thronging Corso to your steep open staircase, and your snug log fire, and meditate on as fair and heavenly a sight as ever blessed a day on this varied earth.

"Rome itself is a place of never-dying and ever-varying interest; but the Campagna of Rome is a pure source of unfailing delight."—*Dean Alford.*

Yet without its varied mountain distances, without the glorious climate to illuminate it, it is almost impossible to say how ugly the Campagna would be. As it is it is perfectly beautiful. For so vast an expanse there are few marked features; only, here and there, the aqueducts, sometimes striding across the plain in mighty lines of arches garlanded against the sky with ivy and smilax, sometimes merely marked by a white line in the grass or a succession of miniature round towers over their openings. Between the aqueducts, run the roads, often following the course of the ancient Roman highways, and, as in the case of the Via Tiburtina, still paved with the blocks of black lava, laid down two thousand years ago, over which the wine-carts rattle with their revolving hoods (*capote*), shelters alike against sun and shower,—often drawn by grand, meek-eyed oxen. Hard by, the black crosses, sprinkled along the dusty wayside amongst the thistles, keep their dismal record of accidents or murders; and refuges of hurdles, erected at intervals, attest the ferocity of the Campagna buffaloes and the necessity of escape from them.

In the winter the plain is crimson and gold with the decaying vegetation; but, as spring advances, it changes so rapidly to green, that it is as if it were suddenly touched with phosphoric light; and, as summer advances, the growth becomes coarse and rampagious to a degree—Virgins thistle, breast-high; rank anchusas; hemlock; huge resedas; acres covered with the tall and stately but poisonous asphodel, here and there a low bush of hawthorn, and a band of green osiers marking where the Anio meanders through a cleft. Almost every building is mediæval, except those which are classical. The most conspicuous are the tall towers of brick and stone, relics for the most part of Orsini and Colonna feuds, and erected as a refuge for the shepherds of one of the great proprietors, against the inroads of his neighbours. Besides these, there are the huts built of reeds, such as Virgil describes, and the rifled tombs, now used as houses, in the doors of which we so often see the shepherd-wives, with folded *panni* shading their withered faces, seated spinning like the pictures of the Fates, while the shepherds themselves, dressed in goat-skins, watch their flocks on the neighbouring turfy hillocks.

"Next to the picturesquely conspicuous towers the most frequent landmarks are the conical shepherds' huts, usually on the higher grounds, inhabited during about half the year by a race of men so cut off from all social and civilizing influences that one might expect to find the lowest brutality, and all the fiercest passions, in a moral soil thus neglected. The shepherd of these parts, in his broad-brimmed black hat, long loose jacket and leggings, both alike of unshorn sheep or goat-skin, might seem the original type whence an idealizing dream devised the mythologic satyr. His temporary dwelling is made of branches of the yellow-flowering Spanish broom, and is open at the pointed apex for the escape of smoke from the wood-fire lit in the middle, around which are ranged beds, something like berths in a ship, and usually for several people, as this hut is inhabited by many inmates, besides dogs or pigs, and at times sheep or goats, also privileged to enjoy its warmth and shelter. Here (it may be within sight of St. Peter's and the Lateran basilica) does this rude servant of the soil spend the long seasons of his monotonous existence, till the summer-sultriness obliges him to migrate with his dogs and sheep. The usual food of these outcast-looking beings is black bread and *ricotta* (ewe's-milk cheese). Yet, despite his wild and savage aspect, this shepherd, on near approach, proves a harmless creature; will sometimes beg in the humblest tone; and has the reputation of being consistently devout, his religion standing him in the stead of knowledge and ideas."—*Heman's Story of Monuments in Rome.*

"Vous apercevez çà et là quelques bouts de voies romaines dans des lieux où il ne passe plus personne, quelques traces desséchées des torrents de l'hiver, qui, vues de loin, ont elles-mêmes l'air de chemins battus et fréquentés, et qui ne sont que le lit d'une onde orageuse, qui s'est écoulée comme le peuple romain. A peine découvrez-vous quelques arbres, mais vous voyez partout des ruines d'aqueducs et de tombeaux qui semblent être les forêts et les plantes indigènes d'une terre composée de la poussière des morts et des débris des empires; souvent, dans une grande plaine, j'ai cru voir de riches moissons; je m'en approchais, et ce n'étaient que des herbes flétries qui avaient trompé mon œil. Sous ces moissons arides, on distingue quelquefois les traces d'une ancienne culture. Point d'oiseaux, point de mugissements de troupeaux, point de villages; un petit nombre de fermes délabrées se montrent sur la nudité des champs; les fenêtres et les portes en sont fermées, il n'en sort ni fumée, ni bruit, ni habitants. Une espèce de sauvage, presque nu, pâle et miné par la fièvre, garde seulement ces tristes chaumières, comme ces spectres qui, dans nos histoires gothiques, défendent l'entrée des châteaux abandonnées. . . .

Vous croiriez peut-être, d'après cette description, qu'il n'y a rien de plus affreux que les campagnes romaines ; vous vous tromperiez beaucoup : elles ont une inconcevable grandeur."—*Chateaubriand.*

In this vast undulating plain, generally occupying some green knoll, washed by a brook at its base, are the sites of many an ancient Latin town which was alternately the enemy and the ally of Rome. Sometimes, as in the case of Ostia, a whole city, with its paved streets, its narrow shops, and its equally miniature temples, has been laid bare. Sometimes, as at Veii, Gabii, and Tusculum, only a fragment of ruin, rising here and there above-ground, marks one of the principal buildings—a theatre or a temple. Often, as at Antemnæ, Fidenæ, Crustumerium, and Collatia, only the undulations of the turf attest where the city has been.

As we advance into the hills, where they were more easily protected, the ancient cities are far more perfect; at Tivoli are beautiful miniature temples of the ancient Tibur; at Sutri is its wonderful rock-hewn amphitheatre; at Aquino are noble remains both of arches and temples; at Cori are the threefold walls which gird, and the rock temples which crown, its hill top.

Further still from the capital, where the classical buildings were always less magnificent, glorious mediæval remains attest the presence of Popes who made the hill-towns the fortified residence of their troubled reigns. The massive remains of the Papal palaces of Anagni, Viterbo, and Orvieto, with the glorious churches of those towns; the gothic palace of Cardinal Vitelleschi at Corneto; the convents of Monte Cassino, Subiaco, Farfa, Grotta Ferrata, Trisulti, Casamari, and Fossanuova; the castles and towers of Tivoli, Bracciano, Ostia, Celano, Avezzano, Borghetto, and

Bolsena; the walls of Civita Lavinia and Nepi,—attest the love and knowledge of art and beauty which flourished in those dark ages.

As we go further from Rome, too, new interests are suggested by the pelasgic and cyclopean remains at Palestrina, Cori, Norba, Segni, Alatri, and Arpino, or by the marvellous Etruscan discoveries of Cervetri, Corneto, Vulci, Norchia, and Bieda.

"The excursions in the neighbourhood of Rome are charming, and would be full of interest if it were only for the changing views they afford of the wild Campagna. But every inch of ground, in every direction, is rich in associations, and in natural beauties. There is Albano, with its lovely lake and wooded shore, and with its wine, that certainly has not improved since the days of Horace, and in these times hardly justifies his panegyric. There is squalid Tivoli, with the river Anio, diverted from its course, and plunging down, headlong, some eighty feet in search of it. With its picturesque Temple of the Sibyl, perched high on a crag; its minor waterfalls glancing and sparkling in the sun; and one good cavern yawning darkly, where the river takes a fearful plunge and shoots on, low down under beetling rocks. There, too, is the Villa d'Este, deserted and decaying among groves of melancholy pine and cypress trees, where it seems to lie in state. Then, there is Frascati, and, on the steep above it, the ruins of Tusculum, where Cicero lived, and wrote, and adorned his favourite house (some fragments of it may yet be seen there), and where Cato was born. We saw its ruined amphitheatre on a grey dull day, when a shrill March wind was blowing, and when the scattered stones of the old city lay strewn about the lonely eminence, as desolate and dead as the ashes of a long-extinguished fire."—*Dickens.*

"Nothing can be more rich and varied, with every kind of beauty, than the Campagna of Rome—sometimes, as around Ostia, flat as an American prairie, with miles of *canni* and reeds rustling in the wind, fields of exquisite feathery grasses waving to and fro, and forests of tall golden-trunked stone-pines poising their spreading umbrellas of rich green high in the air, and weaving a murmurous roof against the sun; sometimes drear, mysterious, and melancholy, as in the desolate stretches between Civita Vecchia and Rome, with lonely hollows and hills without a habitation, where sheep and oxen feed, and the wind roams over treeless and deserted slopes, and silence makes its home; sometimes rolling like an inland sea whose waves have suddenly been checked and stiffened, green with grass, golden with grain, and gracious with myriads of wild flowers, where scarlet poppies blaze over acres and acres, and pink-frilled daisies cover the vast meadows, and pendant vines shroud the picturesque ruins of antique villas, aqueducts, and tombs, or droop from mediæval towers and fortresses.

"Such is the aspect of the Agro Romano, or southern portion of the Campagna extending between Rome and Albano. It is a picture wherever you go. The land, which is of deep rich loam that repays a hundred-fold the least toil of the farmer, does not wait for the help of man, but bursts into spontaneous vegetation and everywhere laughs into flowers. Here is pasturage for millions of cattle, and grain fields for a continent, that now in wild untutored beauty bask in the Italian sun, crying shame on their neglectful owners. Over these long unfenced slopes one may gallop on horseback for miles without let or hindrance, through meadows of green smoothness on fire with scarlet poppies—over hills crowned with ruins that insist on being painted, so exquisite are they in form and colour, with their background of purple mountains—down valleys of pastoral quiet, where great *tufa* caves open into subterranean galleries leading beyond human ken; or one may linger in lovely secluded groves of ilexes and pines, or track the course of swift streams overhung by dipping willows, and swerving here and there through broken arches of antique bridges smothered in green ; or wander through hedges heaped and toppling over with rich luxuriant foliage, twined together by wild vetches, honeysuckles, morning-glories, and every species of flowering vine; or sit beneath the sun-looped shadows of ivy-covered aqueducts, listening to the song of hundreds of larks far up in the air, and gazing through the lofty arches into wondrous deeps of violet-hued distances, or lazily watching flocks of white sheep as they cross the smooth slopes guarded by the faithful watch-dog. Everywhere are deep brown banks of *pozzolana* earth which makes the strong Roman cement, and quarries of tufa and travertine with unexplored galleries and catacombs honey-combing for miles the whole Campagna. Dead generations lie under your feet wherever you tread. The place is haunted by ghosts that outnumber by myriads the living, and the air is filled with a tender sentiment and sadness which makes the beauty of the world about you more touching. You pick up among the ruins on every slope fragments of rich marbles that once encased the walls of luxurious villas. The *contadino* or shepherd offers you an old worn coin, on which you read the name of Cæsar, or a *scarabæus* which once adorned the finger of an Etruscan king, in whose dust he now grows his beans, or the broken head of an ancient jar in marble or terra-cotta, or a lacrymatory of a martyred Christian, or a vase with the Etrurian red that now is lost, or an *intaglio* that perhaps has sealed a love-letter a thousand years ago."—*Story's Roba di Roma*, i. 313.

From the unenclosed nature of the Campagna and the paucity of inhabitants, all the ancient land-marks are more easily traced here than in other parts of Italy.

"The hills of Rome are such as we rarely see in England, low in height but with steep and rocky sides. In early times the natural wood still remained in patches amidst the buildings, as at this day it still grows here and there on the green sides of the Monte Testaccio. Across the Tiber the ground rises to a greater height than that of the Roman hills, but its summit is a level unbroken line, while the heights, which opposite to Rome itself rise immediately from the river, under the names of Janiculus and Vaticanus, then sweep away to some distance from it, and return in their highest and boldest form at the Monte Mario, just above the Milvian bridge and the Flaminian road. Thus to the west the view is immediately bounded; but to the north and north-east the eye ranges over the low ground of the Campagna to the nearest line of Apennines, which closes up, as with a gigantic wall, all the Sabine, Latin, and Volscian lowlands, while over it are still distinctly to be seen the high summits of the central Apennines, covered with snow, even at this day, for more than six months in the year. South and south-west lies the wide plain of the Campagna; its level line succeeded by the equally level line of the sea, which can only be distinguished from it by the brighter light reflected from its waters. Eastward, after ten miles of plain, the view is bounded by the Alban Hills, a cluster of high bold points rising out of the Campagna, like Arran from the sea, on the highest of which, at nearly the same height with the summit of Helvellyn, stood the Temple of Jupiter Latiaris, the scene of the common worship of all the people of the Latin name. Immediately under this highest point lies the crater-like basin of the Alban lake; and on its nearer rim might be seen the trees of the grove of Ferentia, where the Latins held the great civil assemblies of their nation. Further to the north, on the edge of the Alban Hills looking towards Rome, was the town and citadel of Tusculum; and beyond this, a lower summit crowned with the walls and towers of Labicum seems to connect the Alban hills with the line of the Apennines just at the spot where the citadel of Præneste, high up on the mountain side, marks the opening into the country of the Hernicans, and into the valleys of the streams that feed the Liris.

"Returning nearer to Rome, the lowland country of the Campagna is broken by long green swelling ridges, the ground rising and falling, as in the heath country of Surrey and Berkshire. The streams are dull and sluggish, but the hill-sides above them constantly break away into little rocky cliffs, where on every ledge the wild fig now strikes out its branches, and tufts of broom are clustering, but which in old times formed the natural strength of the citadels of the numerous cities of Latium. Except in these narrow dells, the present aspect of the country is all bare and desolate, with no trees nor any human habitation. But anciently, in the time of the early kings of Rome, it was full of independent cities, and in its population and the careful cultivation of its little garden-like farms, must have resembled the most flourishing parts of Normandy or the Netherlands."—*Arnold's Hist. of Rome*, vol. i., ch. iii.

Excursions from Rome have hitherto been usually limited to the Alban Hills and Tivoli, or at most Subiaco. Thus foreigners have lost not only enjoyment of much that is worth seeing, but the benefit of occasional draughts of pure mountain air, which would do much to keep off the fevers to which too many, who strictly confine themselves to the city-sights, are apt to fall victims.

You enter the Campagna and "the ancient dust and mouldiness of Rome, the dead atmosphere in which so many months are wasted, the hard pavements, the smell of ruin and decaying generations, the chill palaces, the convent bells, the heavy incense of altars, the life led in the dark narrow streets, among priests, soldiers, nobles, artists, and women; all the sense of these things rises from the consciousness like a cloud which has imperceptibly darkened over it."—*Hawthorne.*

In the Campagna, taken in its narrower sense, the Malaria is always sufficiently alarming to make it desirable to avoid lingering on its damp grass, and especially to hesitate about sketching in the sunset. Its growth is most mysterious, but it is certainly in no way due, as is often stated, to the misgovernment of the Popes.

"'Latifundia perdidere Italiam' (large farms were the ruin of Italy) is the expression of the elder Pliny; and in reference to this later period does Strabo particularize the sites on the Campagna notoriously dangerous to inhabit :—Ardea, Sætia (now Sezza), Terracina, &c. In reference to this does Cicero complain of the fevers prevailing in its low districts ; and Livy laments the fate of the retired soldiers doomed to reside on this soil—'Se militando fessos in pestilenti atque arido, circa urbem, solo luctari.' Horace also observes of the month of August in the city 'Adducit febres et testamenta resignat.' "—*Hemans' Story of Monuments in Rome.*

Even in the villas at Tivoli, as in those nearer Rome, malaria is greatly to be feared towards sunset.

"What the flaming sword was to the first Eden, such is the malaria to these sweet gardens and groves. We may wander through them of an afternoon, it is true, but they cannot be made a home and a reality, and to sleep among them is death. They are but illusions, therefore, like the show of gleaming waters and shadowy foliage in the desert."—*Transformation.*

But malaria does not penetrate into the hills, and nothing can be more healthy and invigorating than the air in the more distant mountain towns.

The middle of winter should be devoted to the city, and to the nearer Campagna drives, so as to leave many spring days for the hill-excursions, which will then have a charm none who have not felt them can realize.

> " About your feet the myrtles will be set,
>   Grey rosemary, and thyme, and tender blue
> Of love-pale labyrinthine violet ;
>   Flame-born anemones will glitter through
>   Dark aisles of roofing pine-trees ; and for you
> The golden jonquil and starred asphodel
> And hyacinth their speechless tales will tell.
>
> The nightingales for you their tremulous song
>   Shall pour amid the snowy scented bloom
> Of wild acacia bowers, and all night long
>   Through starlight-flooded spheres of purple gloom
>   Still lemon-boughs shall spread their faint perfume,
> Soothing your sense with odours sweet as sleep,
> While wind-stirred cypresses low music keep."—*J. A. S.*

"The spring came; the languid, fragrant, joyous Italian spring, all sunshine and perfume, and singing of birds and blossoming of flowers. The Easter festivals were past, and the strangers dispersed and gone. The snow had faded from the summit of Soracte. The Coliseum hung out its banners of fresh green. The Campagna glowed under the midday sun, like a Persian carpet—one wilderness of poppies and harebells, buttercups, daisies, wild convolvuli, and purple hyacinths. Every crumbling ruin burst into blossom, like a garden. Every cultivated patch within the city walls ran over, as it were, spontaneously, with the delicious products of the spring. Every stall at the shady corner of every quiet piazza was piled high with early fruits: and the flower-girls sat all day long on the steps of the Trinità de' Monti. Even the sullen pulses of the Tiber seemed stirred by a more genial current, as they eddied round the broken piers of the Ponte Rotto. Even the solemn sepulchres of the Appian Way put forth long feathery grasses from each mouldering cranny, and the wild eglantine struck root among the shattered urns of the roadside columbarium. Now, too, the transparent nights, all spangled with fire-flies, were even more balmy than the days. And now the moon shone down on troops of field-labourers encamped under the open sky against the city walls; and the nightingales sang as if inspired, among the shadowy cypresses of the Protestant burial-ground."—*Barbara's History*.

The spring in Italy is the time for active, the summer for passive enjoyment.

"You know not yet the enchantment of an Italian summer amid Italian hills! You know not what it is to breathe the perfume of the orange-gardens—to lie at noon in the deep shadow of an ilex-grove, listening to the ripple of a legendary spring, older than history—to stroll among ruins in the purple twilight! Then up there, far from the sultry city and the unhealthy plains, we have such sunrises and sunsets as you, artists though you be, have never dreamt of—there, where the cool airs linger longest, and the very moon and stars look more golden than elsewhere."—*Barbara's History*.

In the mountain towns, living is exceedingly economical. Even at the hotels there are few places where the charges for *pension* including everything would be more than $4\frac{1}{2}$, or at most 5 francs a day, while in lodgings one may live quite handsomely for 25 francs a week. All prices are proportion-ately small. For instance, in the Abruzzi a whole day's journey by diligence seldom costs more than 6 or 8 francs. Of course this tariff does not apply to Albano, where the price of everything has been raised by foreign interference, but rather to places which are not much frequented, or which are resorted to by Italians of the lower-upper or *mezzo-ceto* classes, who would simply laugh down any overcharge. In some of these places there are charming, happy summer colonies, which migrate to the fresher air like the swallows, as regularly as the hot months come round. .To L'Ariccia especially the artists flock forth, and there and at Olevano they make their summer societies, leading an innocent, merry life enough, and, while rivals in their art, filled with simple kindnesses for one another; the companionship and good-fellowship of the Via Margutta being carried on in these country villages.

"The life of the student in Rome should be one of unblended enjoyment. If he loves his work, or, what is the same, if he throws himself conscientiously into it, it is sweetened to him as it can be nowhere else. His very relaxations become at once subsidiary to it, yet most delightfully recreative. His daily walks may be through the field of art, his resting-place in some seat of the muses, his wanderings along the stream of time bordered by precious monuments. He can never be alone; a thousand memories, a thousand associations accompany him, rise up at every step, bear him along. There is no real loneliness in Rome now any more than of old, when a thoughtful man could say that 'he was never less alone than when alone.' "—*Cardinal Wiseman.*

He who lives long in one of these country places will have an experience of Italian character which no town residence will give; and will be astonished at the amount of quaint folk lore and historical tradition which is handed down orally in a population which can seldom read, and is utterly ignorant of the most notorious principles of modern information. They seldom go beyond the limits of their own *castelli*, except that all have probably paid one visit to Rome in their lifetime, to receive the Easter Benediction from the Holy Father. Their animals are generally like friends to them, and are often trained in a wonderfully human way—especially their pigs, which generally live in the houses, and are the companions of their daily life. A pig at Subiaco danced the tarantella like a human being. If an Italian peasant were told that there was no future state for his domestic animals he would be very incredulous. "Sant' Antonio abbia pietà dell' anima sua," cried Madame de Stael's Italian coachman, as his horse fell down dead; and the *Intendente* of the Duke of Sermoneta, writing lately to announce that a number of his pigs had died in the country, said simply, "Sono andati in Paradiso."

The men are generally far more instructed than the women, whose ideas are for the most part confined to what they hear in the churches, and to the stories of their own village or of the saints.

"Among us, and in many places, the *contadina* is neither more nor less than the wife, the female of the *contadino*, as the hen is the female of the cock; with which, except in sex, it has life, nourishment, habits, all in common. This equality, on the contrary, in certain places becomes destruction and loss to the poor woman. Here, for example, if a faggot of wood and a bunch of chickens have to be carried down to the shore from one of the villages half-way up the mountain, the labour is thus distributed in the family; the wife loads herself with the faggot of wood which weighs half a hundred-weight, and the husband will take the chickens which weigh a mere nothing. In mountainous places it is generally thus. It is curious to hear the *contadini*, when they are trying to lift a weight, if they find it heavy, say, as they quickly put it down again, 'It is woman's work!'"—*Massimo d'Azeglio.*

"From a people so original and so ignorant we may expect many quaint superstitions. Accordingly besides ghosts and haunted houses we hear of the *lupo-manaro*, a kind of were-wolf, most dangerous on rainy nights; of witches whom you may keep out of the house by hanging a broom at the window. The Roman witch seizes eagerly on her favourite steed, and with the muttered charm,

'Sopr' acqua e sopra vento
Portami alla noce di Benevento,'

she is off in a trice to join her Samnite sisters. If a Roman housewife has lost anything, she will repeat Psalm xci., '*Qui habitat,*' quite sure that at the words 'from the snare of the hunter' ('*de laqueo venantium*'—she reads it '*acqua di Venanzio*') the truant will re-appear. Then she has her famous '*Rimedii Simpatici.*' To cure a wart you must tie the finger round with crimson silk ribbon : for a sty, pretend to sew it up with needle and thread : for a boil, get a poor neighbour to beat a frying-pan at your door. Their faith in the lottery and the *libro deli' arte* is too well known for comment ; a similar reverence is paid to the weather-prophecies of the almanac. The book must be true, they argue, for it has the *Imprimatur.*"—*Claude Delaval Cobham, "Essay on Belli."*

In spite of the richness of the land, and in spite of the fact that most of the peasants are themselves land-owners on a very small scale, the most terrible poverty frequently prevails, but this is greater in the Hernican and Equian than in the Alban Hills.

"Can we believe that amid the abundant produce of the land the peasants are poor? Looking at the region, it appears to be an Eldorado of happy inhabitants ; but living with them in the paradise of Nature we meet too often with starvation. All these fruits (twenty figs or twenty walnuts may be bought here for one bajocco, and in good years a bottle of wine for the same price) do not feed the peasant ; he would starve if he had not the meal of the Turkish corn, which is his only food. The fault of this incongruity lies in the agrarian condition. To begin with, you must know that the possessor of land here owes the fourth part of the produce as rent to the lord of the soil. It is the old curse of the latifundia to sink the people in poverty. There are indeed few peasants who do not possess a small vineyard, but it is not sufficient to maintain the family. Usury is unlimited ; even from the poorest ten per cent. is taken. The smallest misfortune, or a bad harvest, brings him into debt. If he borrows money or grain the interest burdens him; the avaricious rich man watches for the time of want to wrest the land from the small proprietor for a nominal price. Barons and monasteries grow rich, the peasant-farmer becomes their vassal and vine-dresser. As a rule the transaction takes place thus,—the debtor only sells the soil; the trees (*gli alberi*, which includes the vines) remain his, he continues to cultivate the vineyard, and retains for himself half or three-quarters of the produce. Scarcely a year passes, and the same vine-owner appears before the purchaser of his land and offers him the trees for sale. Now he becomes farmer for his master, inhabits the vineyard with his family, and continues to cultivate it, receiving a portion of the produce. This may equal or even exceed that of the present proprietor, but yet he will find himself more and more in debt, and have to make over to his master no small proportion of his gains in advance."—*Gregorovius.*

The simple religious faith which exists amongst the mountain peasantry is most touching and instructive. The sound of the angelus bell will collect the whole population of one of the small Abruzzi towns in its churches, and the priests, unlike the spectres which haunt ultra-Protestant story-books, are more frequently simple gentle fathers of their people, consulted by them in every anxiety, and trusted in every difficulty. The open-air life in many of these villages, where all the spinning, lace-making, and other avocations are carried on in the street, brings the people wonderfully together, and unites their interests and associations as those of one great family, and if a poor person dies, it is not unusual to see the whole town attend the funeral, while orphans who have been born in the place, become regarded as universal property, and receive a share of the attentions and care of all. On a summer's evening, when crowds of the inhabitants of a mountain town are sitting out in the shady street at their work, it is not unusual for one of them to take up one of the long melancholy never-ending songs which are handed down here for generations, and for the whole people to join in the choruses. These songs are inexhaustible, varying *from* the short lively catches in two lines called *stornelli*, to long ballads which sometimes succeed one another in more than a hundred verses. A curious collection of the latter, giving their variations according to the different towns and patois in which they are sung, are being published, under the name of "Canti e Racconti del Popolo Italiano," collected by D. Comparetti and A. D'Ancona. But no more complete picture of the manners and characteristics of the lower classes in Rome and its neighbourhood can be found than that which is given in the two thousand three hundred sonnets of Belli (1791—1863), who, himself one of "the people," wrote with the very essence of their feeling. There is a charming volume on "The Folklore of Rome," by R. H. Busk.

Riding is the best means of seeing the Campagna immediately around Rome; indeed there are many interesting places, such as Rustica on the Anio, which cannot be reached in a carriage. But for the longer excursions it is far best to adopt whatever is the usual means of locomotion in the district, generally some high-slung *Baroccino*. In the Abruzzi, diligences are universally used, and, where the distances are so great between one town and another, they are quite a necessity. In some places these are of the most primitive construction, and in mountainous districts are always drawn by oxen placed in front of the horses, while the harness of the latter, thickly adorned with bells, feathers, and little brass figures of saints, is quite an artistic study. Diligence life is a phase of Italian existence which no one should omit trying at least once, or rather that of the public carriages which ply slowly between the different surrounding towns and the capital. In a vehicle of this kind one cannot fail to be thrown into the closest juxtaposition with one's neighbours, and nowhere is the universal national bonhommie and good fellowship more conspicuous. Suppose you are at Tivoli and wish to go to Rome. The diligence starts in the middle of the day. You walk to it from your inn, with a porter carrying your portmanteau. You find it under a dark archway; a lumbering vehicle, something like a heavy though very dilapidated fly, with three lean unkempt horses attached to it by ropes. The company is already assembled and greet you as if you were an old acquaintance. There is a fat monk in a brown habit which does not smell very good, a woman in *panno* and large gold ear-rings, a young office clerk, a girl of sixteen, and a little child of two. The young man sits by the driver, all the rest go inside. There is endless delay in starting, for when you are just going off, the rope-harness gives way and has to be mended. You begin to feel impatient, but find nobody cares in the least, so you think it is not worth while. You get in, and find the interior very mouldy, with tattered sides, and dirty straw on the floor. The most unimaginable baggage is being packed on the roof. The gossippy *conduttore* leans against the portico smoking cigarettes, and regaling Tivoli with the scandal of Rome. An important *stalliere* in rags stands by and demands his fee of one *soldo*. At last the company are desired to mount. The diligence is moving: it is an immense excitement: there is quite a rush of children down the street to see it. The vehicle creaks and groans. Surely the ropes are going to break again; but no, they actually hold firm this time and the carriage starts, rocking from side to side of the rugged pavement, amid the remonstrances of the woman in the ear-rings, whose daughter has not been able to embrace her, and who shrieks out of the window, "Ma, Nino, Nino, non ho baciato la figlia mia."

You do not get far before the fleas become active and a universal scratching begins. The child squeals. Then the monk gives it a lollypop and begins a long story about an image in his convent which winked twice—*ringraziamo Dio* —actually *twice*, on the eve of Ascension Day. You can hardly hear, for you are going down a hill and the carriage rocks so, and the bells make such a noise. Suddenly there is a regular outcry, "Oh, Madonna Santissima!" the young girl is taken worse. . . . "Oh, povera piccina!" You stop for a little while, and are glad to escape even for a minute from the overwhelming smell of cheese and garlic which rises from a basket your next neighbour has placed at your feet. All is perfect good humour, the invalid recovers, you mount once more, the driver sings *stornelli* in a loud ringing voice : the monk hands round his snuff-box : you sneeze, and all the company say " Felicita "—and so on, till, when you reach the walls of Rome, you are all the greatest friends in the world, and you shake hands all round when you part, amid a chorus of " a rivederla Signore ! "

It is melancholy to think how many people are deterred from the great enjoyment which is to be obtained from these Italian mountain excursions by imaginary fears of brigands. Of course it is just within the bounds of possibility that a casualty might occur, but, except perhaps in the neighbourhood of Palestrina or the Pontine Marshes, the chances are exceedingly remote, and as a general rule the more distant places are the safest. Those who stay amongst the cordial, frank, friendly people of most of the mountain towns, or who visit the beautiful prosperous valley of the Liris, would smile at the very idea of an adventure; and, in the nearer Campagna, the buffaloes, and still more the shepherd dogs, are far more to be dreaded by lonely pedestrians than the inhabitants. Tourists who are content to travel simply to live with and like the people they are amongst, and especially who can sign "*pittore*" to the description of their profession required in strangers' books at the inns, are not only likely to be unmolested, but cordially welcomed and kindly treated, however savage the aspect of nature may be in the country in which they are wandering. The times are quite passed when picturesque groups surrounded every carriage which appeared in a remote place, and commanded its occupants to "*saltar fuora*," as the expression was. The brigand stories of the last century are preserved in English country houses, and served up for the benefit of any member of the family who may be travelling south, as if they were events of to-day. But those who entertain these fears do not realize how *very* small the proportion of robberies and murders is in Italy compared to that of their own country—and do not know that no well-authenticated case can be ascertained of a foreigner having been either murdered or carried off by brigands, north of the old Neapolitan states, since the time of railways. Events which would curdle the blood of every Italian throughout the country pass almost unnoticed in England. For instance, what detail of old Italian brigandage was ever half so horrible as the sentence which was appended to the account of the dreadful railway accident at Merthyr Tydvil (May, 1874) in the *Times:*—"We regret to say that the poor women most injured were robbed of their purses even before they could be extricated from the ruins of the carriages!" Or, what tale of Italian ferocity ever equalled that of the Liverpool "roughs" (August, 1874), who, when a respectable citizen refused to give up his money, deliberately kicked him to death, in the presence of his wife and brother, who were themselves terribly injured in endeavouring to defend him. Even from brigands, if they are Italian, a woman would be almost certain to meet with nothing but personal kindness and respect, and a suffering woman could not be sufficiently commiserated or assisted.

An equally false impression exists in England as to middle and upper classes in Central Italy, who are generally represented and believed to be little better than well-dressed clowns, selfish, egotistical, frivolous, uneducated, ground down by superstition, devoid of all the habits of cleanly and civilized life. Such misconceptions will soon vanish from the minds of those who are at the pains to furnish themselves with introductions to the resident gentry on their mountain excursions, and who enjoy the friendly cordial hospitality of the many happy family homes, in which generation after generation have lived honoured and beloved, while in the sons and daughters of the country-houses, as well as in those of many of the Roman palaces, the same cultivation and accomplishments will be found which exist in a similar class in England, illuminated by that native grace and natural quickness and brilliancy which is seldom seen out of Italy.

"Any one who has been at the pains to seek a friendship, and has been lucky enough to find one, among the sons of modern Rome, will not be slow in doing justice to their charms; the faithfulness, warmth, tact, good humour, the grace of manner, the courage and tenderness, and that dignity of manhood which is so well reflected in the strong straight limbs, bright skin, rippling hair, and sunny faces, so well known to the loungers in the Corso, or on the Pincian hill. Let us not judge the Roman harshly. His history has been strangely chequered, and his energies may have varied with his fortunes. Sometimes, like

Rienzi, he may still mistake memories for hopes, idle visions of past greatness for that inspiration which is the earnest of future glory :

'At non omnia perdidit, neque omnes.'"

Claude Delaval Cobham.

With regard to the best seasons for the excursions from Rome, those who reach Central Italy in October will find that month far the best for a tour in the Abruzzi, before the winter snows have set in. Subiaco and its surroundings are gloriously beautiful in November, and are greatly enhanced by the tints of the decaying vegetation, the absence of which is much felt in spring when the valley between Subiaco and Tivoli looks bare and colourless.

During the winter months many of the shorter excursions may be pleasantly made from Rome in a carriage or on horseback, and a tramontana, if not too severe, will be found most agreeable by pedestrians in the valleys of Veii, or on the heights of Tusculum. The railway to Frascati opens many delightful and short excursions, and may always give a perfect country change of a few hours. In March, Alatri, Anagni, Cori, and Segni may be visited, with many other places in that district, but March is an uncertain month because "Marzo è pazzo," for it is the time, say Italians, "when men did kill God."

"A reverend meteorologist accounted for the cold in Lent, by saying that it was a mortification peculiar to the holy season, and would continue till Easter, because it was cold when Peter sate at the High Priest's fire on the eve of the Crucifixion."—*Forsyth*.

But April is the pleasantest month of all, and then should be made the enchanting excursion to Soracte, Caprarola, and the Ciminian Hills—which may be extended to Orvieto, whence those who do not wish to return to Rome may continue their journey northwards.

CHAPTER I.

OSTIA AND CASTEL FUSANO.

(This excursion can easily be managed in the day. Provisions must be taken, as there is no inn at Ostia, and visitors to Castel Fusano must provide themselves the day before with an order (given on presenting a card with a request, at the Chigi Palace in the Corso) to put up their horses there. Two hours suffice to see Ostia, but as much time as possible should be given to Castel Fusano.)

IT was in the freshness of an early morning of most brilliant sunshine, that we drove out of the old crumbling Ostian gate now called Porta San Paolo, which Belisarius built, and where Totila and Genseric entered Rome, and passed beneath the Pyramid of Caius Cestius, which for nineteen hundred years has cast its pointed shadow over the turfy slopes, where foreign Christians, gathered from so many distant lands, now sleep in Christ. This pyramid St. Paul looked upon as he was led out to execution beyond the city walls, and it may be considered as "the sole surviving witness of his martyrdom." A little further and we pass the "Chapel of the Farewell," which marks the site of his legendary leave-taking with St. Peter, and is adorned with a bas-relief of the two aged martyrs embracing for the last time, and inscriptions of the words they are reported to have spoken to one another. Then we reach the great basilica, once surrounded by the flourishing fortified village of Joanopolis, but now standing alone in solitary abandonment, even the monks, who scantily occupy its adjoining convent, being obliged to fly into the town before the summer malaria. Outside, the restored church has no features of age or grandeur, but within, as the eye passes down its unbroken lines of grey columns, surmounted by a complete series of papal portraits, it may rest upon the magnificent mosaics of the tribune, and the grand triumphal arch of Galla Placidia, relics of the venerable basilica which perished by fire on the night of the 15th of July, 1823, on which Pius VII. lay dying, who had long been a monk within its walls, and to whom the watchers by his death-bed never ventured to tell the great catastrophe with which the sky was red, though as his last moments approached, he is believed to have seen it in a troubled vision.

Beyond San Paolo, and indeed all the way from thence to Ostia, the road was once bordered with villas, but now there are only three cottages in the whole distance, which is bare or solemn as the feelings of those who visit it. It leads through the monotonous valley of the Tiber, where buffaloes and grand slow-moving *bovi* feed amid the rank pastures which are white with narcissus. Here and there a bit of tufa rock crops up crested with ilex and laurestinus. A small Roman bridge called Ponte della Refolta is passed. At length, on mounting a slight hill, we come upon a wide view over the pale-blue death-bearing marshes of the Maremma, here called *Campo-morto*, to the dazzling sea, and almost immediately enter a forest of brushwood, chiefly myrtle and phillyrea, from which we only emerge as we reach the narrow singular causeway leading to Ostia itself. It is a strange scene, not unlike the approach to Mantua upon a small scale. On either side stretch the still waters of the pestiferous lagoon, called the Stagno, waving with tall reeds which rustle mournfully in the wind, and white with floating ranunculus. To the left, a serrated outline of huge pine-tops marks the forest of Fusano; to the right we see the grey towers of Porto, the cathedral of Hippolytus, and the tall campanile which watches over the Isola Sacra, where, with a feeling fitting the mysterious sadness of the place, Dante makes souls wait to be ferried over into purgatory. Large sea-birds swoop over the reedy expanse. In front the mediæval castle rises massive and grey against the sky-line. As we approach, it increases in grandeur, and its huge machicolations and massive bastions become visible. The desolate causeway is now peopled with marble figures; heroes standing armless by the wayside, ladies reposing headless amid the luxuriant thistle-growth. Across the gleaming water we see the faint snowy peaks of the Leonessa. On each sandbank, rising above the Stagno, are works connected with the salt mines founded by King Ancus Martius, twenty-five centuries ago, and working still. They have always been important, as is evidenced by the name of one of the gates of Rome, the Porta Salara, through which the inhabitants of the Sabina passed with their purchases of Ostian salt.

Every artist will sketch the Castle of Ostia, and will remember as he works, that Raphael sketched it long ago, and that, from his sketch, Giovanni da Udine painted it in the background of his grand fresco of the victory over the Saracens, in the Stanza of the Incendio del Borgo in the Vatican, for here the enemy who had totally destroyed the ancient town in the fifth century, were as totally defeated in the reign of Leo IV. (A.D. 847—856). Procopius in the sixth century wrote of Ostia as "a city nearly overthrown." The present town is but a fortified hamlet, built by Gregory IV., and originally called by him Gregoriopolis. It was strengthened by Nicholas I. in 858. In the fifteenth century Cardinal d'Estouteville employed Sangallo, who lived here for two years, in building the castle, and Giuliano della Rovere, afterwards Pope Julius II. and then cardinal bishop of Ostia, continued the work. Here he took refuge

Castle of Ostia.

for two years from the persecution of Alexander VI. Afterwards he imprisoned Cæsar Borgia here in 1513, whose escape was connived at by Cardinal Carbajal, to whose care he was intrusted. Nothing remains of the internal decorations but some mouldering frescoes executed by Baldassare Peruzzi and Cesare da Sesto for Cardinal della Rovere, but the outer walls are so covered with the escutcheons of their different papal owners as "to form a veritable chapter of pontifical heraldry." Conspicuous amongst these grand coats of arms are the oak-tree (Robur) of the Della Rovere, and the wreathed column of the

Colonna. On the battlements above, masses of the blue-green wormwood, which is a lover of salt air and scanty soil, wave in the wind. Artists will all regret the destruction of the tall pine, so well known till lately in pictures of Ostia, which stood beside the tower, till it died in 1870.

The tiny town, huddled into the narrow fortified space, which forms as it were an outer bastion of the castle, contains the small semi-Gothic cathedral, a work of Baccio Pintelli, with a rose-window, but scarcely larger than a chapel, and seeming out of keeping with the historical recollections which we have of many mighty cardinal bishops. Some accounts state that this most ancient see was founded by the apostles themselves; others consider that Pope Urban I. (A.D. 222) was its founder, and announce St. Ciriacus as its first bishop. It is the bishop of Ostia who has always been called upon to ordain a pope who has not been in priests' orders at the time of his election, and he bears the title of " Dean of the Sacred College."*

A quarter of a mile beyond the mediæval town we enter upon the ancient city. It is like Pompeii. The long entrance street, now quite unearthed, is paved with great blocks of lava closely dovetailed into one another, and is lined with the low ruins of small houses and shops, chiefly built of brick, set in *opus reticulatum*. Here and there a tall grey sarcophagus stands erect; but no building remains perfect in the whole of the great town, which once contained eighty thousand inhabitants. Thistles flourish everywhere, and snakes and lizards abound, and glide in and out of the hot unshaded stones. After a time we turn into other and

---

* The towns of Ostia, Portus, Silva Candida, Sabina, Præneste, Tusculum, and Albanum, were the sees of seven suffragan bishops, afterwards called cardinal bishops, of whom the Bishop of Rome was in a special sense the Metropolitan.

smaller streets, in some of which there are evident remains of pillared porticoes. A temple of Mithras, supposed to be of the date of the Antonines, has been identified by the inscription on its pavement, "Soli Invict. Mit. D. D. L. Agrius Calendio." Three statues of Mithraic priests were found near its altar. Baths, richly decorated with mosaics, have also been discovered.

In the streets, the marks, the deep ruts of the chariot-wheels—obliged by the narrow space to run always in the same groove, remain in the pavement. The ground is littered with pieces of coloured marble, and of ancient glass tinted with all the hues of a peacock's tail by its long interment. The banks are filled with fragments of pottery, and here and there of human bones. The whole scene is melancholy and strange beyond description. Emerging from the narrow, almost oppressive confinement of the ruined streets, upon higher ground still unexcavated, which stretches away in ashy reaches to the mouths of the Tiber and the sea, we find a massive quadrangular building of brick, which is more stately and perfect than anything else, and is supposed to have been a temple of Jupiter. It contains its ancient altar.

Ancus Martius was the original founder of Ostia, which then stood upon the sea-shore, and for hundreds of years it was the place where the great Roman expeditions were embarked for the subjugation of the provinces. Chief among these were the expedition of Scipio Africanus to Spain, and that of Claudius to Britain. It was in the time of Claudius that the town obtained its chief importance. He dearly loved his sea-port, often stayed here, and it was from hence that he was summoned to Rome by the news of the iniquities which led to the death of Messalina. In his time the sand was already beginning to accumulate at the mouth of the Tiber, and Ostia was soon after ruined, paling before the prosperity of Porto. In consequence of the changes in the mouth of the Tiber, which has no longer the graceful course and the woody banks described by Virgil, it is difficult to ascertain the site of the ancient harbour. It is even disputed through how many channels the river entered the sea; Dionysius, in his "Periegesis," declares that it had only one; Ovid alludes to two.

"Ostia contigerat, qua se Tiberinus in altum
    Dividit, et campo liberiore natat."—*Fast.* iv. 291.

"Fluminis ad flexum veniunt; Tiberina priores
    Ostia dixerunt, unde sinister abit."—*Fast.* iv. 329.

But from these classical recollections the Christian pilgrim will turn with enthusiasm to later memories, as precious and beautiful as any that the Campagna of Rome can afford, and he will see Augustine, with his holy mother, Monica, sitting, as in Ary Scheffer's picture, at "a curtain window," discoursing alone, together, very sweetly, and, "forgetting those things which are behind and reaching forth to those things which are before," inquiring in the presence of the Truth of what sort the eternal life of the saints was to be, and "gasping with the mouths of their hearts" after the heavenly streams of the fountain of life. Then, as the world and all its delights become contemptible in the nearness into which their converse draws them to the unseen, he will hear the calm voice of Monica in the twilight telling her son that her earthly hopes and mission are fulfilled, and that she is only waiting to depart, "since that is accomplished for which she had desired to linger awhile in this life, that she might see him a Catholic Christian before she died." He will remember that five days after this conversation, Monica lay in Ostia upon her death-bed, and waking from a long swoon, and looking fixedly on her two sons standing by her, "with grief amazed," said to Augustine, "Here thou shalt bury thy mother;" and that to those who asked whether she was not afraid to leave her body so far from her own city, she replied, "Nothing is far to God; nor is it to be feared lest at the end of the world He should not recognize whence to raise me up." And here "on the ninth day of her sickness, and the fifty-sixth year of her age, was that religious and holy soul freed from the body." The bones of Monica were moved afterwards to Rome, to the church which was dedicated to her son's memory; but it is Ostia which will always be connected with the last scenes of that most holy life, and at Ostia that Augustine describes the "mighty sorrow which flowed into his heart," the tears and outcries of "the boy Adeodatus,"* as the beloved mother sank into her last sleep; how Euodius calmed their grief by taking up the Psalter, and how all the mourning household sang the psalm, "I will sing of mercy and judgment to thee, O Lord," around the silent corpse; and lastly, how the body was carried to the burial, and they "went and returned without tears—for the bitterness of sorrow could not exude out of the heart."

With these recollections in our minds, let us leave Ostia. It is a curious and deeply interesting, but not a beautiful place, and it is a strange contrast, when we have returned once more to the old fortress, and, turning sharply round its walls, traversed the two miles of desolate campagna between

* The son of Augustine.

it and the pine-wood, to find in Castel Fusano an absolute climax of poetical loveliness. The peasants do all their field labour here in gangs, men and women together, and most picturesque they look, for the costumes which are dying out in Rome are universally worn here, and all the women have their heads shaded by white *panni*, and are dressed in bright pink and blue petticoats and laced bodices. They have hard work to fight against the deep-rooted asphodels, which overrun whole pastures and destroy the grass, and they have also the constantly recurring malaria to struggle against, borne up every night by the poisonous vapours of the marsh, which renders Ostia almost uninhabitable even to the natives in summer, and death to the stranger who attempts to pass the night there.

Approach to Castel Fusano.

A bridge, decorated with the arms of the Chigis, takes us across the last arm of the Stagno, with a huge avenue of pines ending on a green lawn, in the midst of which stands the mysterious, desolate Chigi palace, occupying the site of the beloved Laurentine villa of Pliny. No road, no path even, leads to its portal; but all around is green turf, and it looks like the house where the enchanted princess went to sleep with all her attendants for five hundred years, and where she must be asleep still. Round the house, at intervals, stand gigantic red vases, like Morgiana's oil-jars, filled with yuccas and aloes. Over the parapet wall stone figures look down, set there to scare away the Saracens, it is said, but for centuries they have seen nothing but a few stranger tourists or sportsmen, and the wains of beautiful meek-eyed oxen drawing timber from the forest. All beyond is a vast expanse of wood, huge pines stretching out their immense green umbrellas over the lower trees; stupendous ilexes contorted by time into a thousand strange vagaries; bay-trees bowed with age, and cork-trees grey with lichen—patriarchs even in this patriarchal forest. And beneath these greater potentates such a wealth of beautiful shrubs as is almost indescribable—arbutus, lentisc, phillyrea; tall Mediterranean heath, waving vast plumes of white blossom far overhead, sweet daphne, scenting all around with its pale pink blossoms; myrtle growing in thickets of its own; smilax and honeysuckle, leaping from tree to tree, and forming themselves into a thousand lovely wreaths, and, beneath all, such a carpet of pink cyclamen, that the air is heavy with its perfume, and we may sit down and fill our hands and baskets with the flowers without moving from a single spot. A road, a mile long, paved with blocks of lava plundered from the Via Severiana, leads from the back of the palace to the sea, and we must follow it, partly to see the famous rosemary which Pliny describes, and which still grows close to the shore in such abundance, and partly for the sake of a glimpse of the grand Mediterranean itself (so refreshing after the close air of Roman streets), which rolls in here with long waves upon a heavy sandy shore, where a few fishermen have their huts, built of myrtle from the wood, and bound together with the reeds of the Stagno. But all the forest is delightful, and one cannot wander enough into its deep recesses, where some giant of the wood is reflected in a solitary pool, or where the trees reach overhead into long aisles like a vast cathedral of Nature. If time can be given, it is well worth while to follow on horseback the heavy road which leads continuously through the forest to Porto d'Anzio, by Ardea and Pratica; but in this case it will be necessary to have permission to sleep at Castel Fusano. Such an excursion will give leisure to dwell upon the beauties which are generally seen so hurriedly. Virgil should be taken as a companion, who describes the very pines, which cast such long shadows, in his "Æneid,"—

"Evertunt actas ad sidera pinus,"*

and with the poet as a fellow-traveller, perhaps the very desertion and solitude will act as a charm, and the intense silence, only broken by the songs of the birds and the chirp of the cicala.

* xi. 136.

CHAPTER II.

ALBANO AND LARICCIA.

(The Hotel de Paris (occupying an old palace) at Albano, is perhaps the best, and is comfortable. The Albergo della Posta, belonging to the same landlord, is an old-established inn in the Italian style, and has a few pleasant rooms towards the Campagna. The Hotel de Rome, on the other side of the street, nearer Lariccia and the country, is comfortable and well-furnished; the upper floor is very cold in winter. The Hotel de Russie, near the Roman gate and the Villa Doria, is an old-fashioned inn, with less pretensions. At all the hotels at Albano the charges are very high in comparison with other places near Rome, and quite unreasonably so. It is necessary *on arriving* to make a fixed bargain at all of them, and for *everything*. The charges for carriages are most extortionate and ought to be universally resisted. If no bargain is made at the railway-station, travellers are liable to a charge of 10 or even 15 francs for a carriage to take them to their hotel. Places in the open omnibus, without luggage, cost one franc each. It is far more economical as well as pleasanter for a party of people to take a carriage from Rome to Albano (costing 20 francs), than to go by the railway and be at the mercy of the Albano carriages on arriving. Those who stay long in the place will find it much less expensive to walk across the viaduct to Lariccia and take a carriage from thence, or even to order one from Genzano. Donkeys cost four francs by the day, the donkeyman four francs, and the guide seven francs: these prices include the whole excursion by Monte Cavo and Nemi.)

LOOKING across the level reaches of the Campagna as it is seen above the walls of the city from the Porta Maggiore to the Porta S. Paolo, the horizon is bounded by a chain of hills, or rather very low mountains, so varied in outline, so soft and beautiful in the tender hues of their ever-changing colour, that the eye is always returning to rest upon them, and they soon assume the aspect of loved and familiar friends, equally charming in the sapphire and amethyst hues of autumn, under the occasional snow-mantle of mid-winter, or when bursting afresh into light and life, from the luxuriant green of early spring. Where they break away from the plain, the buttresses of the hills are clothed with woods of olives or with fruit-trees, then great purple hollows vary their slopes, and towns and villages on the projecting heights gleam and glitter in the sun, towns, each with a name so historical as to awaken a thousand associations. And these centre most of all round the white building on the highest and steepest crest of the chain, which marks the summit of the Alban Mount, and the site of the great temple of Jupiter Latiaris—the famous—the beloved sanctuary of the Latin tribes.

"For those who have not been at Rome I will say, that on looking south-east from the gate of S. John Lateran, after a slightly undulating plain of eleven miles, unbroken by any tree, but only by tombs and broken aqueducts, there rises in the mist of beautiful days, a line of blue hills of noble forms, which, leaving the Sabine country, go leaping on in various and graceful shapes, till they reach the highest point of all, called the Monte Cavo. Hence the chain descends afresh, and with moderate declension, and a line long drawn out, reaches the plain, and is lost there not very far from the sea."—*Massimo d'Azeglio.*

"Alba, thou findest me still, and, Alba, thou findest me ever,
 Now from the Capitol steps, now over Titus's Arch,
Here from the large grassy spaces that spread from the Lateran portal,
 Towering o'er aqueduct lines lost in perspective between,
Or from a Vatican window, or bridge, or the high Coliseum,
 Clear by the garlanded line cut of the Flavian ring.
Beautiful can I not call thee, and yet thou hast power to o'ermaster,
 Power of mere beauty ; in dreams, Alba, thou hauntest me still."
A. H. Clough.

Pedestrians will do well to take the old Appian Way in

going to Albano (see *Walks in Rome*, vol. i.), every step of which is full of interest; but carriages will usually follow the Via Appia Nuova, which emerges from the city walls by the Porta S. Giovanni, and after crossing the Via Latina (*Walks in Rome*, i. 124), runs between the stately arches of the Claudian Aqueduct on the left, and the ruined tombs of the Appian Way on the right.

Claudian Aqueduct.

"L'aqueduc et la voie d'Appius marquent un moment d'une grande importance dans la destinée de Rome, ils sont comme une magnifique vignette entre le premier alinéa de l'histoire de la république et les suivants."—*Ampère, Hist. Rom.*, iv. 49.

"Passing out by the San Giovanni gate, you enter upon those broad wastes that lie to the south-east of the city. Going forward thence, with the aqueducts to your left, and the old Appian Way, lined with crumbling sepulchres, reaching for miles in one unswerving line on your far right, you soon leave Rome behind. Faint patches of vegetation gleam here and there, like streaks of light; and nameless ruins lie scattered broadcast over the bleak slopes of this most desolate region. Sometimes you come upon a primitive bullock-waggon, or a peasant driving an ass laden with green boughs; but these signs of life are rare. Presently you pass the remains of a square temple, with Corinthian pilasters—then a drove of shaggy ponies—then a little truck with a tiny pent-house reared on one side of the seat, to keep the driver from the sun—then a flock of rusty sheep—a stagnant pool—a clump of stunted trees—a conical thatched hut—a round sepulchre, half buried in the soil of ages—a fragment of broken arch; and so on, for miles and miles across the barren plain. By and by you see a drove of buffaloes scouring along towards the aqueducts, followed by a mounted herdsman, buskined and brown, with his lance in his hand, his blue cloak floating behind him, and his sombrero down upon his brow—the very picture of a Mexican hunter."—*Miss Edwards, Barbara's History*.

Eleven miles from Rome the Via Appia Nova joins the Via Appia Vecchia at *Le Frattocchie*. The view from hence, looking down the avenue of mouldering sepulchres, is most desolate and striking. The use of the popular term Strada del Diavolo, which we constantly meet with here as applied to the Via Appia, will call to mind the name of the Devil's Dyke as applied to a well-known Roman work in England.

"One day we walked out, a little party of three, to Albano, fourteen miles distant; possessed by a great desire to go there by the ancient Appian Way, long since ruined and overgrown. We started at half-past seven in the morning, and within an hour or so were out upon the open Campagna. For twelve miles we went climbing on, over an unbroken succession of mounds, and heaps, and hills, of ruin. Tombs and temples, overthrown and prostrate; small fragments of columns, friezes, pediments; great blocks of granite and marble; mouldering arches, grass-grown and decayed; ruin enough to build a spacious city from, lay strewn about us. Sometimes loose walls, built up from these fragments by the shepherds, came across our path; sometimes a ditch, between two mounds of broken stones, obstructed our progress; sometimes the fragments themselves, rolling from beneath our feet, made it a toilsome matter to advance; but it was always ruin. Now, we tracked a piece of the old road above the ground; now traced it underneath a grassy covering, as if that were its grave; but all the way was ruin. In the distance, ruined aqueducts went stalking on their giant course along the plain; and every breath of wind that swept towards us stirred early flowers and grasses, springing up, spontaneously, on miles of ruin. The unseen larks above us, who alone disturbed the awful silence, had their nests in ruin; and the fierce herdsmen, clad in sheepskins, who now and then scowled upon us from their sleeping nooks, were housed in ruin. The aspect of the desolate Campagna in one direction, where it was most level, reminded me of an American prairie; but what is the solitude of a region where men have never dwelt, to that of a Desert where a mighty race have left their foot-prints in the earth from which they have vanished; where the resting-places of their Dead have fallen like their Dead; and the broken hour-glass of Time is but a heap of idle dust!

Returning, by the road, at sunset ; and looking, from the distance, on the course we had taken in the morning, I almost felt as if the sun would never rise again, but look its last, that night, upon a ruined world."—*Dickens.*

Le Frattocchie itself was the scene of the fatal meeting (Jan. 20th, B.C. 52) between Clodius and Milo.

"Clodius était allé à Aricia pour une affaire. Le lendemain, il s'était arrêté dans sa villa, voisine du mont Albain, où il devait coucher. La nouvelle de la mort de son architecte le fit partir assez tard. A peine avait-il commencé à suivre la voie Appienne, qu'il se croisa près de Boville avec Milon ; Milon se rendait à Lanuvium, d'où il était originaire, pour y installer dans sa charge un prêtre de la déesse du lieu, Junon Sospita.

"Je crois que les deux ennemis ne s'attendaient pas à se rencontrer. Milon était en voiture avec sa femme ; escorté par ses esclaves, parmi lesquels se trouvaient deux gladiateurs renommés. Dans la situation où il se trouvait vis-à-vis de Clodius, cette escorte n'avait rien d'extraordinaire.

"Clodius était à cheval, suivi de trois amis, et d'une trentaine d'esclaves. Les deux ennemis s'étaient dépassés sans se rien dire. Une querelle s'engagea entre ceux qui formaient leur suite.

"Selon Cicéron, un grand nombre des gens de Clodius attaquèrent Milon d'un lieu qui dominait la route. Son cocher fut tué. Milon sauta à terre pour se défendre ; les gens de Clodius coururent vers la voiture pour attaquer Milon, et commencèrent à frapper ses esclaves à coups d'épée. Ce fut alors que le gladiateur Birra, attaquant Clodius par derrière, lui perça l'épaule.

"Les serviteurs de Clodius, beaucoup moins nombreux, s'enfuirent et emportèrent leur maître dans une hôtellerie ; l'hôtellerie fut assiégée par les hommes de Milon, l'hôte tué. Clodius, arraché de cet asile, fut ramené sur la route, et là percé de coups. Milon ne fit rien pour l'empêcher. On dit plus tard qu'après le meurtre il était allé dans la villa de son ennemi, qui était tout proche, pour chercher son enfant et l'égorger ; que, ne le trouvant pas, il avait torturé ses esclaves ; mais ces accusations n'ont aucune vraisemblance.

"La suite de Clodius s'était dispersée. Un sénateur qui passait par là trouva son corps gisant sur la route et le fit reporter dans sa maison du Palatin."—*Ampère, Hist. Rom.*, iv. 577.

Some ruins at a short distance to the left are supposed to

mark the site of the city of *Appiola*, destroyed by Tarquin, who used its spoil to erect the Circus Maximus.

A little to the right are the ruins of *Bovillæ*, whose foundation is attributed to Latinus Silvius of Alba. The remains consist of insignificant fragments of the circus and theatre. Bovillæ was the first station on the Appian Way :—

"Et cum currere debeas Bovillas,
Interjungere quæris ad Camœnas."
Martial. ii., *Ep.* 6.

The title of Suburbanæ distinguished it from another town of the same name :—

" Orta suburbanis quædam fuit Anna Bovillis,
Pauper, sed multæ sedulitatis, anus."
Ovid. Fast. iii. 667.

" Quidve suburbanæ parva minus urbe Bovillæ."
Propertius, iv., *Eleg.* i.

Florus speaks of Bovillæ as one of the first towns subdued by the Romans : Plutarch tells how it was taken and plundered by Marcus Coriolanus. In the time of Cicero, who speaks of it as a "municipium," it was already almost deserted.* The Julian Gens had a chapel here, where their images were preserved, and games were performed in their honour. Here the body of the Emperor Augustus rested for a month as it was being brought from Nola, and here the knights assembled to conduct it to the city. The position of Bovillæ receives an additional identification from the description which Cicero gives of the circumstances which led to the murder of Clodius, when he speaks of it as " Pugna Bovillana."†

Beyond Le Frattocchie the Via Appia ascends continuously.

* Orat. pro Plancio. † Ad Atticum. v. 15.

"Now the Campagna is left behind, and Albano stands straight before you, on the summit of a steep and weary hill. Low lines of white-washed wall border the road on either side, enclosing fields of *fascine*, orchards, olive-yards, and gloomy plantations of cypresses and pines. Next come a range of sand-banks, with cavernous hollows and deep under-shadows; next, an old cinque-cento gateway, crumbling away by the road-side; then a little wooden cross on an overhanging crag; then the sepulchre of Pompey; and then the gates of Albano, through which you rattle into the town, and up to the entrance of the Hotel de Russie."—*Miss Edwards, Barbara's History*.

Immediately before entering the town, we pass, on the left, a lofty tomb, always known as the *Tomb of Pompey*. Plutarch mentions his sepulchre as being near his villa at Albanum, though according to the epigram of Varro Atacinus, quoted by the scholiast on Persius ii. 36, Pompey had no tomb:—

"Marmoreo Licinus tumulo jacet; at Cato parvo;
Pompeius nullo; quis putet esse Deus."

To those who receive their previous impressions of Albano from water-colour drawings and from the engravings of Pinelli, the sight of the place will be full of disappointment. The town consists, for the most part, of an ill-paved street a mile in length, of shabby white-washed houses, without feature, and the inhabitants have little beauty and wear no distinctive costume. All the interest of the place is to be found in the lovely scenery which surrounds it, and most lovely it is; and for costumes and primitive habits of the peasantry we must penetrate further, to the Volscian and Hernican hills. Yet, except in the building of a few better-class hotels, Albano has made no progress in late years, and is ill-provided with all the comforts of civilized life: the few there are being supplied to strangers at prices which are enormous for Italy.

"Albano—a place of more than 6000 souls, the episcopal see of a Cardinal who represented his sovereign in the spiritual government of Rome—has not a bookseller's shop, no sort of library for public use, no journal except sterile official papers, though a large Cathedral Chapter, seminary, and public schools, the residence of a Gonfaloniere and a governor, attest the importance—numerous hotels and rather gay caffès, announce the fashionable—reputation of this town. Under the old government, twelve convents, in Albano and its vicinity, dispensed charities, usually in the form of soup and bread, to all applicants, either daily or on stated days. Yet the town itself has always been swarming with beggars, who usually appeal to compassion with promises of so many Aves in return! The native youth of the place, seeming for the most part artizans or labourers in tolerably good condition, spend their evenings generally, as the visitor may perceive, at the caffès playing cards."—*Hemans' Catholic Italy.*

But the beauty of the villas, and the variety of excursions in the neighbourhood, make Albano the most enchanting of summer residences for those who can bear the heat of Italian *villeggiature*. Large airy apartments may be obtained in many of the old palaces, where, in the great heat, the scarcity of furniture is scarcely a disadvantage. But those who sojourn here, will do well to conform to Italian habits— to dine early and then take a siesta, followed by the delicious Italian refection of lemonade, fruits, &c., which is known as *Merenda*, and sallying out in the gorgeous beauty of the evening to walk or drive in the "galleries" which overhang the lake, or in the woods towards Nemi.

"Ah, dearest, you know not yet the enchantment of a summer amid Italian hills, and you know not what it is to breathe the perfume of the orange gardens—to lie at noon in the deep shadow of an ilex grove, listening to the ripple of a legendary spring, older than history—to stroll among ruins in the purple twilight! Then up here at Albano, far from the sultry city and the unhealthy plain, we have such sunrises and sunsets as you, artist though you be, have never dreamt of—here, where the cool airs linger longest, and the very moon and stars look more golden than elsewhere."—*Barbara's History.*

"When the sun draws down to the horizon the people flock forth from their houses. All the chairs and benches in front of the *caffè* are filled—the streets are thronged with companies of promenaders—every door-step has its little group—the dead town has become alive. Marching through the long green corridors of the "gallerie" that lead for miles from Albano or Castel Gandolfo to Genzano, whole families may be seen loitering together, and pausing now and then to look through the trunks of the great trees at the purple flush that deepens every moment over the Campagna. The *cicale* now renew their song as the sun sets, and croak dryly in the trees their good-night. The *contadini* come in from the vineyards and olive-orchards, bearing ozier-baskets heaped with grapes, or great bundles of brush-wood on their heads. There is a crowd around the fountain, where women are filling their great copper vases with water, and pausing to chat before they march evenly home under its weight like stout *caryatides*. Broad-horned white oxen drag home their creaking wains. In the distance you hear the long monotonous wail of the peasant's song as he returns from his work, interrupted now and then with a shrill scream to his cattle. White-haired goats come up the lanes in flocks, cropping as they go the over-hanging bushes—and mounting up the bank to pluck at the flowers and leaves, they stare at you with yellow glassy eyes, and wag their beards. The sheep are huddled into their netted folds. Down the slopes of the pavement jar along ringing files of wine-carts going towards Rome, while the little Pomeranian dog who lives under the triangular hood in front is running about on the piled wine-casks, and uttering volleys of little sharp yelps and barks as the cars rattle through the streets. If you watch the wine-carriers down into the valley you will see them pull up at the wayside fountains, draw a good flask of red wine from one of the casks, and then replace it with good fresh water.

"The *grilli* now begin to trill in the grass, and the hedges are alive with fire-flies. From the ilex groves and the gardens nightingales sing until the middle of July; and all summer long glow-worms show their green emerald splendour on the grey walls, and from under the road-side vines. In the distance you hear the laugh of girls, the song of wandering promenaders, and the burr of distant tambourines, where they are dancing the *saltarello*. The *civetta* hoots from the old tombs, the *barbigiano* answers from the crumbling ruins, and the plaintive, monotonous *ciou* owls call to each other across the vales. The moonlight lies in great still sheets of splendour in the piazza, and the shadows of the houses are cut sharply out in it, like blocks of black marble. The polished leaves of the laurel twinkle in its beams and rustle as the wind sifts through them. Above, the sky is soft and tender; great, near, palpitant stars flash on you their changeful splendour of emerald, topaz, and ruby.

The Milky Way streams like a torn veil over the heavens. The villa fronts whiten in the moonlight among the grey smoke-like olives that crowd the slopes. Vines wave from the old towers and walls, and from their shadow comes a song to the accompaniment of a guitar—it is a tenor voice, singing 'Non ti scordar, non ti scordar di me.'

"Nothing can be more exquisite than these summer nights in Italy. The sky itself, so vast, tender, and delicate, is like no other sky. As you stand on one of the old balconies or walls along the terraces of the Frescati villas, looking down over the mysterious Campagna, and listening to the continuous splash of fountains and the song of nightingales, you feel Italy—the Italy of Romeo and Juliet. Everything seems enchanted in the tender splendour. The stars themselves burn with a softer, more throbbing and impulsive light. The waves of the cool, delicate air, passing over orange and myrtle groves, and breathing delicately against the brow and cheeks, seem to blow open the inmost leaves of the book on which youth painted its visionary pictures with the colours of dreams. In a word, we say this is Italy—the Italy we dreamed of—not the Italy of fleas, couriers, mendicants, and postilions, but of romance, poetry, and passion."—*Story's Roba di Roma*, i. 298.

As soon as the visitor is settled in his hotel he will probably wander up to the end of the street, where he will at once find himself amid the greatest attractions of the place. Just below the road, upon the right, is the tomb of Aruns, son of Porsenna. It is a huge square base with four cones rising from it, and a central chamber, in which an urn with ashes was discovered some years ago. Aruns was killed by Aristodemus of Cumæ before Ariccia, which his father had sent him to besiege: his tomb is identified by the description which Pliny gives of that of Porsenna, but it was long supposed to be the monument of the Horatii and Curiatii.

Below the tomb of Aruns, the old road to Ariccia winds through the hollow, amid rocks and trees, which, alas, have lately been pollarded. Still the glen must always be full of beauty, and is the constant summer resort of landscape-painters.

"From Albano we had to go on foot for the short and beautiful remainder of the way through Ariccia. Reseda and golden cistus grew wild by the road-side; the thick, juicy olive-trees cast a delicious shade. I caught a glimpse of the distant sea; and upon the mountain-slopes by the wayside, where a cross stood, merry girls skipped dancing past us, yet never forgetting piously to kiss the holy cross. The lofty dome of the church of Ariccia I imagined to be that of S. Peter, which the angels had hung up in the blue air among the dark olive-trees."—*Improvisatore.* *H. C. Anderson.*

L'Ariccia.

The ravine is now called *Vallericcia*, and was once a sheet of water called Lacus Aricinus. Near the road are some small remains supposed to be those of a temple of Diana.

"The ceremonies of the temple of Aricia were, according to Strabo, barbaric and Scythian, like those of the Tauric Diana. The priest (Rex Nemorensis) was always a fugitive who had slain his predecessor, and always had in his hand a drawn sword, to defend himself from a similar fate. There was a tree near the temple, whence if a fugitive could approach and carry off a bough, he was entitled to the duel, or monomachia, with the Rex Nemorensis.

"A most curious basso-relievo was found in the neighbourhood some years ago,* representing several personages, among whom is the priest, lately in possession, lying prostrate, with his entrails issuing from a

---

* Now at Palma in Majorca.

wound, inflicted by his successor, who stands over him with his sword ; there are also several females in long robes, in the Etruscan style, who seem to invoke the gods. This basso-relievo and the passage of Strabo seem to explain each other."—*Sir W. Gell.*

Hippolytus or Urbius, the legendary founder of Ariccia, was joined with Diana in the worship of the inhabitants, and is commemorated with her by many of the Latin poets.

"Jamque dies aderat ; profugis cum regibus altum
Fumat Aricinum Triviæ Nemus, et face multa
Conscius Hippolyti splendet lacus."
Stat. Silv. iii. 1.

" Ecce suburbanæ templum nemorale Dianæ,
Partaque per gladios regna nocente manu."
Ovid. Art. Am. i. 259.

" Nympha, mone, Nemori stagnoque operata Dianæ ;
Nympha, Numæ conjux, ad tua festa veni.
Vallis Aricinæ sylva præcinctus opaca
Est lacus, antiqua religione sacer.
Hic jacet Hippolytus furiis direptus equorum," &c.
Ovid. Fast. iii. 261.

" Lucus eum, nemorisque tui Dictynna recessus
Celat : Aricino Virbius ille lacu est."
Ovid. Fast. vi. 755.

" . . . . nam conjux urbe relicta
Vallis Aricinæ densis latet abdita sylvis :
Sacraque Oresteæ gemitu questuque Dianæ
Impedit. Ah quoties Nymphæ nemorisque lacusque,
Ne faceret, monuere."
Ovid. Metam. xv. 487.

" Ibat et Hippolyti proles pulcherrima bello,
Virbius ; insignem quem mater Aricia misit,
Eductum Egeriæ lucis, humentia circum
Littora, pinguis ubi et placabilis ara Dianæ."
Virgil. Æn. vii. 761.

" At Trivia Hippolytum secretis alma recondit
Sedibus, et nymphæ Egeriæ nemorique relegat ;
Solus ubi in silvis Italis ignobilis ævum
Exigeret, versoque ubi nomine Virbius esset."
Virgil. Æn. vii. 774.

> "Jam nemus Egeriæ, jam te ciet altus ab Alba
> Jupiter, et soli non mitis Aricia regi."
> *Val. Flac. Arg.* ii. 304.

> " . . . . quos miserat altis
> Egeriæ genitos immitis Aricia lucis,
> Ætatis mentisque pares ; at non dabat ultra
> Clotho dura lacus aramque videre Dianæ."
> *Sil. Ital.* iv. 368.

The steep ascent from Vallericcia to the town is also commemorated by the poets.

> . . "accedo Bovillas
> Clivumque ad Virbi ; præsto est mihi Manlius hæres."
> *Persius. Sat.* vi. 56.

> " Irus tuorum temporum sequebaris.
> Migrare Clivum crederes Aricinum."
> *Martial.* xii. *Ep.* 32.

The steepness of the hill from the earliest times afforded great advantages to the beggars.

> " Dignus Aricinos qui mendicaret ad axes,
> Blandaque devexæ jactaret basia rhedæ."
> *Juvenal. Sat.* iv. 117.

The rich country upon which we look down was as famous in ancient as in modern times for the produce of its vineyards.

> " Est mihi nonum superantis annum
> Plenus Albani cadus."
> *Horace. Od.* iv. 11.

> " Hic herus, Albanum, Mæcenas, sive Falernum
> Te magis appositis delectat ; habemus utrumque."
> *Sat.* ii. 8.

> " Hoc de Cæsareis mitis vindemia cellis
> Misit, Iuleo quæ sibi monte placet."
> *Martial.* xiii. 106.

Aricia was also celebrated for its leeks :—

> " Bruttia quæ tellus, et mater Aricia porri."
> *Colum. R. Rust.* x.

THE PALAZZO CHIGI.

> "Mittit præcipuos nemoralis Aricia porros."
> *Martial.* xiii. 16.

Some fragments of the ancient wall may be seen before entering the gate of Aricia with its forked Guelfic battlements. The city itself is of very ancient origin, being first mentioned in the story of Tarquinius Superbus, when Turnus Herdonius, its king, was drowned in the Aqua Ferentina. It was the birth-place of Atia, mother of Augustus, and as such is extolled by Cicero in his third Philippic.

Aricia was a station on the Via Appia:—

> "Nous arrivons avec Horace à Lariccia. Là nous disons comme lui:
> 'Egressum magna me excepit Aricia Roma'
> (*Sat.* i., *S.* i.)
> enchantés de ces délicieux aspects dont Horace, moins occupé que nous ne le sommes du pittoresque, n'a point parlé. La ville moderne de Lariccia s'est perchée, comme il arrive souvent, dans la citadelle de la ville ancienne. M. Pierre Rosa, cet explorateur infatigable et sagace de la campagne romaine, et qui excelle à découvrir les ruines que son aïeul Salvator Rosa aimait à peindre, a cru retrouver les restes de la petite auberge (*Sat.* i., *S.* i.) où Horace a logé (*hospicio modico*), et même des vases contenant l'orge destinée aux montures des voyageurs."—
> *Ampère, Emp. Rom.* i. 365.

Lariccia is now chiefly remarkable for the huge *Palace of the Chigi family*, built by *Bernini* for Alexander VII. It is noble and imposing in its proportions, as it rises on huge buttresses from the depths of the ravine. In the interior are some interesting rooms hung with exceedingly curious stamped leather, and a chamber containing portraits of the twelve nieces of Alexander VII., who were so enchanted at the elevation of their uncle, that they all took the veil immediately to please him. Apartments are let here in the summer months, and are very delightful.

Opposite the palace is the beautifully proportioned *Church of the Assumption*, also built (1664) by *Bernini*, with a dome painted by *Antonio Raggi*, and a few very indifferent pictures. A fountain covered with mimulus stands in front of the portico. The palace and church form the beautiful group of Lariccia so well known from pictures. Between them the town is now entered from Albano by a grand viaduct, 700 feet long, whence the view is exquisitely lovely, on the left over the Campagna, on the right looking into the depths of the immemorial wood known as the *Parco Chigi*.

"Le pont monumental remplit un profond ravin pour mettre de plain-pied la route d'Aricia à Albano. Il passe donc par-dessus tout un paysage vu en profondeur, et ce paysage est rempli par une forêt vierge jétée dans un abîme. Une forêt vierge fermée de murs, c'est là une de ces fantaisies que les princes peuvent seuls se passer. Il y a cinquante ans que la main de l'homme n'a abattu une branche et que son pied n'a tracé un sentier dans le forêt Chigi. Pourquoi? *Chi lo sa?* vous disent les indigènes.

"Au reste, ce caprice-là, qui serait bien concevable de la part d'un propriétaire artiste, est une agréable surprise pour l'artiste qui passe. Sur les flancs du ravin s'echelonnent les têtes vénérables des vieux chênes soutenant dans leur robuste branchage les squelettes penchés de leurs voisins morts, qui tombent en poussière sous une mousse desséchée d'un blanc livide. La lierre court sur ces ruines végétales, et sous l'impénétrable abri de ces réseaux de verdure vigoureuse et de pâles ossements, un pêle-mêle de ronces, d'herbes, et de rochers va se baigner dans le ruisseau sans rivages practicables. Si l'on n'était sur une grande route, avec une ville derrière soi, on se croirait dans une forêt du nouveau monde."—*George Sand, La Daniella*.

"It had been wild weather when I left Rome, and all across the Campagna the clouds were sweeping in sulphurous blue, with a clap of thunder or two, and breaking gleams of sun along the Claudian aqueduct, lighting up the infinity of its arches like the bridge of chaos. But as I climbed the long slope of the Alban Mount, the storm swept finally to the north, and the noble outline of the domes of Albano, and graceful darkness of its ilex grove, rose against pure streaks of alternate blue and amber; the upper sky gradually flushing through the last fragments of rain-cloud in deep, palpitating azure, half æther and half dew The noonday sun came slanting down the rocky slopes of La Riccia, and their masses of entangled and tall foliage, whose autumnal tints were mixed with the wet verdure of a thousand evergreens, were penetrated with it as with rain. I cannot call it colour, it was conflagration. Purple, and crimson, and scarlet, like the curtains of God's tabernacle, the rejoicing trees sank into the valley in showers of light, every separate leaf quivering with burning and buoyant life; each, as it turned to reflect or transmit the sunbeam, first a torch, and then an emerald. Far up into the recesses of the valley, the green vistas arched like the hollows of mighty waves of some crystalline sea, with the arbutus flowers dashed along their flanks for foam, and silver flakes of orange spray tossed into the air around them, breaking over the gray walls of rock into a thousand separate stars, fading and kindling alternately as the weak wind lifted and let them fall. Every glade of grass burned like the golden floor of heaven, opening in sudden gleams as the foliage broke and closed above it, as sheet-lightning opens in a cloud at sunset; the motionless masses of dark rock—dark though flushed with scarlet lichen—casting their quiet shadows across its restless radiance, the fountain underneath them filling its marble hollow with blue mist and fitful sound ; and over all—the multitudinous bars of amber and rose, the sacred clouds that have no darkness, and only exist to illumine, were seen in fathomless intervals between the solemn and orbed repose of the stone pines, passing to lose themselves in the last, white, blinding lustre of the measureless line where the Campagna melted into the blaze of the sea."—*Ruskin's Modern Painters.*

The most delightful lanes fringed with cyclamen and forget-me-not, lead under the arch at the back of the Chigi palace and skirt the walls of the wood to the *Convent of the Cappuccini,* from whose lovely ilex groves there are glorious views in every direction. The convent occupies the site of part of the villa of Domitian, whither Juvenal describes the saturnine emperor as summoning the imperial council from Rome in the winter of A.D. 84.

"Anxiously they asked each other, What news? What the purport of their unexpected summons? What foes of Rome had broken the prince's slumbers,—the Chatti or the Sicambri, the Britons or the Dacians? While they were yet waiting for admission, the menials of the palace entered, bearing aloft a huge turbot, a present to the emperor, which they had the mortification of seeing introduced into his presence, while the doors were still shut against themselves. A humble fisherman had found the monster stranded on the beach, beneath the fane of Venus at Ancona, and had hurried to receive a reward for so rare an offering to the imperial table. When at last the councillors were admitted, the question reserved for their deliberations was no other than this, whether the big fish should be cut in pieces, or served up whole on some enormous platter, constructed in its honour. The cabinet was no doubt sensibly persuaded that the question allowed at least of no delay, and with due expressions of surprise and admiration voted the dish, and set the potter's wheel in motion."—*Merivale's Romans under the Empire.*

> "Surgitur, et misso proceres exire jubentur
> Consilio, quos Albanam dux magnus in arcem
> Traxerat attonitos et festinare coactos."
>
> *Sat.* iv. 145.

This palace of Domitian is frequently alluded to in the poets:—

> "Hoc tibi Palladiæ seu collibus uteris Albæ,
> Cæsar, et hinc Triviam prospicis, inde Thetin;
> Mittimus."
>
> *Martial,* v. *Ep.* I.

> "Sed quis ab excelsis Trojanæ collibus Albæ,
> Unde suæ juxta prospectat mœnia Romæ,
> Proximus ille Deus."
>
> *Statius, Silv.* v. 2.

One of the best subjects for a picture is the view from under the great ilex-trees in front of the convent gate towards Albano and the sea. A door in the wall on the right of the lane which leads down towards Albano, admits one to the remains of the *Roman Amphitheatre,* now used as folds for goats, who crowd the rugged recesses of its caverned masonry, and group themselves picturesquely on its old walls. This was the scene of some of the worst cruelties of Domitian. The other Roman remains in Albano are insignificant, the ruins of the *Prætorian Camp* near the Church of S. Paolo, and some fragments of Roman ornamentation built into the Church of Sta. Maria della Rotonda being the chief of them.

Turning the rocky corner beyond the Cappuccini we come at once upon one of the loveliest scenes in this land of beauty, and look down upon

> "—the still glassy lake that sleeps
> Beneath Aricia's trees." *

At the other end of the lake stands, on the hill-side, Castel Gandolfo, embossed against the delicate hues of the distant Campagna. Beneath us, buried in verdure, is the famous Emissarium; on the opposite shore was the site of Alba Longa; and on the right, beyond the convent of Palazzuola, rise Rocca di Papa, and the Alban Mount. The lake itself, which occupies the crater of an extinct volcano, is 6 miles in circuit, $2\frac{1}{3}$ miles long, and $1\frac{3}{4}$ miles wide. Concerning its origin, a legend was related to one of the translators of *Niebuhr's History*, by a peasant boy, who guided him to Frescati, as follows :—

"'Where the lake now lies, there once stood a great city. Here, when Jesus Christ came into Italy, He begged alms. None took compassion on Him but an old woman, who gave Him two handfuls of meal. He bade her leave the city : she obeyed: the city instantly sank ; and the lake rose in its place.' To set the truth of the story beyond dispute, the narrator added, *Sta scritto nei libri.*"—*Niebuhr's Hist. of Rome.*

"The lakes of Alba and Nemi, like others in the neighbourhood of Rome, are of a peculiar character. In their elevation, lying nestled as it were high up in the bosom of the mountains, they resemble what in Cumberland and Westmoreland are called tarns ; but our tarns, like ordinary lakes, have their visible feeders and outlets, their head which receives the streams from the mountain-sides, and their foot by which they discharge themselves, generally in a larger stream, into the valley below. The lakes of Alba and Nemi lie each at the bottom of a perfect basin, and the unbroken rim of this basin allows them no visible outlet.

* *Macaulay's Lays.*

Again, it sometimes happens that lakes so situated have their outlet under-ground, and that the stream which drains them appears again to the day after a certain distance, having made its way through the basin of the lake by a tunnel provided for it by nature. This is the case particularly where the prevailing rock is the mountain or metalliferous limestone of Derbyshire, which is full of caverns and fissures; and an instance of it may be seen in the small lake or tarn of Malham in Yorkshire, and another on a much larger scale in the lake of Copais in Bœotia. But the volcanic rocks, in which the lake of Alba lies, do not afford such natural tunnels, or at least they are exceedingly small, and unequal to the discharge of any large quantity of water; so that if any unusual cause swells the lake, it can find no adequate outlet, and rises necessarily to a higher level. The Roman tradition reported that such a rise took place in the year 357; it was caused probably by some volcanic agency, and increased to such a height, that the water at last ran over the basin of the hills at its lowest point, and poured down into the Campagna. Traces of such an outlet are said to be still visible; and it is asserted that there are marks of artificial cutting through the rock, as if to enlarge and deepen the passage. This would suppose the ordinary level of the lake in remote times to have been about two hundred feet higher than it is at present; and if this were so, the actual tunnel was intended not to remedy a new evil, but to alter the old state of the lake for the better, by reducing it for the time to come to a lower level. Possibly the discharge over the edge of the basin became suddenly greater, and so suggested the idea of diverting the water altogether by a different channel. But the whole story of the tunnel, as we have it, is so purely a part of the poetical account of the fall of Veii, that no part of it can be relied on as historical. . . . . Admitting that it was wholly worked through the tufa, which is easily wrought, still the labour and expense of such a tunnel must have been considerable; and in the midst of an important war, how could either money or hands have been spared for such a purpose? Again, was the work exclusively a Roman one, or performed by the Romans jointly with the Latins, as an object of common concern to the whole confederacy? The Alban lake can scarcely have been within the domain of Rome; nor can we conceive that the Romans could have been entitled to divert its waters at their pleasure without the consent of the neighbouring cities. But if it were a common work; if the Latins entered heartily into the struggle of Rome with Veii, regarding it as a struggle between their race and that of the Etruscans; if the overflow of the waters of their national lake, the lake which bathed the foot of the Alban mountain, where their national temple stood, and their national solemnities were held, excited an interest in every people of the Latin name, then we may understand how their joint labour and joint contributions may have accomplished the work even in the midst of war ; and the Romans, as they disguised on every occasion the true nature of their connexion with the Latins, would not fail to represent it as exclusively their own."—*Arnold's Hist. of Rome*, vol. I. ch. xxiii.

Following the beautiful avenue of ilexes, known as the *Galleria di Sopra*, as far as the Convent of S. Francesco, we shall find a little path winding down through thickets of cistus and genista to the water's edge, where we may see the remains of the famous *Emissarium*, constructed B.C. 394. The extreme beauty of the spot is worthy of the romantic story of its origin.

"For seven years and more the Romans had been besieging Veii. Now the summer was far advanced, and all the springs and rivers were very low ; when on a sudden the waters of the Lake of Alba began to rise ; and they rose above its banks, and covered the fields and the houses by the water-side ; and still they rose higher and higher, till they reached the top of the hills which surrounded the lake as with a wall, and they overflowed where the hills were lowest ; and behold the water of the lake poured down in a mighty torrent into the plain beyond. When the Romans found that the sacrifices which they offered to the gods and powers of the place were of no avail, and their prophets knew not what counsel to give them, and the lake still continued to overflow the hills and to pour into the plain below, then they sent over the sea to Delphi, to ask counsel of the oracle of Apollo, which was famous in every land.

"So the messengers were sent to Delphi. And, meanwhile, the report of the overflowing of the lake was much talked of ; so that the people of Veii heard of it. Now there was an old Veientian, who was skilled in the secrets of the Fates, and it chanced that he was talking from the walls with a Roman centurion whom he had known before in the days of peace ; and the Roman spoke of the ruin that was coming upon Veii, and was sorry for the old man his friend ; but the old man laughed and said : ' Ah ! ye think to take Veii ; but ye shall not take it till the waters of the Lake of Alba are all spent, and flow out into the sea no more.' When the Roman heard this he was much moved by it, for he knew that the old man was a prophet ; and the next day he came again to talk with the old man, and he enticed him to come out of the city, and to go aside with him to a lonely place, saying that he had a certain matter of his own concerning which he desired to know the secrets of fate: and while they were talking together, he seized the old man, and carried him off to the Roman camp, and brought him before the generals; and the generals sent him to Rome to the Senate. Then the old man declared all that was in the Fates concerning the overflow of the Lake of Alba; and he told the Senate what they were to do with the water, that it might cease to flow into the sea: 'If the lake overflow, and its waters run out into the sea, woe unto Rome; but if it be drawn off, and the waters reach the sea no longer, then it is woe unto Veii.' But the Senate would not believe the old man's words, till the messengers should come back from Delphi.

"After a time the messengers came back, and the answer of the god agreed in all things with the words of the old man at Veii. For it said, 'See that the waters be not confined within the bason of the lake; see that they take not their own course and run into the sea. Thou shalt let the water out of the lake, and thou shalt turn it to the watering of thy fields, and thou shalt make courses for it till it be spent and come to nothing.' Then the Romans believed the oracle, and they sent workmen, and began to bore through the side of the hills to make a passage for the water. And the water flowed out through this passage underground; and it ceased to flow over the hills; and when it came out from the passage into the plain below, it was received into many courses which had been dug for it, and it watered the fields, and became obedient to the Romans, and was all spent in doing them service, and flowed to the sea no more. And the Romans knew that it was the will of the gods that they should conquer Veii."—*Arnold's Hist. of Rome.*

"L'emissaire fonctionne encore aujourd'hui; par lui les eaux du lac *arrosent la campagne romaine* et vont se jeter *non dans la mer* mais dans *le Tibre:* l'oracle a donc été obéi, aussi Véies a été prise."— *Ampère, Hist. Rom.* ii. 526.

The opening of the Emissarium is enclosed within a Nymphæum of imperial date, such as is beautifully described in the lines of Virgil :—

"Fronte sub adversa scopulis pendentibus antrum ;
Intus aquæ dulces, vivoque sedilia saxo ;
Nympharum domus."

Æn. i. 167.

A *custode* (who resides at Castel Gandolfo) is required to

open the grating. Italians always set fire to little paper boats, which they call "fates," and float them down through the darkness, where they may be seen burning for an immense distance. Near the Nymphæum are many ruins of other Roman buildings known by the country people as Bagni di Diana, Grotte delle Ninfe, &c. All probably are remains of the summer retreats of Domitian.

"Quand, par un beau jour de printemps, on contemple le lac endormi dans une coupe de verdure et réfléchissant les gracieuses ondulations de ses bords, à la pensée de Domitien on voit apparaître le bateau où Pline le Jeune nous le montre troublé par du bruit des rames, dont chaque coup le fait tressaillir. Il fallait cesser de ramer et le remorquer. 'Alors,' dit Pline, 'immobile dans ce bateau muet, il semblait traîné comme à une expiation.'"—*Ampère, L'Emp. Rom.* ii. 135.

Clambering up the hill again, we find the height crested by the fine trees overhanging the wall of the *Villa Barberini*. The beautiful grounds of this villa may always be visited by strangers, and present an immense variety of lovely views, from a foreground, half cultivated and half wild, ending in a grand old avenue of umbrella-pines. The ruins, which we see here in such abundance, are supposed to be remains of the Villa of Pompey, or of the "insane structures," as Cicero calls them, belonging to the villa of Clodius. As we wander here we cannot but call to mind the whole grand invocation of Cicero in his speech in behalf of Milo against the owner of this villa.

"And you, hills and groves of Alba, you, I say, I entreat and implore, and you, the ruined shrines of the Albans, so closely knit with all that is revered by the people of Rome, altars which this fellow in his headlong madness had dared to strip and rob of their holy groves, and bury beneath the insane piles of his own buildings. Then it was your shrines, your rites that were honoured, your influence which prevailed, which he had insulted with crime of every kind, and thou, from thy lofty peak, great Jupiter Latiaris, whose lake and woods and fields he had often defiled with every abominable wickedness and crime, at last thou openedst thine eyes to punish him : to you, late though you might deem it, his punishment was a just and due atonement."

Words fail to paint the glories of Italian sunset as seen from the Villa Barberini.

" Various as the Campagna is in outline it is quite as various in colour, reflecting every aspect of the sky, and answering every touch of the seasons. Day after day it shifts the slide of its wondrous panorama of changeful pictures—now tender in the fresh green and flower-flush of spring—now golden in the matured richness of summer—and now subdued and softened into purple-browns in the autumn and winter. Silent and grand, with shifting opal hues of blue, violet, and rose, the mountains look upon the plain. Light clouds hide and cling to their airy crags, or drag along them their trailing shadows. Looking down from the Alban Hill one sees in the summer noons wild thunder-storms, with sloping spears of rain and flashing blades of lightning, charge over the plain and burst here and there among the ruins, while all around the full sunshine basks upon the Campagna, and trembles over the mountains. Towards twilight the landscape is transfigured in a blaze of colour—the earth seems fused in a fire of sunset—the ruins are of beaten gold—the meadows and hollows are as crucibles where delicate rainbows melt into every tone and gradation of colour—a hazy and misty splendour floats over the shadows, and earth drinks in the glory of the heavens. Then softly a grey veil is drawn over the plain, the shadow creeps up the mountain-side, the purples deepen, the fires of sunset fade away into cold ashes—and sunset is gone almost while we speak. The air grows chill, and in the hollows and along the river steal long white snakes of mist—fires from the stubble begin to show here and there—the sky's deep orange softens slowly into a glowing citron, with tinges of green, then refines into paler yellows, and the great stars begin to look out from the soft deep-blue above. Then the Campagna is swallowed up in dark, and chilled with damp and creeping winds."—*Story's Roba di Roma*, i. 324.

Close to the entrance of the villa, is the town-gate of *Castel Gandolfo,* the favourite summer residence of the popes for the last two hundred and fifty years, and the only portion of their property outside the Vatican walls, left untouched since the Sardinian occupation. The place was the fortress of the Gandolfi family in the 12th century, when Otho Gandolfi was senator of Rome. In 1218, it passed to the Savelli, who held it for four hundred years, triumphantly defying all attempts to wrest it from them. In 1596 it was raised into a duchy for Bernardino Savelli by Sixtus V., but poverty obliged him to sell the property to the government for 150,000 scudi, an enormous sum in those days. Clement VIII., by a decree of 1604, incorporated it with the temporal domain of the Holy See, and included it expressly in the bull of Pius V. *de non infeudandis bonis Ecclesiæ*. It was reserved for Urban VIII. in 1604 to adopt it as a residence, and to build the palace from designs of Carlo Maderno, Bartolomeo Breccioli, and Domenico Castelli. Urban came every year to Castel Gandolfo, and a large number of his bulls are dated from hence. The pontifical palace was enlarged by Alexander VII., and completed by Clement XIII. The interior is furnished in the simplest manner and is little worth visiting. Pius IX. spent part of each summer here, before the invasion; and every afternoon saw him riding on his white mule in the old avenues or on the terraced paths above the lake, followed by his cardinals in their scarlet robes—a most picturesque and mediæval scene.

The *Church of S. Thomas of Villanuova*, close to the palace, was built 1661, by Bernini, for Alexander VII. Its altar-piece is by *Pietro da Cortona*.

Not many tourists penetrate to the other side of the lake, yet here, it is established with tolerable certainty, was the *Site of Alba Longa*, the mother city of Rome. As the town was entirely destroyed by Tullus Hostilius, who removed its inhabitants to Rome, and established them on the Cœlian, its situation was long a disputed point with topographers, and was generally asserted to be that now occupied by Palazzuola, but Sir W. Gell discovered traces of an ancient road leading up the hills from the plain to the further shore of the lake, and suddenly terminating there at a turn of the precipice. This caused an examination of the spot to which it led, and resulted in the discovery of vast blocks of masonry and portions of columns buried beneath the underwood, probably fragments of the temples of the gods which Strabo tells us were spared by the Romans amid the general destruction. A knoll to the north was also found to be covered with ruins.

Alba was the metropolis of the cities of Latium before the building of Rome. Its foundation is ascribed by the Latin poets to Ascanius, and its name to the white sow of Eneas, and her thirty little pigs.

"Ex quo ter denis urbem redeuntibus annis
Ascanius clari condet cognominis Albam."
Æn. viii. 47.

"Et stetit Alba potens, albæ suis omine nata."
Propert. iv. *El.* i.

" . . . . . Tum gratus Iülo,
Atque novercali sedes prælata Lavino,
Conspicitur sublimis apex ; cui candida nomen
Scrofa dedit."
Juv Sat. xii. 70.

Lycophron however (*Cassandra*, v. 1255) says that the sow was black.

"La truie figure encore dans les armes de la petite ville d'Albano, et un bas-relief qui la représente au milieu de sa famille, encastré dans le mur d'une maison du-dessus d'une fontaine, a donné à une rue de Rome le nom de rue *de la Truie* (Via della Scrofa) ; allusion bien moderne à un bien antique souvenir."—*Ampère, Hist. Rom.* i. 196.

Since attention was first turned to this spot, every succeeding discovery has curiously confirmed the opinion that it is the true site of Alba.

"The characteristics of the city of Alba, says Dionysius of Halicarnassus, were, 'that it was so built, with regard to the mountain and the lake, that it occupied a space between them, each seeming like a wall of defence to the city.' . . . Livy (Lib. i. c. 3) has a passage, which is too descriptive of Alba Longa to be omitted: 'Ascanius, abundante Lavinii multitudine . . . novam ipse aliam sub Albano monte condidit; quæ ab situ *porrectæ in dorso urbis*, Longa Alba adpellata.' Dionysius also (Lib. i.) informs us that the name Longa was added 'on account of the shape (τοῦ σχήματος) of its ground plan;' Varro, that it was called Longa, 'propter loci naturam;' and Aurelius Victor, 'eamque ex formâ, quòd ita in longum porrecta est, Longam cognominavit."

. . . "There is a tradition, that the palace of the kings of Alba stood on a rock, and so near the edge of the precipice, that when the impiety of one of its monarchs provoked Jupiter to strike it with his lightning, a part of the mass was precipitated into the lake, carrying the impious king along with the ruins of his habitation. Now this tradition is apparently confirmed by a singular feature in a part of the remains of this city; for directly under the rock of the citadel towards the lake, and where the palace, both for security and prospect, would have been placed, is a cavern about fifty feet in depth, and more than one hundred in width, a part of the roof of which has evidently fallen in, and some of its blocks remain on the spot. This may be visited from below without difficulty, by a small path used by goat-herds and wood-cutters, leading across four deep ravines to Palazzuola."—*Sir W. Gell.*

It is a beautiful walk or drive back to Albano, through the *Galleria di Sotto*, shaded by huge ilexes which were planted by Urban VIII., or are even of older date. These gigantic trees, acquainted for centuries, often lean together against the walls as if in earnest conversation; often, faint from old age, are propped on stone pillars, supported by which, they hang out towards the Campagna. At the end of the avenue we come upon Pompey's Tomb, beneath which are some of the *Capanne* or shepherds' huts of reeds, described by Virgil. On the opposite side of the Via Appia stands the

Villa Alticri, consecrated now to the Italian heart as having

Galleria di Sotto, Albano.

been the residence of the noble and self-devoted cardinal, who died a martyr to his self-sacrifice in the cholera of 1867.

The disease appeared quite suddenly during the first week in August. At that time Albano was especially crowded with visitors of high and low degree, from the Royal Family of Naples and the principal members of the Roman aristocracy, to the thrifty Jewish salesman from the Ghetto, intent on combining a stroke of business with change of air. On a beautiful Monday afternoon various parties were given in the gardens of the principal villas, and as Albano had always hitherto been exempt from attacks of pestilence, no alarm was felt, though there were already cases of cholera at Rome. Suddenly a cloud, bringing a strange chill, seemed to rise out of the Campagna; cloaks and wraps were brought out for those who were feasting in the gardens, but the chill passed away as quickly as it had come, and was succeeded by great heat. Almost immediately the pestilence began. People were attacked on the garden-seats as they sat. Before morning there were 115 cases and 15 deaths. All who could, fled to Rome and the neighbouring towns. "The prevailing features of the scene were the processions of priests with the consecrated host, litters conveying the sick to the hospital, and carts conveying the dead to the cemetery. The usual agents in the latter operation, being by no means adequate in number to the amount of doleful work thus devolved upon them, were aided by the soldier of a company of Zouaves, who had been sent to Albano for change of air after recovery from fever, and who arrived opportunely on the very morning when their aid was so much needed. Telegraphic messages were sent to Rome repeatedly in the course of the day, requesting medical aid, instructions, and vehicles. Cardinal Altieri, being bishop of Albano, came out from the capital to encourage the towns-people by his presence, and take the direction of affairs. In the course of the afternoon many people arrived from Rome in a state of great anxiety about their families or relatives, whom they had left at Albano, and whom they were desirous of conveying elsewhere as soon as possible. Means of transport to the capital by the high road became suddenly scarce, and the drivers of omnibuses down to the station availed themself of the opportunity of exacting double fare from the panic-stricken fugitives who surrounded the vehicles." At the entrance of the Olmata of Genzano, a cordon was established, and no one was allowed to pass without undergoing fumigation. On the same day the Royal Family of Naples was attacked, some of the servants died, and one of the princes was taken ill.

On the second morning "the dead-carts rolled drearily about the town, stopping here and there to take up rude wooden boxes, rather than coffins, for conveyance to the cemetery of the Madonna della Stella. Many of the shops were shut up, their owners having either died or emigrated. Fruit-stalls were abolished." All who could, endeavoured to reach a purer air if possible, but it was already difficult, as "the authorities of Ariccia had placed *guardiani* with guns to prevent any one crossing the great viaduct from Albano, and all the neighbouring towns, except Rome, had drawn the same inextricable cordon." The attacks of the disease were so sudden that if a carriage containing five fugitives took the way towards Rome, three were frequently dead before it reached the walls of the city.

By the third morning 120 deaths from cholera had occurred in the village of Albano. People fled in every direction. "Along the road were families migrating in all sorts of waggons and vehicles: the country farm-houses were resorted to all round, though it was the fever season, and it seemed as if there would soon be none left to kill in Albano. But unfortunately most of the fugitives took away the germ of the malady with them, and died wherever they might chance to have taken refuge." On the evening of the 8th, the Queen-Dowager of Naples died, after an illness of only four hours' duration, and on the same day the Princess Colonna, having fled to Genzano to the palace of Duke Cesarini, to whom her eldest daughter was engaged, was seized with cholera at luncheon, and died in a few hours.

Meanwhile Cardinal Altieri was unremitting in his attentions to the sick and dying, giving himself too little rest either by night or day, but on the Friday he was himself seized with the malady, and died on Sunday the 11th. On the same day Mr John Macdonald, brother of the well-known sculptor, died soon after effecting his escape to Rome. Frightful mortality began amongst the regiment of Zouaves who had so courageously devoted themselves to the dead, and almost all of them perished—chiefly, it is said, because, owing to the rapid succession of deaths, and the impossibility of finding grave-diggers, the corpses buried on the first day in one large grave had to be packed to give more space!

On the 13th the cholera catastrophe at Albano had reached such a degree that the most necessary relations of social existence might be said to be annihilated. With the exception of the Gonfaloniere, who took flight early, all the local authorities were either ill or dead, and the Pope had sent out Monsignor Apolloni, as special commissary, to assume the government of the town. The last of the bakers who had the courage to remain in Albano and carry on his trade died on the 12th, so that to prevent the surviving inhabitants from starving, bread and other provisions had to be sent out from Rome.

After the 14th the cholera began to abate, having carried off more than one-tenth of the population.—*From the Letters of the " Times Correspondent."*

The monument of Cardinal Altieri is the only object of interest in the *Cathedral*, which stands in a small square behind the principal street. It is inscribed:—

Ludovicus de Alteriis, Card. S.E.R. Episc. Albanus,

Pastor bonus cum in medium gregem dira sæviente lue advolasset, præclarum vitæ cursum morte magnanima consummavit sanctissime,

III Id. Aug. MDCCCLXVII. Vixit annos LXII.

Celebrated among the bishops of Albano was Pietro Aldobrandini (S. Pietro Igneo), who walked through fire at Settimo in 1067, to prove a charge of simony against Pietro di Pavia, bishop of Florence.

The festa of S. Pancrazio—the patron of Albano—is kept here with great solemnity.

"From the cathedral issued, at an early hour, a procession whose length almost corresponded to that of the town itself. There were little girls in tinsel finery, with butterfly-wings, intended to represent angels, and chubby little boys who toddled along in the disguise of Carmelite friars, curiously contrasting with the gravity of friars full grown, bearded

capuchins, venerable canons, and full-armed soldiers. There was the
Gonfaloniere with his two councillors; the local magistracy, in long
robes of black silk and velvet lined with silver tissue, with flat black caps,
looking not unlike some of Titian's portraits; and another conspicuous
group, very different, formed by young girls in long white satin dresses,
with veils covering not only the head but the lower part of the face,
each attended by a buxom matron in the gayest local costume—a bright-
coloured bodice, white linen veil folded square over the brow, and ample
folds of muslin round the largely-developed bust, their full-blown charms
further set off by a profusion of gold ornaments chiselled in a style resembling those in Etruscan museums — precisely such figures as Pinelli
and many other artists have delighted to introduce in *genre* pictures illus-
trative of Italian life and scenery. The younger females were those
selected to receive small dowries out of a fund appropriated to charity,
such donations being annually conferred at the religious seasons in
Albano. Next to the female group came about a hundred members of
a lay fraternity in their peculiar costume with hoods, carrying large
crucifixes and banners painted on both sides with sacred figures life-size,
and, finally, the principal group of clergy, the first in dignity supporting
under a crimson canopy a bust of silver-gilt containing the skull of S.
Pancrazio."—*Hemans' Catholic Italy.*

On the right of the main street, on entering the Roman
gate, is the *Villa Doria*, whose grounds, abounding in ancient
ilex groves, and in fragments of ruin of imperial date, are of
the most extreme beauty.

About a mile below the town the ruins of the *Castello
Savelli* crown a conical hill above the plain, and form a
pleasant object for a short excursion. The great family
of the Savelli continued to be lords of Albano till the
middle of the sixteenth century, when tragical circumstances
led to their extinction. The young and handsome heir of
the house was betrothed to the daughter of the Marchese
del Vasto of Naples, who had a dowry of 800,000 crowns.
But while waiting for his bride to attain her thirteenth year,
when the marriage was to be solemnized, he became passion-
ately in love with a beautiful young girl of Albano, of
humble but respectable parentage. Her father, fearing the

addresses of his young lord, hastened her marriage with one Cristoforo, a vassal of the Savelli. But the young count continued to persecute her with his attentions, took a house immediately opposite to the married pair, and wrote constantly in the hope of softening the object of his love. She remained faithful to her husband, to whom she showed all the letters of the count: but Cristoforo constantly mistrusted her, and was full of jealousies. One day he borrowed her flounced petticoat (guardinfante) and other attire, and forced her to write a letter to Savelli appointing an assignation, persuading her that he only intended to humiliate him by a disappointment.

Savelli arrived at the rendezvous and was received by Cristoforo in his wife's dress, who shot him through the heart, cut his throat, and dragged the corpse to the front of the Savelli palace, where he left it weltering in its blood. On the discovery of the murder all the inhabitants of Albano were shut up in their houses to prevent flight. Cristoforo had made good his escape, but his innocent wife and all her family were arrested and frequently put to the torture, in the hope of extorting the whereabouts of the fugitive, of which they were really ignorant. After six months' imprisonment, the relatives were set at liberty, but the wife was condemned to death, and was only saved by the intervention of the Duchess of Parma, who received her into her service, from whence she was transferred to that of the Duchess of Modena.

The bereaved father never recovered the shock of his son's murder, and died in a lunatic asylum, and the only survivor of the Savelli having no heir, all the property of that ancient race passed to the family of Chigi.

CHAPTER III.

MONTE CAVO, NEMI, AND CIVITA LAVINIA.

(Donkeys should be taken for the excursion from Albano to Monte Cavo and Nemi, except by very good walkers—price, four francs each, the donkey-man four francs, the guide seven francs, for the day. Civita Lavinia will form a pleasant separate drive for the afternoon from Albano—a carriage ought not to cost more than seven or eight francs.

Those who ascend Monte Cavo from Rome, and return thither in the same day, may take the morning train to Frascati, or, still better, drive thither, and send on their carriages to the Hotel de Russie at Albano (as being the hotel nearest to the "galleries" and the Roman gate). They may then take donkeys at Frascati (price, five francs for the day), and ascend Monte Cavo by Rocca di Papa. After passing some time at the temple, they may descend by the Madonna del Tufo, Palazzuola, and skirting the Alban Lake, visit Castel Gandolfo, and ride through the "galleries" to Albano. Good walkers may also see Nemi the same day, but this is too great a hurry to be commended. The rest is an easy day's work, and allows time for returning to Rome in the evening from Albano, where the horses will have rested for many hours. Those who do not bring a carriage from Rome, and intend returning by the railway, must recollect that the Albano station is $2\frac{1}{3}$ miles distant from the town, and that fatigue and distance, as well as expense, are thus greatly increased.)

ASCENDING the stony path which leads from Albano to the Cappuccini, and reaching the corner whence we overlook the glassy lake, sleeping in its deep wooded hollow, let us turn to the right by the tempting path which winds through the woods and rocks, between banks which in spring are quite carpeted with cyclamen, violets, hepaticas, and every shade of anemone, while higher up, amid the richly flowering laurestinus and genista, patches of brilliant pink "honesty" glow in the sunshine. At every turn the flowers become lovelier, and the fore-grounds more as if they were waiting for an artist to paint them, till, passing between some jagged masses of rock, which have fallen down from the higher cliffs long ago, but have been half buried for centuries under luxuriant drapery of ferns and moss, we reach, above the southern end of the lake, the Franciscan monastery of *Palazzuola*.

Here we may allow our donkeys to rest for a few minutes on the little rounded platform which so beautifully overlooks the lake, and stop to examine a *Consular Tomb* cut in the rock, which overhangs the garden of the convent, and which resembles in style many of the tombs in Etruria. It is attributed to Caius Cornelius Scipio Hispallus, consul and pontifex-maximus, though he died at Cumæ, on the very slight ground that he was first attacked with his fatal illness, paralysis, while on a pilgrimage to the temple of the Alban Mount, in B.C. 176.

A path winding upwards through the woods leads from hence to the little sanctuary of the *Madonna del Tufo*, much frequented by the country people, whence a beautiful terrace fringed with ilexes extends to the picturesque village of *Rocca di Papa*, which occupies an isolated sugar-loaf rock standing out from the rest of the mountain-side and crowned by the ruins of a castle, which for two centuries was a stronghold of the Colonnas, but afterwards (1487) passed into the hands of the Orsini.

"All know that, in those ages, the poor and weak had the choice of being assassinated in two ways, but they were obliged to choose ; either assassinated by casual wandering brigands, or by established brigands, settled in the fortresses. Generally the preference was given to the second, and thus around the fortresses was formed a trembling settlement of hovels and huts of contadini, which were afterwards changed into villages, towns, and cities, a preference which speaks to the praise of those poor calumniated barons of the middle-ages."—*Massimo d'Azeglio.*

"Rocca di Papa est un cône volcanique couvert de maisons superposées jusqu'au faîte, qui se termine par un vieux fort ruiné. Les caves d'une zone d'habitations s'appuient sur les greniers de l'autre ; les maisons se tombent continuellement sur le dos ; le moindre vent fait pleuvoir des tuiles et craquer des supports. Les rues, peu à peu verticales, finissent par des escaliers qui finissent eux-mêmes par des blocs de lave supportant une ruine difficile à aborder, et flanquée d'un vieil arbre qui se penche sur la ville, comme une bannière à la pointe d'un clocher.

"Tout cela est vieux, crevassé, déjeté et noir comme la lave dont est sorti ce réceptacle de misère et de malpropreté. Mais, vous savez, tout cela est superbe pour un peintre. Le soleil et l'ombre se heurtent vivement sur des angles de rochers qui percent de toutes parts à travers les maisons, sur des façades qui se penchent l'une contre l'autre, et tout à coup se tournent le dos pour obéir aux mouvements du sol, âpre et tourmenté, qui les supporte, les presse et les sépare. Comme dans les faubourgs de Gênes, des arceaux rampants relient de temps en temps les deux côtés de la ruelle étroite, et ces ponts servent eux-mêmes de rues aux habitants du quartier supérieur.

"Tout donc est précipice dans cette ville folle, refuge désespéré des temps de guerre, cherché dans le lieu le plus incommode et le plus impossible qui se puisse imaginer. Les confins de la steppe de Rome sont bordés, en plusieurs endroits, de ces petits cratères pointus, qui ont tous leur petit fort démantelé et leur petite ville en pain de sucre, s'écroulant et se relevant sans cesse, grâce à l'acharnement de l'habitude et à l'amour du clocher.

"Cette obstination s'explique par le bon air et la belle vue. Mais cette vue est achetée au prix d'un vertige perpétuel, et cet air est vicié par l'excès de saleté des habitations. Femmes, enfants, vieillards, cochons et poules grouillent pêle-mêle sur le fumier. Cela fait des groupes bien pittoresques, et ces pauvres enfants, nus au vent et au soleil, sont souvent beaux comme des amours. Mais cela serre le cœur quand-même. Je crois d'ailleurs que je m'habituerais jamais à les voir courir sur ces abîmes. L'incurie des mères, qui laissent leurs petits, à peine âgés d'un an, marcher et rouler comme ils peuvent sur ces talus effrayants, est quelque chose d'inouï qui m'a semblé horrible. J'ai demandé s'il n'arrivait pas souvent des accidents.

"'Oui,' m'a-t-on répondu avec tranquillité, 'il se tue beaucoup d'enfants et même de grandes personnes. Que voulez-vous, la ville est dangereuse!'"—*George Sand, La Daniella.*

Rocca di Papa is frequently used as a summer residence by English who are detained all the year round in the neighbourhood of Rome: but it is not desirable, being so exposed to the sun, with very little shade. The place derives its present name from the residence here of the anti-pope John, in A.D. 1190.

By the steep path which scrambles up the rocks above the house-tops of Rocca di Papa, we reach a wide grassy plain known as the *Campo di Annibale* from a tradition that Hannibal encamped there when marching against Rome.*
In spring it is covered with snow-drops, *pan-di-neve* the Italians call them. Hence we enter the forest, and under the green boughs and gnarled stems of the over-arching trees, in the hollow way lined with violets and fumitory, we find the great lava blocks of the pavement of the Via Triumphalis still entire.

> "Quaque iter est Latiis ad summam fascibus Albam:
> Excelsa de rupe procul jam conspicit urbem."
> *Lucan.* iii. 87.

The marks of chariot-wheels still remain. Pope Alexander VII. was the last person who enjoyed a triumph here in the footsteps of Julius Cæsar, and he was drawn up in a carriage. The stones are frequently marked V. N., signifying Via Numinis.

"Le lac d'Albano était entouré d'une forêt. Ovide est sur ce point d'accord avec Tite Live (v. 15), et la tradition qui donne à plusieurs rois fabuleux d'Alba le nom de *Sylvius, Homme des bois,* semble confirmer par les témoignages les plus anciens la vérité de ce double témoignage.

"Aujourd'hui, on ne trouve un bout de forêt que plus haut, en

---

* See *Livy*, xxvi. cap. 10.

gravissant le Mont-Albain (Monte-Cavi), à l'endroit où, sous les grands chênes, apparaissent tout à coup, parmi les feuilles tombées, les dalles de la voie Triomphale."—*Ampère, Hist. Rom.* i. 47.

" Up this same Alban Mount, to the temple of Jupiter Latiaris, which was for Alba what the Capitol was for Rome, the dictators of Alba and Latium undoubtedly led their legions when they returned in triumph. This solemnity, in which the triumphant generals appeared in royal robes, was unquestionably derived from the period of the monarchy : nor would the Latin commanders deem themselves inferior to the Romans, or bear themselves less proudly, when they were not subject to the imperium of the latter, or show less gratitude to the gods. Indeed their triumph was preserved in that which the Roman generals solemnized on the Alban Mount: for that the first who assumed this honour (C. Papirius Maso) was renewing an earlier usage, is at least far more probable, than that he should have ventured to assume a distinction of his own devising. He triumphed here, not properly as a Roman consul, but as commander of the Latin cohorts, belonging partly to the towns of ancient Latium, partly to the colonies which sprang out of that state after it was broken up, and which represented it. At this distance from Rome he was secured from interruption by his imperium: and the honour was bestowed on him by the acclamation of the Latins, seconded by that of the Italian allies, and perhaps expressing itself by the otherwise inexplicable salutation of *imperator*, given to generals after a victory ; a salutation which, at least after the Latins and their allies had all received the freedom of the city, was used by the Roman legions ; as they may have joined in it previously, when its origin was forgotten. In early times, if fortune was propitious, Latin triumphs might be celebrated, for wars conducted by Latin generals under their own auspices. and even, by virtue of their equality in the league, with Latin legions under their command."—*Niebuhr's Hist. of Rome,* ii. 36.

The top of the mount is a grassy platform, in the centre of which is a Passionist Convent, built in 1788 by Cardinal York, who destroyed the ruins of the famous temple for the purpose. The only remains are some massive fragments of wall and the huge blocks of masonry which surround a grand old wych-elm tree in front of the convent. The Latin Feriæ had been always celebrated on the Alban Mount ; and there Tarquin erected the temple of Jupiter Latiaris, probably with the idea of doing something popular, in using a site

Remains of the Temple of Jupiter Latiaris, Monte Cavo.

once consecrated to the protecting god of the Latin confederation :

"Et residens celsâ Latiaris Jupiter Albâ."
Lucan. Phars. i. 198.

Piranesi says that the temple was 240 ft. long and 120 wide—the having the width half the length being according to Etruscan taste. Servius had already built a temple for the Latins (that of Diana) upon the Aventine—but :

"Le Monte Albain, qui s'élève à trois mille pieds au-dessus de la mer et domine tout la Latium, allait mieux au Superbe, visant dans tous ses monuments et dans tout son règne à la grandeur et à la magnificence, que l'humble Aventin, l'un des séjours de le *plebs* latine favorisée par Servius et méprisée par Tarquin."—*Ampère, Hist. Rom.* i. 214.

Instead of sacrificing a bull on the Capitol, on the summit of the Alban Mount Crassus sacrificed a sheep—*ovem*—hence *ovation*.

"La route des Ovations est celle qu'on suit aujourd'hui pour arriver au sommet du Mont Albain. Une partie, qui est très-bien conservée, frappe le voyageur quand elle lui apparait tout à coup au sein d'une forêt solitaire. Il est encore imposant ce souvenir, même du petit triomphe."
—*Ampère, Hist. Rom.* iv. 416.

On the Alban Mount, Juno, in the *Æneid*, stood to contemplate the country, in the same way that tourists do in our days :—

> " At Juno, e summo, qui nunc Albanus habetur,
> Tum neque nomen erat, nec honos aut gloria monti,
> Prospiciens tumulo, campum adspectabat, et ambas
> Laurentum Troümque acies, urbemque Latini."
>
> *Æn.* xii. 134.

And truly the view is worthy of the eyes of a goddess, though the heights of Monte Pila close it in towards the south.

" From the summit of the Alban Mount, by the light of the setting sun, the eye can reach Corsica and Sardinia ; and the hill which still bears the name of Circe looks like an island beneath the first rays of her heavenly sire. The line of the long street of Alba, stretching between the mountain and the lake, may still be made out distinctly. Monte Cavo was the Capitoline hill of Alba; its summits required to be fortified, to secure the town from above : and there is great probability in the conjecture, that, as the citadel at Rome was distinct from the Capitoline temple, the Rocca di Papa was the citadel of Albano."—*Niebuhr's Hist. of Rome*, i. 199.

Hence, by the green lanes of *La Fajola*, once notorious for their brigands, and by winding pathlets through delicious woods, and narrow ways between green meadows (somewhat difficult to find without a guide), passing a farm of the Corsini, we descend upon the second lake of our pilgrimage.

> "Lo, Nemi! navelled in the woody hills
> So far, that the uprooting wind which tears
> The oak from his foundation, and which spills
> The ocean o'er his boundary, and bears
> Its foam against the skies, reluctant spares

The oval mirror of thy glassy lake ;
And, calm as cherish'd hate, its surface wears
A deep cold settled aspect nought can shake,
All coiled into itself and round, as sleeps the snake."
                                    Byron's Childe Harold.

"Ovide dit, en parlant du lac de Nemi : ' Là est un lac ceint d'une épaisse forêt.'

'. . . . . . Sylva præcinctus opacâ
Est lacus.' (*Fast.* iii. 263.)

Il y'avait donc en cet endroit une forêt. Cette forêt était assez considérable pour faire donner au sanctuaire de la Diane d'Aricie le nom de *Nemus*. Ce bois n'existe plus, mais il a laissé son nom au lac charmant et au village pittoresque de *Nemi*."—*Ampère, Hist. Rom.* i. 48.

Nemi.

The village of *Nemi* (far more worth visiting than Genzano) is beautifully situated on the edge of a steep cliff above the lake, and is surmounted by a fine old castle which, after passing through the hands of the Colonna, Borgia, Piccolomini, Cenci, Frangipani, and Braschi, is now the property of Prince Rospigliosi.

"The water is surrounded in parts by rocks of the hardest basaltic lava, in others by conglomerated cinders and scoriæ, and in some places by banks of tufa. Its circumference is about five miles, and the level of the water higher than that of the Alban lake. The story of the ship discovered at the bottom of this lake, and said by some authors to have belonged to the time of Tiberius, by others to that of Trajan, is well known. Biondi, Leon Battista Alberti, and particularly Francesco Marchi, a celebrated architect and military engineer of the sixteenth century, who went down into the lake himself, have spoken of it. Fresh investigations have been carried on of late, at which I was present, and I assert that the pretended ship was nothing more than the wooden piles and timbers used in the foundations of a building. The beams were of fir and larch, and were joined by metal rails of various sizes. The pavement, or at least the lowest stratum of the remains, was formed of large tiles placed upon a kind of grating of iron, on which the name Caisar in ancient letters was marked.

"The name Caisar seems to explain the history of the building. For Suetonius, in his *Life of Julius Cæsar*, as an illustration of the Dictator's extravagance, asserts, that after having built a villa on the lake of Nemi at an enormous expense, he had the whole destroyed because it did not quite suit his taste. It is my belief that the pretended ship was nothing else than the piles and wooden framework upon which this villa was supported, and that after the upper part was destroyed the foundation under the water still remained, partly covered by fragments of the demolished building above."—*Nibby*.

Nemi occupies the site of the ancient town of Nemus.

"Albanus lacus, et socii Nemorensis ab unda."
Propert. iii. *El.* 22.
"Nemus . . . glaciale Dianæ."
Stat. Silv. iv. 4.

Diana must have had a grove and temple here as well as at Ariccia. The fountain into which she is supposed to have changed the nymph Egeria after the death of Numa is pointed out on the way to Genzano.

"Non tamen Egeriæ luctus aliena levare
Damna valent; montisque jacens radicibus imis
Liquitur in lacrymas: donec pietate dolentis
Mota soror Phœbi gelidum de corpore fontem
Fecit, et æternas artus tenuavit in undas."
Ovid. Metam. xv. 547.

Genzano, which forms so conspicuous a feature in the view

from Nemi, is reached by a circuitous walk along the ridges of the hills. The slopes beneath the town are occupied by the gardens of Duke Sforza-Cesarini (which an order or even "a silver key" will generally open to visitors). The scenery of this beautiful hill-side is photographed in the description of H. Christian Andersen.

"The lake of Nemi slept calmly in the great round crater, from which at one time fire spouted up to heaven. We went down the amphitheatre-like, rocky slope, through the great beech wood and the thick groves of plane trees, where the vines wreathed themselves amongst the tree-branches. On the opposite steep lay the city of Nemi, which mirrored itself in the blue lake. As we went along we bound garlands, entwining the dark green olive and fresh vine-leaves with the wild golden cistus. Now the deep-lying blue lake and the bright heavens above us were hidden by the thick branches and the vine-leaves, now they gleamed forth again as if they were only one united infinite blue. Everything was new and glorious to me; my soul trembled for its great joy. There are even still moments in which the remembrance of these feelings comes forth again like the beautiful mosaic fragments of a buried city.

"The sun burned hotly, and it was not until we were by the water-side, where the plane trees raise aloft their ancient trunks from the lake, and bend down their branches, heavy with enwreathing vines, to the watery mirror, that we found it cool enough to continue our work. Beautiful water-plants nodded here as if they dreamed under the cool shadow, and they too made part of our garlands. Presently, however, the sunbeams no longer reached the lake, but only played upon the roofs of Nemi and Genzano; and the gloom descended upon where we sate. I went a little distance from the others, yet only a few paces, for my mother was afraid that I should fall into the lake where it was deep and the banks were steep. Not far from the small stone ruins of an old temple of Diana there lay a huge fig-tree which the ivy had already begun to bind fast to the earth; I climbed upon this, and wove a garland whilst I sang from a canzonet,—

> Ah, rossi, rossi fiori,
> Un mazzo di viole!
> Un gelsomin d'amore."

The *Palazzo Cesarini* contains nothing of interest, but is associated with one of those dramas of real life which are seldom found out of Italy. A Duchess Cesarini dreamt before her confinement that she should give birth to twins, one of whom would endanger the happiness of the other. Determined to obviate this misfortune, she bribed the midwife to convey one of the children away as soon as it was born, and bring it up as a peasant. This was done, and the young Cesarini served as a shepherd, supposing himself to be a shepherd's son, till after he came of age. Then his adopted shepherd-mother happened to hear that the young Duke Cesarini and his father and mother were dead and that there was no heir to the fortunes and title, and going to the palace with the midwife, she was able to produce indisputable proofs to the astonished heirs-at-law which established the claims of the shepherd-boy, who was sent to Paris to be educated and became the late Duke Cesarini.

Genzano is now chiefly celebrated for the festival of the *Infiorata*, which takes place on the eighth day after Corpus Domini, and is wonderfully appropriate to this land of flowers.

"I dreamed till the sun shone in at my window, and awoke me to the beautiful feast of flowers.

"How shall I describe the first glance into the street—that bright picture as I then saw it? The entire, long, gently-ascending street was covered with flowers; the ground colour was blue; it looked as if they had robbed all the gardens, all the fields, to collect flowers enough of the same colour to cover the street; over these lay in long stripes, green, composed of leaves, alternately with rose-colour, and at some distance from this was a similar stripe, as it were a broad border to the whole carpet. The middle of this represented stars and suns, which were formed by a close mass of yellow, round, and star-like flowers; more labour still had been spent upon the formation of names—here flower was laid upon flower, leaf upon leaf. The whole was a living flower-carpet, a mosaic floor, richer in pomp of colouring than anything which Pompeii can show. Not a breath of air stirred—the flowers lay immoveable, as if they were heavy, firmly-set precious stones. From all the windows were hung upon the walls large carpets, worked in leaves and flowers, representing holy pictures. Here Joseph led the ass on which sat the Madonna and the child; roses formed the faces, the feet, and the arms, gilly-flowers and anemones their fluttering garments; and crowns were made of white water-lilies, brought from Lake Nemi. Saint Michael fought with the dragon; the holy Rosalia showered down roses upon the dark blue globe, wherever my eye fell flowers related to me Biblical legends; and the people all round about were as joyful as myself. Rich foreigners, from beyond the mountains, clad in festal garments, stood in the balconies, and by the side of the houses moved along a vast crowd of people, all in full holiday costume, each in the fashion of his country. The sun burnt hotly, all the bells rang, and the procession moved along the beautiful flower-carpet; the most charming music and singing announced its approach, choristers swung the censer before the Host, the most beautiful girls in the country followed, with garlands of flowers in their hands, and poor children, with wings to their naked shoulders, sang hymns, as of angels, while awaiting the arrival of the procession at the high altar. Young fellows wore fluttering ribands around their pointed hats, upon which a picture of the Madonna was fastened; silver and gold rings hung to a chain round their necks, and handsome bright-coloured scarfs looked splendidly upon their black velvet jackets. The girls of Albano and Frascati came, with their thin veils elegantly thrown over their black, plaited hair, in which was stuck the silver arrow; those of Velletri, on the contrary, wore garlands around their hair, and the smart handkerchief, fastened so low down in the dress as to leave visible the beautiful shoulder and the round bosom. From Abruzzi, from the Marshes, from every other neighbouring district, came all in their peculiar national costume, and produced altogether the most brilliant effect. Cardinals, in their mantles woven with silver, advanced under canopies adorned with flowers, then monks of various orders, all bearing burning tapers. When the procession came out of church, an immense crowd followed."—*The Improvisatore.*

We were at Genzano on Good Friday, when all the boys of the place were busy, not only "grinding Judas's bones" in the ordinary fashion, i.e. by rattling them together in a box, but were banging large planks of wood and broad strips of bark up and down upon the church steps, with almost frantic fury, to show what good Christians they were.

We took a little carriage in the piazza of Genzano in which we rattled merrily down the hill-side for about two miles to

Civita Lavinia, occupying the site of the ancient Lanuvium,

Breaking Judas' bones. Genzano.

and remarkable as the birth-place of the Emperors Antoninus Pius and Commodus, of T. Annius Milo the enemy of Clodius, of Roscius the comedian, L. Murœna who was defended by Cicero, and P. Sulpicius Quirinus who was Cyrenius the Governor of Syria, mentioned in St. Luke's Gospel. Lanuvium was celebrated for the worship of Juno Sospita, and when it took part with the other Latin cities against Rome and was defeated, its inhabitants were not only unpunished, but admitted to the rights of Roman citizens, on condition that the temple of their goddess should be common to the Romans also.

"Quos Castrum, Phrygibusque gravis quondam Ardea misit,
Quos celso devexa jugo Junonia sedes
Lanuvium."
Sil. Ital. viii. 361.

"Lanuvio generate, inquit, quem Sospita Juno
Dat nobis, Milo, Gradivi cape victor honorem."
xiii. 364.

"Inspice, quos habeat nemoralis Aricia Fastos
 Et populus Laurens, Lanuviumque meum :
 Est illic mensis Junonius."
Ovid. Fast. vi. 59.

"Livy mentions the Juno of Lanuvium more than once. Lib. xxi. 62, he says, 'among other prodigies, it was affirmed that the spear of Lanuvian Juno vibrated spontaneously, and that a raven flew into the temple;' and again: 'forty pounds of gold were sent to Lanuvium, as an offering to the goddess.' In another place he says (xxiii. 31), 'the statues at Lanuvium in the temple of Juno Sospita, shed blood, and a shower of stones fell round the temple;' and in Lib. xxiv. 10: 'the crows built nests in the temple of Juno Sospita at Lanuvium.' Cicero also, in Orat. pro Mur. ad fin., speaks of the sacrifices made by the consuls to Juno Sospita, in connection with the 'municipium honestissimum' of Lanuvium. In Propertius we read,

 'Lanuvium annosi vetus est tutela draconis.'

There were great treasures in the temple, which Augustus borrowed, as well as those of the Capitol, of Antium, Nemus, and Tibur."
Sir W. Gell.

From Civita Lavinia.

Civita Lavinia is approached by a terrace commanding a grand view across the Pontine Marshes to the Circean mount. It stands on the edge of the promontory and is surrounded by dark walls of peperino, in many places apparently of great antiquity. At the western extremity is a building which Gell imagines may be the cella of the temple of Juno. Curious old mediæval houses are everywhere built upon the walls, and are highly picturesque, and near the gateway is a very fine machicolated tower. In the little piazza is a magnificent sarcophagus, now used as a fountain. Some remains of the theatre were found in 1831, on the western slope below the town, and the ancient paved road may still be traced in its descent towards the cities of the plain.

(Standing out from the main line of hills, below Genzano are two projecting spurs. The higher is *Monte Due Torre*, once crowned by two towers, of which only one is now standing, the other lying in ruins beside it. The lower, covered with vineyards and fruit gardens, and only marked at the summit by a low tower and some farm buildings, is now called *Monte Giove*, but is almost universally allowed to have been the famous Corioli, the great Volscian city, which gave the title of Coriolanus to its captor, C. Marcius, and which was once at the head of a confederation almost too strong for Rome.

"There was a war between the Romans and the Volscians: and the Romans attacked the city of Corioli. The citizens of Corioli opened their gates, and made a sally, and drove the Romans back to their camp. Then Caius ran forwards with a few brave men, and called back the runaways, and he stayed the enemy and turned the tide of battle, so that the Volscians fled back into the city. But Caius followed them, and when he saw the gates still open, for the Volscians were flying into the city, then he called to the Romans, and said, 'For us are yonder gates set wide rather than for the Volscians; why are we afraid to rush in?' He himself followed the fugitives into the town, and the enemy fled before him; but when they saw that he was but one man they turned against him; but Caius held his ground, for he was strong of hand, and light of foot, and stout of heart, and he drove the Volscians to the furthest side of the town, and all was clear behind him, so that the Romans came in after him without any trouble and took the city. Then all men said, 'Caius and none else has won Corioli,' and Cominius the general said, 'Let him be called after the name of the city.' So they called him Caius Marcius Coriolanus."—*Arnold's Hist. of Rome.*

The farm-house on Monte Giove now stands desolate amongst its vineyards, and there are no remains of the ancient city above-ground. It is supposed that the present name of the hill commemorates a temple of Jupiter which may have remained to later times, for the Romans usually spared the temples of the cities they destroyed. In imperial times the town had quite disappeared.

" There was a time when Tibur and Præneste, our summer retreats, were the objects of hostile vows in the Capitol, when we dreaded the shades of the Arician groves, when we could triumph without a blush over the nameless villages of the Sabines and Latins, and even Corioli could afford a title not unworthy of a victorious general."—*Florus, temp. Hadrian.*)

In returning to Albano (from Civita Lavinia) we pass through the triple avenue of elms called the *Olmata*, planted in 1643 by Giuliano Cesarini, as an approach to his palace of Genzano. Then, on the left, we pass the handsome Church of *La Madonna del Galloro*, beneath which the substructions which raised the Via Appia above the level of the plain, deserve observation.

CHAPTER IV.

FRASCATI, TUSCULUM, AND COLONNA.

(Trains leave Rome at 11.30 and 12.5, returning at 5.40 and 6.18. This gives time for a pleasant sight of Frascati, and for a ride or walk to Tusculum and the Villa Mondragone, or to Tusculum and Grotta Ferrata. There is an excellent small inn at Frascati—the Albergo di Londra—very clean and comfortable. Donkeys cost 5 francs for the whole day, or $2\frac{1}{2}$ francs for the half day; but a distinct agreement must be made.)

IT is only half-an-hour by rail to Frascati, and the change is so complete and reviving, that it is strange more sojourners at Rome do not take advantage of it. Only one excursion to Frascati is generally made during a Roman winter, which gives little time where there is so much to be seen.

Even the railway journey is most delightful and characteristic. The train runs close to the aqueducts, the Paoline first, and then the ruined Claudian. As we pass outside the Porta Furba, the artificial sepulchral mound, called *Monte de Grano*, is seen on the left, and then the vast ruins called *Sette Basse*, belonging to a suburban villa of imperial date,[*] and, as the light streams through their ruined windows,

---

[*] The carriage-road to Frascati passes close to both of these, and then by the beautiful stone-pines on the farm of *Torre Nuova* belonging to Prince Borghese, where archæologists place Papinia, the villa of Attilius Regulus.

forming a beautiful foreground to the delicate distances of mountain and plain.

As we approach nearer, Colonna is seen on the left upon its knoll, then Monte Porzio, and beneath it the site of the Lake Regillus. When the lights and shadows are favourable, the difference between the two craters of this volcanic chain of hills now becomes strikingly evident.

"The Alban hills form a totally distinct group, consisting of two principal extinct volcanic craters, somewhat resembling in their relation to each other the great Neapolitan craters of Vesuvius and Somma. One of them lies within the embrace of the other, just as Vesuvius lies half enclosed by Monte Somma. The walls of the outer Alban crater are of peperino, while those of the inner are basaltic. Both are broken away on the northern side towards Grotta Ferrata and Marino, but on the southern side they are tolerably perfect.

"The outer crescent-shaped crater beginning from Frascati extends to Monte Porzio and Rocca Priora, and then curves round by Monte Algido, Monte Ariano, and Monte Artemisio. The inner crescent includes the height of Monte Cavo, and surrounds the flat meadows known by the name of Campo d'Annibale. Besides these two principal craters, the ages of which are probably as distinct as those of Vesuvius and Somma, there are traces of at least four others to be found in the lakes of Castel Gandolfo, commonly called the Alban lake, and of Nemi, and in the two small cliff-encircled valleys of the Vallis Aricina and Larghetto."—*Burn, The Roman Campagna.*

The effect of the Campagna here, as everywhere, is quite different upon different minds. The French almost always find it as depressing as the English do captivating and exhilarating.

"Frascati est à six lieues de Rome, sur les monts Tusculans, petite chaîne volcanique qui fait partie du système des montagnes du Latium. C'est encore la Campagne de Rome, mais c'est la fin de l'horrible désert qui environne la capitale du monde catholique. Ici la terre cesse d'être inculte et la fièvre s'arrête. Il faut monter pendant une demi-heure, au pas des chevaux, pour atteindre la ligne d'air pur qui circule au-dessus de la région empestée de la plaine immense ; mais cet air pur est moins dû à l'élévation du sol qu'à la culture de la terre et a l'écoulement des eaux, car Tivoli, plus haut perché du double que Frascati, n'est pas à l'abri de l'influence maudite.

"Aux approches de ces petites montagnes, quand on a laissé derrière soi les longs aqueducs ruinés et trois ou quatre lieues de terrains ondulés, sans caractère et sans étendue pour le regard, on traverse de nouveau une partie de la plaine dont le nivellement absolu présente enfin un aspect particulier assez grandiose. C'est un lac de pâle verdure qui s'étend sur la gauche jusqu'au pied du massif du mont Gennaro. Au baisser du soleil, quand l'herbe fine et maigre de ce gigantesque pâturage est un peu échauffée par l'or du couchant et nuancée par les ombres portées des montagnes, le sentiment de la grandeur se révèle. Les petits accidents perdus dans ce cadre immense, les troupeaux et les chiens, seuls bergers qui, en de certaines parties de la steppe, osent braver la *malaria* toute la journée, se dessinent et s'enlèvent en couleur avec une netteté comparable à celle des objets lointains sur la mer. Au fond de cette nappe de verdure, si unie que l'on a peine à se rendre compte de son étendue, la base des montagnes semble nager dans une brume mouvante, tandis que leurs sommets se dressent immobiles et nets dans le ciel."—*George Sand, La Daniella.*

Beyond Ciampino, the railroad ascends out of the Campagna into the land of corn and olives. Masses of pink nectarine and almond-trees bloom in spring amid the green. On the right, we pass the great ruined castle of *Borghetto*, which belonged to the Savellis in the 10th century. At the station, an open omnibus with awnings (fare, 50 centesimi), and carriages, are waiting to save travellers the mile of steep ascent to the town. Here, passing near the Villa Sora, once the residence of Gregory XIII. (1752-85), and skirting the wall of the Villa Torlonia, we are set down in the noisy little piazza before the cathedral, and are at once surrounded by donkey boys vociferating upon the merits of their respective animals.

The cathedral (S. Pietro) only dates from 1700, but we must enter it to visit the monument (near the door), which Cardinal York put up to his brother Prince Charles Edward, who died Jan. 31, 1788. It is inscribed :—

"Hic situs est Carolus Odoardus cui Pater Jacobus III. Rex Angliæ, Scotiæ, Franciæ, Hiberniæ, Primus Natorum, paterni Juris et regiæ dignitatis successor et hæres, qui domicilio sibi Romæ delecto Comes Albaniensis dictus est.

"Vixit Annos LVII. et mensem ; decessit in pace, pridie Kal. Feb. Anno MDCCLXXXVII."

There is an older cathedral, *Duomo Vecchio*, now called SS. Sebastiano e Rocco, chiefly of the 14th century, and near it a fountain erected in 1480 by Cardinal d'Estouteville, the French Ambassador. The streets are dirty and ugly; but the little town is important as being the centre of the villas which give Frascati all its charm. Most of these date only from the 17th century, and, with the exception of the Villa Mondragone, the buildings are seldom remarkable, but they are situated amid glorious groves of old trees, often relics of a natural forest, and amid these are grand old fountains and water-falls, which, though artificial, have been long since adopted by Nature as her own, while from the terraces the views over the Campagna are of ever-varying loveliness. In many of these villas, far too large for any single occupants, vast airy suites of apartments may be hired for the summer *villeggiatura*, and, though scantily furnished, are a delightful retreat during the hot season.

"At Frascati and Albano there are good lodgings to be had. Noble old villas may be hired on the Alban slopes for a small rent, with gardens going to ruin, but beautifully picturesque—old fountains and water-works painted with moss, and decorated with maiden hair, vines, and flowers—shady groves where nightingales sing all the day—avenues of lopped ilexes that, standing on either side like great chandeliers, weave together their branches overhead into a dense roof—and long paths of tall, polished laurel, where you may walk in shadow at morning and evening. The air here is not, however, 'above suspicion ;' and one must be careful at night-fall lest the fever prowling round the damp alleys seize you as its prey. The views from these villas are truly exquisite. Before you lies the undulating plain of the Campagna, with every hue and changing tone of colour ; far off against the horizon flashes the level line of the Mediterranean ; the grand Sabine hills rise all along on the west, with Soracte lifting from the rolling inland sea at their base ; and in the distance swells the dome of St. Peter's. The splendours of sunset as they stream over this landscape are indescribable, and in the noon the sunshine seems to mesmerise it into a magic sleep."—*Story's Roba di Roma.*

"Les collines Tusculanes ne sont, d'ici à leur point le plus élevé, qu'un immense jardin partagé entre quatre ou cinq familles princières. Et quels jardins ! celui de Piccolomini ne compte plus. Vendu à des bourgeois qui font argent de leur propriété, il n'a de beau que ce que l'on n'a pu lui ôter. Mais la villa Falconieri, qui le borne à l'est, et la villa Aldobrandini, qui le borne au couchant, la villa Conti, qui touche à cette dernière ; plus haut, la Ruffinella, et, en revenant vers l'est, la Taverna et Mondragone, tout cela se tient et communique, si bien que j'en aurais pour trois heures à vous décrire ces lieux enchantés, ces futaies monstrueuses, ces fontaines, ces bosquets et ces escarpements semés de ruines romaines et pélasgiques ; ces ravins de lierre, de liseron, et de vigne sauvage, où pendent des restes de temples, et où tombent des eaux cristallines. Je renonce au détail qui viendra peut-être par le menu ; je ne peux que vous donner une notion de l'ensemble.

"Le caractère général est de deux sortes : celui de l'ancien goût italien, et celui de la nature locale qui a repris le dessus, grâce à l'indifférence ou à la décadence pécuniaire des maîtres de ces folles et magnifiques résidences. Si vous voulez une exacte description de ces résidences, telles qu'elles étaient encore il y a cent ans, vous la trouverez dans les spirituelles lettres du président de Brosses, un des hommes qui, malgré son apparente légèreté, a le mieux vu l'Italie de son temps. Il s'est beaucoup moqué des *jeux* d'eaux et girandes, des statues grotesques et des concerts hydrauliques de ces villégiatures de Frescati. Il a eu raison. Lorsqu'il voyait dépenser des sommes folles et des efforts d'imagination puérile pour créer ces choses insensées, il s'indignait de cette décadence du goût dans le pays de l'art, et il riait au nez de tous ces vilains faunes et de toutes ces grimaçantes naïades outrageusement mêlés aux débris de la statuaire antique. Il appelait cela gâter l'art et la nature à grands frais d'argent et de bêtise, et je m'imagine que, dans ce temps-là, quand tous ces fétiches étaient encore frais, quand ces eaux sifflaient dans ces flûtes, que les arbres étaient taillés en poires, les gazons bien tondus et les allées bien tracées, un homme de sens et de liberté comme lui devait, à bon droit, s'indigner et se moquer.

"Mais s'il revenait ici, il y trouverait un grand et heureux changement : les Pans n'ont plus de flûte, les nymphes n'ont plus de nez. A beaucoup de dieux badins, il manque davantage encore, puisqu'il rien reste qu'une jambe sur le socle. Le reste gît au fond des bassins. Les eaux ne soufflent plus dans des tuyaux d'orgue ; elles bondissent encore dans des conques de marbre et le long des grandes girandes ; mais elles y chantent de leur voix naturelle. Les rocailles se sont tapissées de vertes chevelures, qui les rendent à la vérité. Les arbres ont repris leur essor puissant sous un climat énergique, et sont devenus des colosses encore jeunes et pleins de santé. Ceux qui sont morts ont dérangé la symétrie des allées ; les parterres se sont remplis de folles herbes ; les fraises et les violettes ont tracé des arabesques aux contours des tapis verts ; la mousse a mis du velours sur les mosaïques criardes : tout a pris un air de révolte, un cachet d'abandon, un ton de ruine et un chant de solitude.

"Et maintenant, ces grands parcs jetés aux flancs des montagnes forment, dans leurs plis verdoyants, des vallées de Tempé, où les ruines rococo et les ruines antiques dévorées par la même végétation parasite donnent à la victoire de la nature un air de gaieté extraordinaire. Comme en somme, les palais sont d'une coquetterie princière ou d'un goût charmant ; que ces jardins, surchargés de détails puérils, avaient été dessinés avec beaucoup d'intelligence sur les ondulations gracieuses du sol, et plantés avec un vrai sentiment de la beauté des sites ; enfin, comme les sources abondantes y ontété habilement dirigées pour assainir et vivifier cette région bocagère, il ne serait pas rigoureusement vrai de dire que la nature y a été mutilée et insultée. Les brimboriens fragiles y tombent en poussière ; mais les longues terrasses d'où l'on dominait l'immense tableau de la plaine, des montagnes et de la mer ; les gigantesques perrons de marbre et de lave qui soutiennent les ressauts du terrain, de qui ont, certes, un grand caractère ; les allées couvertes qui rendent ces vieux Édens praticables en tout temps ; enfin tout ce qui, travail élégant, utile et solide, a survécu au caprice de la mode, ajoute au charme de ces solitudes, et sert à conserver, comme dans des sanctuaires, les heureuses combinaisons de la nature et la monumentale beauté des ombrages. Il suffit de voir, autour des collines de Frascati, l'aride nudité des monts Tusculans, ou l'humidité malsaine des vallées, pour reconnaître que l'art est parfois bien nécessaire à l'œuvre de la création."
—*George Sand, La Daniella.*

Nothing can describe the charm of the villa life at Frascati,—the freshness of the never-ceasing fountains, the deep shade of the thick woods, the splendour of the summer fruits, and, above all, the changing glories of the view, which is unlike any other in the world, over the vast plain, in which the world's capitol seems almost to be lost in the immensity and luminousness of the pink haze.

Opposite to the gate of the town, opens that of the *Villa Torlonia*—the Pincio of Frascati—and the great resort of its inhabitants. The villa itself is not worth visiting, but the view from its terrace is most beautiful, and a grand waterfall tumbles down a steep behind the house, through the magnificent ilex-groves. This type of villa is well pourtrayed by Miss Edwards.

"We went down a broad walk, wide enough for a carriage drive, and completely roofed in by thick trees. Weeds grew unheeded in the gravel, and last year's leaves lay thick on the ground. Here and there, in the green shade, stood a stone seat brown with mosses ; or a broken urn ; or a tiny antique altar, rifled from a tomb—and presently we reached a space somewhat more open than the rest, with a shapeless mass of reticulated brick-work and a low arch guarded by two grim lions, in the midst. Here the leaves had drifted more deeply, and the weeds had grown more rankly than elsewhere ; and a faint oppressive perfume sickened on the air. We pushed our way through the grass and brambles, and looked down into the darkness of that cavernous archway. A clinging damp lay on the old marble lions, and on the leaves and blossoms of the trailing shrubs that overgrew them. A green lizard darted by on a fragment of broken wall. A squirrel ran up the shaft of a stately stone pine that stood in the midst of the ruins.

"At length we emerged upon a terrace that bounded the gardens on this side. The Campagna and the hills lay spread before us in the burning sun-set, and a shining zone of sea bounded the horizon. Long shadows streamed across the marble pavement, and patches of brilliant light pierced through the carved interstices of the broken balcony. A little fountain dripped wearily in the midst, surmounted by a headless Triton, and choked with water-weeds ; whilst all along the parapet, with many a gap, the statues of the Cæsars stood between us and the sun."—*Barbara's History.*

Below the Villa Torlonia, the *Villa Pallavicini*, with an ilex-crested terrace, projects over the plain. Above it, is the *Villa Aldobrandini*, standing grandly upon a succession of terraces, designed by Giacomo della Porta, and finished

Palazzo Aldobrandini, Frascati.

by Giovanni Fontana for Cardinal Pietro Aldobrandini, nephew of Clement VIII. The villa is adorned internally with frescoes by *Cav. d'Arpino*. Behind it a succession of waterfalls tumble through a glorious old ilex-grove, into a circle of fantastic statues. The scene may once have been ridiculous, but Nature has now made it most beautiful.

"At the Villa Aldobrandini, or Belvidere, we were introduced to the most multifarious collection of monsters I ever hope to behold. Giants, centaurs, fauns, cyclops, wild beasts, and gods, blew, bellowed, and squeaked, without mercy or intermission; and horns, pan's-pipes, organs, and trumpets, set up their combined notes in such a dissonant chorus, that we were fain to fly before them; when the strains that suddenly burst forth from Apollo and the Nine Muses, who were in a place apart, compelled us to stop our ears, and face about again in the opposite direction.

"When this horrible din was over, we were carried back to admire the now silent Apollo and the Muses,—a set of painted wooden dolls, seated on a little mossy Parnassus, in a summer-house,—a plaything we should have been almost ashamed to have made even for the amusement of children. All these creatures, in the mean time, were spouting out water. The lions and tigers, however, contrary to their usual habits, did nothing else; and the 'great globe itself,' which Atlas was bearing on his shoulders, instead of 'the solid earth,' proved a mere aqueous ball, and was overwhelmed in a second deluge."—*Eaton's Rome.*

Those who are not good walkers, should engage donkeys for the excursion to Tusculum, to which a steep ascent leads from the piazza of the town, between the walls of the villas Aldobrandini and Falconieri. Just beyond the latter, an inscription marks the humble retreat of the learned Cardinal Baronius. A steep hill leads to the Convent of the Cappuccini, but our path passes through the shady and delightful walks of the *Villa Rufinella*, which is now the property of Prince Lancellotti, having formerly belonged to the Buonapartes. The casino was built by Vanvitelli. The chapel contains monuments of the Buonaparte family. During the residence of Lucien Buonaparte here (Nov. 1818), this villa was the scene of one of the boldest acts of brigandage known in the Papal States. A party of robbers, who had their rendezvous at Tusculum, first seized the old priest of the family as he was out walking, and having plundered and stripped him, bound him hand and foot. As they surmised, when the dinner-hour arrived, and the priest was missing, a servant was sent out in search of him, and left the door open, through which five bandits entered, and attacking the servants they met, forced them to silence by threats of instant death. One maid-servant, however, escaped, and gave warning to the party in the dining-room, who all had time to hide themselves, except the Prince's secretary, who had already left the room to discover the cause of the noise, and who was carried off, together with the butler, and a *facchino*. The old priest meanwhile contrived to escape and conceal himself in some straw.

The next day the *facchino* was sent back to treat with the Prince, and to say that unless he sent a ransom of 4000 crowns the prisoners would be immediately put to death. He sent 2000 and an order on his banker for the remainder. The brigands, greatly irritated, returned the order torn up with a demand for 4000 crowns more, and with this the Prince was forced to comply in order to preserve the lives of his attendants. The brigands escaped scot free !

A tomb which is passed at the entrance of Frascati towards the Villa Rufinella is said to be that of Lucullus, who is known to have had a villa here. This stood near the Villa of Cicero, who was accustomed to borrow books and fetch them with his own hand (*De Fin.* iii. 2) from the library of his friend. The scholiast on Horace describes the Villa of Cicero as being "ad latera superiora" of the hill, and its site is generally believed to have been that now occupied by the Villa Rufinella, and that the Casino stands on the site of his Academica, which had shady walks like those of Plato's Garden—forefathers of the walks which we still see.

The Tusculan Disputations of Cicero take their name from this beloved villa of his, which he bitterly complained of the Roman consuls valuing at only "quingentis millibus" —between £4000 and £5000. A complete picture of the villa may be derived from the many allusions to it in the works of Cicero, thus :—

"We learn that it contained two *gymnasia* (*Div.* i. *s.*), an upper one called the Lycæum, in which, like Aristotle, he was accustomed to walk and dispute in the morning (*Tusc. Disp.* ii. 3), and to which a library was attached (*Div.* ii. 3) ; and a lower one called the Academy (*Tusc. Disp.* ii. 3). Both were adorned with beautiful statues in marble and bronze (*Ep. ad Att.* i. 8, 9, 10). The villa likewise contained a little atrium (atriolum, *Ib.* i. 10 *ad Quint. Fr.* iii. 1), a small portico with exedria (*ad Fam.* vii. 23), a bath (*Ib.* xiv. 20), a covered promenade ('tecta ambulatiuncula,' *ad Att.* xiii. 29), and a horologium (*ad Fam.* xvi. 18). The villa, like the town and neighbourhood, was supplied by the Aqua Crabra (*De Leg. Agr.* iii. 31)."—*Smith's Dict. of Greek and Roman Geography.*

In his Essay on Old Age, Cicero describes the delights of country life as enjoyed in a villa of this kind.

"Where the master of the house is a good and careful manager, his wine-cellar, his oil-stores, his larder, are always well stocked; there is a fulness throughout the whole establishment; pigs, kids, lambs, poultry, milk, cheese, honey,—all are in abundance. The produce of the garden is always equal, as our country-folk say, to a second course. And all these good things acquire a double relish from the voluntary labours of fowling and the chase. What need to dwell upon the charm of the green fields, the well-ordered plantations, the beauty of the vineyards and olive-groves? In short, nothing can be more luxuriant in produce, or more delightful to the eye, than a well-cultivated estate."— *Trans. by Lucas Collins.*

Leaving the Villa Rufinella by shady avenues of laurel and laurestinus, the path to Tusculum emerges on the hillside, where, between banks perfectly carpeted with anemones and violets in spring, a street paved with polygonal blocks has been laid bare. On the left are remains of the small *Amphitheatre;* all the seats have perished, and it is only recognizable by its form. Beyond, also on the left, are the ruins of a villa, called, without authority, *Scuola di Cicerone.*

The path leads directly up to the most important of the ruins, the *Theatre,* which was excavated in 1839 by Maria Christina, Queen-dowager of Sardinia. With the exception of the walls of the *scena,* the lower walls are almost perfect, and the fifteen rows of seats in the lower circle (*cavea*) remain intact, though the upper rows have perished. The spectators, facing the west, had a magnificent view over the plains of Latium, with Rome in the distance. Close to the

Theatre of Tusculum.

Theatre are the remains of a piscina, and the fountain supplied from it.

"Je parvins au sommet de la montagne, en m'égarant dans de superbes bosquets. Puis, je me trouvai sur un long plateau dont le versant est aussi nu et aussi désert que celui que l'on monte depuis Frascati est ombragé et habité. Devant moi se présentait une petite voie antique, bordée d'arbres, qui, suivant à plat la crête douce de la montagne, devait me conduire à Tusculum.

"J'arrivai bientôt en vue d'un petit cirque de fin gazon, bordé de vestiges de constructions romaines. Un peu au-dessous, je pénétrai, à travers les ronces, dans la galerie souterraine par laquelle, au moyen de trappes, les animaux féroces, destinés aux combats, surgissaient tout à coup dans l'arène, aux yeux des spectateurs impatients. Ce cirque n'a de remarquable que sa situation. Assis sur le roc, au bout le plus élevé d'une étroite gorge en pente, qui s'en va rejoindre, en sauts gracieux et verdoyants, les collines plus basses de Frascati et en suite la plaine, il est là comme un beau siège de gazon, installé pour offrir au voyageur le plaisir de contempler à l'aise cette triste vue de la Campagne de Rome, qui devient magnifique, encadrée ainsi. Le remplement de la colline autour du cirque le préserve des vents maritimes. Ce serait un emplacement délicieux pour une villa d'hiver.

"J'y pris quelques moments de repos. Pour la première fois depuis que j'ai quitté Gênes, il faisait un temps clair. Les montagnes lointaines étaient d'un ton superbe, et Rome se voyait distinctement au fond de la plaine. Je fus étonné de l'emplacement énorme qu'elle occupe, et de l'importance du dôme de Saint-Pierre, qui, tout le monde vous l'a dit, ne fait pas grand effet, vu de plus près.

"En quittant cet amphithéâtre, je suivis, dans le désert, un chemin jonché de mosaïques des marbres les plus précieux, de verroteries, de tessons de vases étrusques et de gravats de plâtre encore revêtus des tons de la fresque antique. Je ramassai un assez beau fragment de terre cuite, représentant le combat d'un lion et d'un dragon. Je dédaignai de remplir mes poches d'autres débris ; il y en avait trop pour me tenter. La colline n'est qu'un amas de ces débris, et la pluie qui lave les chemins en met chaque jour à nu de nouvelles couches. Ce sol, quoique souvent fouillé en divers endroits, doit cacher encore des richesses.

"Le plateau supérieur est une vaste bruyère. C'était jadis, probablement, le beau quartier de la ville, car cette steppe est semée de dalles ou de moellons de marbre blanc. Le chemin était, sans doute, la belle rue patricienne. Des fondations de maisons des deux côtés attestent qu'elle était étroite, comme toutes celles des villes antiques. Au bout de cette plaine, le chemin aboutit au théâtre. Il est petit, mais d'une jolie coupe romaine. L'orchestre, les degrés de l'hémicycle sont entiers, ainsi que la base des constructions de la scène et les marches latérales pour y monter. L'avant-scène et les voies de dégagement nécessaires à l'action scénique sont sur place et suffisamment indiquées par leurs bases, pour faire comprendre l'usage de ces théâtres, la place des chœurs et même celle du décor.

"Derrière le théâtre est une piscine parfaitement entière sauf la voûte. On est là en pleine ville romaine. On n'a plus qu'à atteindre le faîte de la montagne pour trouver la partie pélasgique, la ville de Télégone, fils d'Ulysse et de Circé.

"Là, ces ruines prennent un autre caractère, un autre intérêt. C'est la cité primitive, c'est-à-dire la citadelle escarpée ; repaire d'une bande d'aventuriers, berceau d'une societé future. Les temples et les tombeaux des ancêtres y étaient sous la protection du fort. La montagne, semée de bases de colonnes qui indiquent l'emplacement des édifices sacrés, et bordée de blocs bruts dont l'arrangement dessine encore des ramparts, des poternes, et des portes, s'incline rapidement vers d'autres gorges bientôt relevées en collines et en montagnes plus hautes. Ce sont les monts Albains. Dans une de ces prairies humides où paissent les troupeaux, était le lac Régille, on ne sait pas où précisément. Le sort de la jeune Rome, aux prises avec celui des antiques nationalités du Latium, a été décidé là, quelque part, dans ces agrestes solitudes. Soixante-dix mille hommes ont combattu pour *être* ou *n'être pas*, et le destin de Rome, qui en ce terrible jour, écrasa les forces de trente cités latines, a passé sur l'Agro Tusculan comme l'orage, dont la trace est vite effacée par l'herbe et les fleurs nouvelles."—*George Sand, La Daniella.*

Behind the theatre rises the steep hill which was once crowned by the *Arx* of Tusculum, which was of great strength in early times. It was besieged by the Æquians in B.C.

457, and only taken when the garrison were starved out. In B.C. 374 it was successfully defended against the Latins. Dionysius mentions the advantage it received from its lofty position, which enabled its defenders to see a Roman army as it issued from the Porta Latina. The view is indeed most beautiful, over plain and mountains, the foreground formed by the remains of

> —"the white streets of Tusculum,
> The proudest town of all," *

scattered sparsely amongst the furze and thorn-bushes, but the ruins which now exist belong chiefly not to early times but to the mediæval fortress of the Dukes of Tusculum.

Including the Arx, the town of Tusculum was about 1¼ mile in circuit. The Roman poets ascribe the foundation of the city to Telegonus, the son of Circe and Ulysses.

> "Inter Aricinos Albanaque tempora constant,
> Factaque Telegoni moenia celsa manu."
> *Ovid. Fast.* iii. 91.

> "Et jam Telegoni, jam moenia Tiburis udi
> Stabant, Argolicæ quod posuere manus."
> *Ovid. Fast.* iv. 71.

> "At Cato, tum prima sparsus lanugine malas,
> Quod peperere decus Circæo Tuscula dorso
> Moenia, Laërtæ quondam regnata nepoti,
> Cunctantem impellebat equum."
> *Sil. Ital.* vii. 691.

> "Linquens Telegoni pulsatos ariete muros,
> Haud dignam inter tanta moram."
> *Sil. Ital.* xii. 535. †

Tusculum was remarkable for the steadiness of its friendship for Rome, which was only interrupted in B.C. 379, when in consequence of a number of Tusculans having been

---

* Macaulay, *Lays of Ancient Rome.*
† See also Horace, Epode i. 29, and Statius, Silv. i. 3, 83.

found amongst the prisoners made in the Volscian campaign, war was declared, and Camillus was sent against the city.

"But the Tusculans would not accept this declaration of hostilities, and opposed the Roman arms in a manner that has scarcely been paralleled before or since. When Camillus entered their territory he found the peasants engaged in their usual avocations ; provisions of all sorts were offered to his army, the gates of the town were standing open ; and as the legions defiled through the streets in all the panoply of war, the citizens within, like the countrymen without, were seen intent upon their daily business, the schools resounded with the hum of pupils, and not the slightest token of hostile preparation could be discerned. Then Camillus invited the Tusculan dictator to Rome. When he appeared before the senate in the Curia Hostilia, not only were the existing treaties with Tusculum confirmed, but the Roman franchise was shortly afterwards bestowed upon it, a privilege at that time rarely conferred." —*Smith's Dict. of Greek and Roman Geography.*

"In the times of the Latin League, from the fall of Alba to the battle of the Lake Regillus, Tusculum was the most prominent town in Latium. It suffered, like the other towns in Latium, a complete eclipse during the late. Republic and the Imperial times ; but in the ninth, tenth, eleventh, and twelfth centuries, under the Counts of Tusculum, it became again a place of great importance and power, no less than seven popes of the house of Tusculum having sat in the chair of S. Peter. The final destruction of the city is placed by Nibby, following the account given in the records of the Podestà of Reggio, in 1191, on the 1st of April, in which year the city was given up to the Romans by the Emperor Henry VI., and, after the withdrawal of the German garrison, was sacked and razed to the ground. Those of the inhabitants who escaped collected round the Church of S. Sebastian, at the foot of the hill, in the district called Frascati, whence the town of Frascati took its origin and name."—*Burn, The Roman Campagna.*

> "We had wandered long among those hills,
> Watching the white goats on precipitous heights,
> Half-hid among the bushes, or their young
> Tending new-yeaned : and we had paused to hear
> The deep-toned music of the convent bells,
> And wound through many a verdant forest path,
> Gathering the crocus and anemone,
> With that fresh gladness, which when flowers are new

In the first spring, they bring us, till at last
We issued out upon an eminence,
Commanding prospect large on every side;
But largest where the world's great city lay,
Whose features, undistinguishable now,
Allowed no recognition, save where the eye
Could mark the white front of the Lateran
Facing this way, or rested on the dome,
The broad stupendous dome, high over all.
And as a sea around an island's roots
Spreads, so the level champaign round the town
Stretched every way, a level plain, and green
With the new vegetation of the spring;
Nor by the summer ardours scorched as yet,
Which shot from southern suns, too soon dry up
The beauty and the freshness of the plains;
But to the right the ridge of Apennine,
Its higher farther summits all snow-crowned,
Rose, with white clouds above them, as might seem
Another range of more aërial hills.

These things were at a distance, but more near
And at our feet signs of the tide of life,
That once was here, and now had ebbed away—
Pavements entire, without one stone displaced,
Where yet there had not rolled a chariot-wheel
For many hundred years; rich cornices,
Elaborate friezes of rare workmanship,
And broken shafts of columns, that along
This highway side lay prone; vaults that were rooms,
And hollowed from the turf, and cased in stone,
Seats and gradations of a theatre,
Which emptied of its population now
Shall never be refilled : and all these things,
Memorials of the busy life of man,
Or of his ample means for pomp and pride,
Scattered among the solitary hills,
And lying open to the sun and showers,
And only visited at intervals
By wandering herds, or pilgrims like ourselves
From distant lands; with now no signs of life,
Save where the goldfinch built his shallow nest

> 'Mid the low bushes, or where timidly
> The rapid lizard glanced between the stones—
> All saying that the fashion of this world
> Passes away; that not Philosophy
> Nor Eloquence can guard their dearest haunts
> From the rude touch of desecrating Time.
> What marvel, when the very fanes of God,
> The outward temples of the Holy One,
> Claim no exemption from the general doom,
> But lie in ruinous heaps; when nothing stands,
> Nor may endure to the end, except alone
> The spiritual temple built with living stones?"
>
> *Archbishop Trench.*

Descending from the Arx, a path to the right leads through woods full of flowers to the *Camaldoli*, but nobody can pass the cross at the foot of the hill on which the convent stands, upon pain of excommunication. Here Cardinal Passionei lived in retirement, and occupied himself by collecting eight hundred inscriptions found amongst the ruins of Tusculum.

The whole of the inhabitants of the Camaldoli were carried off during an audacious outbreak of brigandage in the reign of Pius VII., but escaped during a skirmish with the Papal troops sent to their rescue. Since then the buildings have been surrounded with defensive walls with loopholes for the discharge of fire-arms. The aspect of the place is beautifully described by Cardinal Wiseman.

"The English college possesses a country house, deliciously situated in the village of Monte-Porzio. Like most villages in the Tusculan territory, this crowns a knoll, which in this instance looks as if it had been kneaded up from the valleys beneath it, so round, so shapely, so richly bosoming does it swell upwards; and so luxuriously clothed is it with the three gifts whereby 'men are multiplied' (Ps. iv. 8), that the village and its church seem not to sit upon a rocky summit, but to be half sunk into the lap of the olive, the vine, and the waving corn, that reach the very houses. While the entrance and front of this villa are upon the regular streets of the little town, the garden side stands upon the very verge of the hill-top; and the view, after plunging at once to the depths of the valley, along which runs a shady road, rises up a gentle acclivity, vine and olive clad, above which is clasped a belt of stately chestnuts, the bread-tree of the Italian peasant, and thence springs a round craggy mound, looking stern and defiant, like what it was—the citadel of Tusculum. Upon its rocky front the English students have planted a huge cross.

"Such is the view which presents itself immediately opposite to the spectator, if leaning over the low parapet of the English garden. Just where the vineyards touch the woods, as if to adorn both, there lies nestling what you would take to be a very neat and regular village. A row of houses, equidistant and symmetrical, united by a continuous dwarf wall, and a church with its towers in the midst, all of dazzling whiteness, offer no other suggestion. The sight would certainly deceive one, but not so the ears. There is a bell that knows no sleeping. The peasant hears it as he rises at day-break to proceed to his early toil; the vine-dresser may direct every pause for refreshment by its unfailing regularity through the day; the horseman returning home at evening uncovers himself as it rings forth the 'Ave;' and the muleteer singing on the first of his string of mules, carrying wine to Rome, at midnight is glad to catch its solemn peal, as it mingles with the tinkle of his own drowsy bells. Such an unceasing call to prayer and praise can only be answered, not by monks nor by friars, but by anchorites.

"And to such does this sweet abode belong. A nearer approach does not belie the distant aspect. It is as neat, as regular, as clean, and tranquil as it looks. It is truly a village divided by streets, in each of which are rows of houses exactly symmetrical. A small sitting-room, a sleeping cell, a chapel completely fitted up, in case of illness, and a wood and lumber room, compose the cottage. This is approached by a garden, which the occupant tills, but only for flowers, assisted by his own fountain abundantly supplied. While singing None in the choir, the day's meal is deposited in a little locker within the door of the cell, for each one's solitary refection. On a few great festivals they dine together; but not even the Pope, at his frequent visits, has meat placed before him. Everything, as has been said, is scrupulously clean. The houses inside and out, the well-furnished library, the stranger's apartments (for hospitality is freely given), and still more the church, are faultless in this respect. And so are the venerable men who stand in the choir, and whose noble voices sustain the church's magnificent psalmody with unwavering slowness of intonation. They are clad in white from head to foot, their thick woollen drapery falling in large folds; and the shaven head, but flowing beard, the calm features, the cast-down eyes, and often venerable aspect, make every one a picture, as solemn as Zurbaran ever painted, but without the sternness which he sometimes imparts to his recluses. They pass out of the church, to return home, all silent and unnoticing; but the guest-master will tell you who they are. I remember but a few. This is a native of Turin, who was a general in Napoleon's army, fought many battles, and has hung up his sword beside the altar, to take down in its place the sword of the Spirit, and fight the good fight within. The next is an eminent musician, who has discovered the hollowness of human applause, and has unstrung his earthly harp, and taken up the 'lyre of the Levite,' to join his strains to those of angels. Another comes 'curved like a bridge's arch,' as Dante says, and leaning on a younger arm, as he totters forward, one whose years are ninety, of which seventy have been spent in seclusion, except a few of dispersion, but in peace: for he refuses any relaxation from his duties. Then follows a fourth, belonging to one of the noblest Roman families, who yet prefers his cottage and his lentil to the palace and the banquet."—*Life of Pius VII.*

Below the Camaldoli we reach the gates of the *Villa Mondragone*, the Queen of Frascati villas. It belongs to the family of Borghese, but is used as a Jesuit College. The casino, built, from designs of Vansanzio, by Cardinal Altemps in the reign of Gregory XIII., is exceedingly magnificent, but still more so is the view from the vast and stately terrace in front, adorned with a grand fountain and tall columns.

"Imaginez-vous un château qui a trois cent soixante quatorze fenêtres, un château compliqué comme ceux d'Anne Radcliffe, un monde d'énigmes à débrouiller, un enchaînement de surprises, un rêve de Piranèse.

"Ce palais fut bâti au seizième siècle. On y entre par un vaste corps de logis, sorte de caserne destinée à la suite armée. Lorsque, plus tard, le pape Paul V. en fit une simple *villégiature*, il relia un des côtés de ce corps de garde au palais par une longue galérie, de plein-pied avec la cour intérieure, dont les arcades élègantes s'ouvraient, au couchant, sur un escarpement assez considerable, et laissent aujourd'hui passer le vent et la pluie. Les voûtes suintent, la fresque est devenue une croûte des stalactites bizarrées; des ronces et des orties poussent dans le pavé disjoint; les deux étages superposés au-dessus de cette galerie s'écroulent tranquillement. Il n'y a plus de toiture; les entablements du dernier étage se penchent et s'appaissent aux risques et périls des passants, quand passants il y a, autour de cette thébaïde.

"Cependant, la villa Mondragone, restée dans la famille Borghèse, à laquelle appartenait Paul V., était encore une demeure splendide, il y a une cinquantaine d'années, et elle revête aujourd'hui un caractère de désolation riante, tout à fait particulier à ces ruines prématurées. C'est durant nos guerres d'Italie, au commencement du siècle, que les Autrichiens l'ont ravagée, bombardée, et pillée. Il en est résulté ce qui arrive toujours en ce pays-ci après une secousse politique : le dégoût et l'abandon. Pourtant la majeure partie du corps de logis principal, la *partemedia*, est assez saine pour qu'en supprimant les dépendances inutiles, on puisse encore trouver de quoi restaurer une délicieuse *villégiature*."
—*George Sand, La Daniella.*

Joining the grounds of the Mondragone are those of the *Villa Taverna*, built in the 16th century, from designs of Girolamo Rainaldi. It was much used, until the change of Government, as a summer residence by the Borgheses.

A beautiful road along the ridge of the hill-side leads back to Frascati, or we may go on to the right towards Colonna, about four miles distant.

Not far below the Villa Mondragone is the volcanic *Lake of Cornufelle*. There is no longer any water here, but its bed is a crater about half a mile in diameter, and is evidently the place described by Pliny, where there was a grove of beeches (probably horn-beams—*carpini*) dedicated to Diana, one of which was so much admired by Passienus, the orator and consul, that he used to embrace it, sleep under it, and pour wine upon it. This is the spot described in Macaulay's Lays, as that

"—where, by Lake Regillus,
Under the Porcian height,
All in the lands of Tusculum,
Was fought the glorious fight."

And Arnold says :—

"The lake of Regillus is now a small and weedy pool surrounded by

crater-like banks, and with much lava or basalt about it, situated at
some height above the plain, on the right hand of the road as you descend from the high ground under La Colonna (Labicum), to the ordinary level of the Campagna, in going to Rome."—*Hist. of Rome,* i. 120.

"The Battle of the Lake Regillus, as described by Livy, is not an en-
gagement between two armies : it is a conflict of heroes, like those in
the *Iliad.* All the leaders encounter hand to hand ; and by them the
victory is thrown now into one scale, now into the other ; while the
troops fight without any effect. The dictator Postumius wounds King
Tarquinius, who at the first onset advances to meet him. T. Æbutius,
the master of the horse, wounds the Latin dictator : but he himself too
is disabled, and forced to quit the field. Mamilius, only aroused by his
hurt, leads the cohort of the Roman emigrants to the charge, and breaks
the front lines of the enemy ; this glory the Roman lays could not allow
to any but fellow-citizens, under whatever banner they might be fighting. M. Valerius, surnamed Maximus, falls as he is checking their
progress. Publius and Marcus, the sons of Publicola, meet their death
in rescuing the body of their uncle, but the dictator with his cohort
avenges them all, repulses the emigrants, and puts them to flight. In
vain does Mamilius strive to retrieve the day : he is slain by T. Herminius, the comrade of Cocles. Herminius again is pierced through with
a javelin, while stripping the Latin general of his arms. At length the
Roman knights, fighting on foot before the standards, decided the
victory : then they mounted their horses, and routed the yielding foe.
During the battle the dictator had vowed a temple to the Dioscuri.
Two gigantic youths on white horses were seen fighting in the van :
and from its being said, immediately after the mention of the vow, that
the dictator promised rewards to the first two who should scale the wall
of the enemy's camp, I surmise that the poem related, nobody challenged
these prizes, because the way for the legions had been opened by the
Tyndarids. The pursuit was not yet over, when the two deities appeared at Rome, covered with dust and blood. They washed themselves
and their arms in the fountain of Juturna beside the temple of Vesta,
and announced the events of the day to the people assembled in the
Comitium. On the other side of the fountain the promised temple was
built. The print of a horse's hoof in the basalt on the field of battle
remained to attest the presence of the heavenly combatants."—*Niebuhr's
Hist. of Rome,* i. 557.

On the right is the hill of *Monte Porzio,* said to have derived its name from the Porcian Villa of Cato the younger.
It is crowned by a large village, built by Gregory XIII.

(Buoncompagni), whose arms adorn its gateway. The church was consecrated by Cardinal York in 1766.

Beyond this, on the right, is *Monte Compatri*, a large village, cresting another hill, and belonging to the Borgheses. Further on is *Rocca Priora*, now identified with Corbio, the first place attacked by the Latin confederates in behalf of Tarquin, who, when they had expelled the garrison, hence ravaged all the surrounding country.

Rocca Priora stands high up on the *Monte Algido*, the second of the heights of which the Alban Hills are composed. On one of its peaks are remains which are referred to a temple of Diana mentioned by Horace.

> "Quæque Aventinum tenet Algidumque,
> Quindecim Diana preces virorum
> Curet."
>
> *Carm. Sæc.* 69.

The plain which separated the Mons Algidus from the heights near Tusculum was frequently a battle-field. In B.C. 458 Cincinnatus gained here his great victory over the Æquians under Clœlius Gracchus; and here, in B.C. 428, Postumius Tubertus conquered the combined armies of the Æquians and Volscians.

> "Scilicet hic olim Volscos Æquosque fugatos
> Viderat in campis, Algida terra, tuis."
>
> *Ovid. Fast.* vi. 721.

Horace mentions the cold climate of Algidus :—

> "Gelido prominet Algido."
>
> *Carm.* i. 21.

> 'Nivali pascitur Algido."
>
> iii. 23.

And its black woods :—

> "Nigræ feraci frondis in Algido."
>
> iv. 4.

Silius Italicus, however, speaks of the pleasures of a residence here :—

> " . . Nec amœna retentant
> Algida."
>
> xii. 536.

On the left we now reach an insulated hill crowned by the picturesque little mediæval town of *Colonna*, for seven centuries the stronghold of the great family of that name, but now belonging to Prince Rospigliosi.

Colonna occupies the site of Labicum, which, according to Virgil, existed before the foundation of Rome, for he represents its warriors as joining the army of Turnus :—

> "Auruncæque manus, Rutuli, veteresque Sicani,
> Et Sacranæ acies, et picti scuta Labici."
>
> *Æn.* vii. 795.

Hannibal approached Rome from hence :—

> "Jamque adeo est campos ingressus et arva Labici,
> Linquens Telegoni pulsatos ariete muros."
>
> *Sil. Ital.* xii. 534.

Silius alludes to the fertility of its lands :—

> ". . . atque habiles ad aratra Labici."
>
> viii. 368.

Through the Middle Ages, Colonna was the scene of endless sieges, and consequently perhaps suffered more than any other town in the neighbourhood of Rome.

"The private story of the Colonna and Ursini is an essential part of the annals of modern Rome. The name and arms of Colonna have been the theme of much doubtful etymology; nor have the orators and antiquarians overlooked either Trajan's Pillar, or the columns of Hercules, or the pillar of Christ's flagellation, or the luminous column that guided the Israelites in the desert. Their first historical appearance in the year 1104, attests the power and antiquity, while it explains the simple meaning, of the name. By the usurpation of Cavi, the Colonna provoked the arms of Paschal II. ; but they lawfully held, in the Campagna of Rome, the hereditary fiefs of Zagarolo and *Colonna ;* and the latter of these towns was probably adorned with some lofty pillar, the relic of a villa or temple. They likewise possessed one moiety of the neighbouring city of Tusculum ; a strong presumption of their descent from the counts of Tusculum, who in the 10th century were the tyrants of the apostolic see. According to their own and the public opinion, the primitive and remote source was derived from the banks of the Rhine ; and the sovereigns of Germany were not ashamed of a real or fabulous affinity with a noble race, which in the revolutions of seven hundred years has been often illustrated by merit, and always by fortune. About the end of the 13th century, the most powerful branch was composed of an uncle and six brothers, all conspicuous in arms, or in the honours of the Church. Of these, Peter was elected senator of Rome, introduced to the Capitol in a triumphant car, and hailed in some vain acclamations with the title of Cæsar ; while John and Stephen were declared Marquis of Ancona and Count of Romagna by Nicholas IV., a patron so partial to their family, that he has been delineated, in satirical portraits, imprisoned as it were in a hollow pillar. After his decease, their haughty behaviour provoked the displeasure of the most implacable of mankind. The two cardinals, the uncle and the nephew, denied the election of Boniface VIII. ; and the Colonna were oppressed for a moment by his temporal and spiritual arms. He proclaimed a crusade against his personal enemies ; their estates were confiscated ; their fortresses on either side of the Tiber were besieged by the troops of S. Peter, and those of the rival nobles ; and after the ruin of Palestrina or Præneste, their principal seat, the ground was marked with a plough-share, the emblem of perpetual desolation. Degraded, banished, proscribed, the six brothers, in disguise and danger, wandered over Europe without renouncing the hope of deliverance and revenge. In this double hope, the French court was their surest asylum ; they prompted and directed the enterprise of Philip ; and I should praise their magnanimity, had they respected the misfortune and courage of the captive tyrant. His civil acts were annulled by the Roman people, who restored the honours and possessions of the Colonna ; and some estimate may be formed of their wealth by their losses, of their losses by the damages of one hundred thousand gold florins, which were granted them against the accomplices and heirs of the deceased pope. All the spiritual censures and disqualifications were abolished by his prudent successors ; and the fortune of the house was more firmly established by this transient hurricane. The boldness of Sciarra Colonna was signalized in the captivity of Boniface, and long afterwards in the coronation of Lewis of Bavaria ; and by the gratitude of the Emperor the pillar in their arms was encircled with a royal crown. But the first of the family in fame and merit was the elder Stephen, whom Petrarch loved and esteemed as a hero superior to his own times, and not unworthy of ancient Rome. Persecution and exile displayed to the nations his abilities in peace and war ; in his distress, he was an object, not of pity, but of reverence ; the aspect of danger provoked him to avow his name and country : and when he was asked, ' Where is now your fortress?' he laid his hand on his heart, and answered, ' Here.' He supported with the same virtue the return of prosperity : and, till the ruin of his declining age, the ancestors, the character, and the children of Stephen Colonna, exalted his dignity in the Roman republic and at the court of Avignon."—*Gibbon's Roman Empire*, ch. lxix.

The ancient *Via Labicana*, now the high road to Naples by Valmontone, runs at the foot of the hill upon which Colonna is situated.

An excellent new road leads from Frascati to Palestrina, passing for the most part through the remains of the fine old chestnut forest, with which these mountain slopes were once covered. The road ascends first to Monte Porzio, which most picturesquely crowns an olive-clad hill with its gaily painted houses. Hence, by a beautiful terrace, with glorious views through the vineyards into the Sabina, we climb up to Monte Compatri, above which stands the great *Convent of S. Silvestro*. We are now high above Colonna, and Monte Porzio becomes very effective rising against the faint distances of the vast plain in which Rome is asleep. From Monte Compatri the new road descends, and falls into the high road from Rome before reaching the Villa Doria at S. Cesareo. On the left, Zagarolo is seen, in a striking position at the end of a ravine. We pass some Roman tombs hewn in the rocks of the hollow way ; the

Via Prenestina with its ancient paving-blocks appears by the side of the road; and, passing a great Casino called *Il Parco dei Barberini*, we reach the foot of the hill, up which Palestrina clambers, at the inn of S. Rocco.

CHAPTER V.

GROTTA FERRATA AND MARINO.

(This is a very pleasant excursion from Rome, and may be taken between two trains from the Frascati station; or, both Grotta Ferrata and Marino may be visited in driving from Frascati to Albano.)

THE great castellated monastery of Grotta Ferrata is only about two miles from Frascati on the slopes of the Alban hills. It is the only Basilian monastery in the Papal States, and its monks perform the service in Greek according to the Greek ritual. The story of its foundation is that of S. Nilus.

S. Nilus was a Calabrian Greek, born near Tarentum. He did not embrace a religious life till his old age, when his wife, to whom he was tenderly attached, was dead, and then he became a Greek monk of the order of S. Basil, and soon was elected abbot of his convent. Driven by the Saracens from the east of Italy, he fled with his brotherhood to Monte Cassino, where the abbot received them kindly, and appointed them a residence in the neighbourhood. While he was here, Aloare, widow of Pandolfo, Prince of Capua, who had incited her two sons to the murder of their cousin, came to S. Nilus to beseech absolution for her crime. He refused, unless she would yield up one of her sons to the family of the murdered man, but she could not make up her mind to the sacrifice, upon which S. Nilus denounced her sin as unforgiven and foretold her punishment. Shortly after, one of the princes was assassinated in a church by his brother, who was himself put to death by order of Hugh Capet, King of France.

S. Nilus next took up his abode at Rome in the convent of S. Alexis, where he wrought many miracles, among others the cure of an epileptic boy. Rome was at this time distracted with internal dissensions, and had been besieged by the Emperor Otho III., who had persuaded Crescentius, Consul of Rome, by his false promises, to deliver up S. Angelo, and had there murdered him; and, putting out the eyes of Pope John XVI., had set up Gregory V. in his place. S. Nilus alone ventured to oppose the marauders, rebuking them as the enemies of God, and writing to the Emperor, "Because ye have broken faith, and because ye have had no mercy for the vanquished, nor compassion for those who had no longer the power to injure or resist, know that God will avenge the cause of the oppressed, and ye shall both seek for mercy and shall not find it." He then fled to Gaeta, and afterwards to a cave at the spot now called Grotta Ferrata.

Two years after, Gregory V. died miserably, and Otho, on his knees at Grotta Ferrata, implored the intercession of Nilus, promising a rich endowment for his convent. But his offers were all sternly refused by the saint, who said with solemnity, that he asked nothing from him but that he would repent of his sins and save his own soul. A few weeks after, Otho was obliged to fly from the people, and was poisoned by the widow of Crescentius. Nilus had betaken himself in

1004 to the solitudes of Grotta Ferrata because of the certainty of canonization if he remained at Gaeta. Here, asleep in a grotto, he had a dream of the Virgin, who commanded him to build a church on that spot, placing a golden apple in the foundations, as a pledge of her protection. Nilus built the church, but first placed in the grotto, where he had received the mandate, a picture of the Virgin which he had brought with him from Gaeta, and guarded it with an iron railing, which gave it the name of Grotta Ferrata. S. Nilus died in the same year with Otho, commanding that his burial-place should be concealed, in order that no undue honours might be paid to his remains; but over the cavern where he had lived, his friend and successor Bartolomeo began to raise the church and castellated convent of Grotta Ferrata, in which, in memory of the Greek Nilus, the rule of S. Basil should always be followed, and mass celebrated in the Greek language. The Count of Tusculum protected the work, which rose rapidly, and the church was consecrated by John XIX., only twenty years after the death of its founder. Several of the popes resided here, especially the boy Pope Benedict IX. (nephew of the Count of Tusculum), who had resigned the honours of the Papacy, of which he was most unworthy, in 1033, at the entreaty of the first Abbot, S. Bartholomew. Pope Julius II. (Della Rovere) had been Abbot here, and began the buildings on which the Rovere oak may still be seen. He, the warlike Pope who commanded at the siege of Mirandola, built, as Abbot, the picturesque fortifications of the monastery. Benedict XIV. ordained that the Abbot, Prior, and Fathers of Grotta Ferrata should always celebrate in the Greek rite. The last Abbot Commendator was Cardinal Gonsalvi, who renounced the baronial jurisdiction which had hitherto belonged to the abbots in 1816.

Grotta Ferrata, at a distance, looks more like a castle than a monastery. It is surrounded by walls with heavy machicolations and low bastion towers. Within, the greater part of the two courts have been modernized, but the church retains its campanile of the tenth century. In the atrium is a black cross supposed to mark the exact height of our Saviour, and a model of the golden apple given by the Virgin to S. Nilus and buried in the foundations of the belfry. Over the western door (now enclosed) is the inscription:—

οἴκου Θεοῦ μέλλοντες εἰσβαίνειν πύλην
ἔξω γένοισθε τῆς μέθης τῶν φροντίδων
ἵν' εὐμενῶς εὕροιτε τὸν κριτὴν ἔσω.

[Ye who would enter here the house of God
Cast out the leaven of pride and worldly thought
That kindly ye may find the Judge within.]

Above, is a very interesting mosaic of 1005, representing the Saviour between the Virgin and S. J. Baptist, with a small standing figure supposed to represent the Abbot S. Bartholomew. The doors are beautifully carved. At the end of the right aisle is a curious piece of perforated carving found in the Campagna, and believed to have belonged to a screen between the nave and choir through which the voices of the monks could reach the congregation: it is inscribed with the names of the thirteen first abbots. At the end of the left aisle is the tomb of Pope Benedict IX., with the imperial eagle in mosaic, and above it two angels with torches in their hands. In the middle of the floor is an enormous dish of porphyry: it was broken by the French in their attempts to remove it. Over the entrance of the choir is a second mosaic, of the Twelve Apostles, with the

Saviour, typified by the Lamb, represented *below*, not *on* the throne. The high altar, decorated with two angels of the Bernini school, sustains a reliquary of bronze with agate pillars, which was intended for S. Peter's, but, being found too small, was given to Grotta Ferrata by Cardinal Barberini.

From the left aisle we enter the famous chapel of the first Abbot, S. Bartholomew. It is a parallelogram with a small dome over the east end. The wall on the left is occupied by the famous frescoes of S. Nilus praying before the crucifix; the visit of Otho III. to S. Nilus; and, in the choir, the healing of the demoniac by S. Nilus. The frescoes on the right represent Nilus and Bartholomew, who by their prayers avert a thunder-storm from the crops which husbandmen are gathering in; the building of the Monastery; and, in the choir, the vision of the Madonna who gives the golden apple. At the sides of the altar are: S. Eustace, because he was the protector of the Farnese family, and S. Edward, because of the name of the Cardinal who built the chapel. In the dome, beneath the figure of the Almighty, are the Roman saints, Agnese, Cecilia, and Francesca Romana. All the frescoes are by *Domenichino*. The altarpiece, representing Nilus and Bartholomew with the Virgin, is by *Ann. Caracci*. At the west end of the chapel is a curious urn used as a baptismal font.

"About the year 1610, when Cardinal Odoardo Farnese was Abbot of Grotta Ferrata, he undertook to rebuild a defaced and ruined chapel, which had in very ancient times been dedicated to the interesting Greek saints S. Adrian and his wife S. Natalia. The chapel was accordingly restored with great magnificence, rededicated to S. Nilus and his companion, S. Bartolomeo, who are regarded as the two first Abbots; and Domenichino, then in his twenty-eighth year, was employed to represent on the wall some of the most striking incidents connected with the foundation of the monastery.

"The walls, in accordance with the architecture, are divided into compartments, varying in form and size. In the first large compartment, he has represented the visit of Otho III. to S. Nilus ; a most dramatic composition, consisting of a vast number of figures. The Emperor has just alighted from his charger, and advances in a humble attitude to claim the benediction of the saint. The accessories in this grand picture are wonderful for splendour and variety, and painted with consummate skill. The whole strikes us like a well-got-up scene. The action of a spirited horse, and the two trumpeters behind, are among the most admired parts of the picture. It has always been asserted that these two trumpeters express, in the muscles of the face and throat, the quality of the sounds they give forth. This, when I read the description, appeared to me a piece of fanciful exaggeration ; but it is literally true. If painting cannot imitate the power of sound, it has here suggested both its power and kind, so that we *seem* to hear. Among the figures is that of a young page, who holds the Emperor's horse, and wears over his light flowing hair a blue cap with a plume of white feathers ; according to tradition, this is a portrait of a beautiful girl, with whom Domenichino fell violently in love while he was employed on the frescoes. Bellori tells us that, not only was the young painter rejected by the parents of the damsel, but that when the picture was uncovered and exhibited, and the face recognized as that of the young girl he had loved, he was obliged to fly from the vengeance of her relatives.

"The great composition on the opposite wall represents the building of the monastery after the death of S. Nilus by his disciple and coadjutor S. Bartolomeo. The master builder, or architect, presents the plan, which S. Bartolomeo examines through his spectacles. A number of masons and workmen are busied in various operations, and an antique sarcophagus, which was discovered in the foundation, and is now built into the wall of the church, is seen in one corner ; in the background, is represented one of the legends of the locality. It is related that when the masons were raising a column, the ropes gave way, and the column would have fallen on the heads of the assistants, had not one of the monks, full of faith, sustained the column with his single strength.

"One of the lesser compartments represents another legend. The Madonna appears in a glorious vision to S. Nilus and S. Bartolomeo in this very Grotta Ferrata, and presents to them a golden apple, in testimony of her desire that a chapel should rise on this spot. The golden apple was reverently buried in the foundation of the belfry, as we now bury coins and medals when laying the foundation of a public edifice.

"Opposite is the fresco which ranks as one of the finest and most expressive of all Domenichino's compositions. A poor epileptic boy is brought to S. Nilus to be healed; the saint, after beseeching the Divine favour, dips his finger into the oil of a lamp burning before the altar, and with it anoints the mouth of the boy, who is instantly relieved from his malady. The incident is simply and admirably told, and the action of the boy, so painfully true, yet without distortion or exaggeration, has been, and I think with reason, preferred to the epileptic boy in Raphael's Transfiguration.

"In a high, narrow compartment, Domenichino has represented S. Nilus before a crucifix: the figure of our Saviour extends his arm in benediction over the kneeling saint, who seems to feel, rather than perceive, the miracle. This also is beautiful.

"S. Nilus having been a Greek monk, and the convent connected with the Greek order, we have the Greek fathers in their proper habits—venerable figures pourtrayed in niches round the cornice. The Greek saints, S. Adrian and S. Natalia; and the Roman saints, S. Agnes, S. Cecilia, and S. Francesca, are painted in medallions.

"A glance back at the history of S. Nilus and the origin of the chapel will show how significant, how appropriate, and how harmonious is this scheme of decoration in all its parts. I know not if the credit of the selection belongs to Domenichino; but, in point of vivacity of conception and brilliant execution, he never exceeded these frescoes in any of his subsequent works; and every visitor to Rome should make this famous chapel a part of his pilgrimage."—*Jameson's Monastic Orders*, p. 35.

Grotta Ferrata formerly possessed the finest Greek library in Italy, but its treasures were removed, partly to the Vatican by Sixtus V., and partly to the Barberini collection by Urban VIII.

In the Palace of the Abbots, in Jan. 1824, died Cardinal Gonsalvi, the famous minister and friend of Pius VII., having survived his master only five months. His body, being opened after death, in consequence of unfounded suspicions, proved that he died from entirely natural causes.

About $3\frac{1}{2}$ miles from Grotta Ferrata, on the way to

Albano, is the very picturesque mediæval town of *Marino*, which has been identified, from inscriptions which have been found there, as occupying the site of Castrimonium, a town fortified by Sylla, and which continued to be a "municipium" to the time of Antoninus Pius. As, in the Middle Ages, Colonna was a principal fortress of the family of that name, so Marino was the stronghold of the great rival family of the Orsini, from whom, however, it was wrested in the 14th century by the Colonnas, who built the walls which still remain.

Beyond the town is the beautiful glen called *Parco Colonna*, once the "Lucus Ferentinæ," which was the meeting-place of the Latin league after the destruction of Alba. A pleasant walk leads up the valley through the green wood fresh with rushing streams and carpeted with flowers, to a pool formed by several springs, with an old statue and remains of 17th-century grottoes. One of the small springs on the right is pointed out as the "Caput Aquæ Ferentinæ," where Turnus Herdonius of Aricia, who had inveighed against the pride of Tarquinius Superbus and warned his countrymen against placing any trust in him, having been accused of plotting the death of the King and condemned by the great council of the Latins, was drowned in the shallow water, being held down by a hurdle, upon which stones were piled.*

* *Livy*, i. 50—52.

CHAPTER VI.

VEII.

(An excursion should be made to Veii before the weather becomes too hot for enjoyment in walking about its steep ravines. A sunny day in February is the best time to choose.)

IT is a drive of about an hour and a half from Rome to Veii. At first we follow the Via Cassia, one of the three roads which led to Cisalpine Gaul, and which passed through the centre of Etruria: Cicero says—"Etruriam discriminat Cassia." It is now one of the pleasantest drives near the city, with its high upland views over the wide plains of the Campagna to the towns which sparkle in the sun under the rifted purple crags of the Sabina, or down bosky glades studded with old cork-trees. whose rich dark green forms a charming contrast to the burnt grass and poetic silvery thistles. Three miles from Rome, on a bank on the left of the road, is the fine sarcophagus adorned with griffins in low relief, which is popularly known as *Nero's tomb*, and is really that of Publius Vibius Marianus and his wife Reginia Maxima. Beyond this, on the right, is the castellated farm-house of *Buon-Ricovero*, picturesquely situated with pine trees upon a grassy knoll.

About 10 miles from Rome we reach the dismal post-house of *La Storta*, where, in *vetturino* days, horses were changed for the last time before reaching the city. Just beyond this the by-road to Veii turns off on the right. As we wind along the hill-sides, we see below us the picturesque little mediæval town of Isola Farnese.

"From La Storta it is a mile and a half to Isola by the carriage road; but the visitor, on horse or foot, may save half a mile by taking a pathway across the downs. When Isola Farnese comes into sight, let him halt awhile to admire the scene. A wide sweep of Campagna lies before him, in this part broken into ravines or narrow glens, which, by varying the lines of the landscape, redeem it from the monotony of a plain, and by patches of wood relieve it of its usual nakedness and sterility. On a steep cliff, about a mile distant, stands the village of Isola—a village in fact, but in appearance a large château, with a few out-houses around it. Behind it rises the long, swelling ground, which once bore the walls, temples, and palaces of Veii, but is now a bare down, partly fringed with wood, and without a single habitation on its surface. At a few miles distance rises the conical tufted hill of Musino, the supposed scene of ancient rites, the Eleusis, the Delphi, it may be, of Etruria. The eye is then caught by a tree-crested mound or tumulus, standing in the plain beyond the site of the city; then it stretches away to the triple paps of the Monticelli, and to Tivoli, gleaming from the dark slopes behind; and then it rises and scans the majestic chain of Apennines, bounding the horizon with their dark-grey masses, and rests with delight on La Leonessa and other well-known giants of the Sabine range, all capt with snow. Oh, the beauty of that range! From whatever part of the Campagna you view it, it presents those long, sweeping outlines, those grand, towering crests—not of Alpine abruptness, but consistently with the character of the land, preserving, even when soaring highest, the true Italian dignity and repose—the *otium cum dignitate* of Nature."
—*Dennis' Cities and Cemeteries of Etruria.*

The fortress, which clings more than half-dismantled to the crumbling tufa-rock, was built by the barons of the Middle Ages, was constantly taken and retaken in the Orsini and Colonna feuds, and was eventually ruined by Cæsar Borgia when he took it after a twelve days' siege.

Here we must leave our carriage and find and engage the

Isola Farnese.

custode who opens the painted tomb. A deep lane between high banks of tufa overhung by bay and ilex, leads into the ravine, where a brook called Fosso de' due Fossi (from the two little torrents, Storta and Pino, of which it is formed) tumbles over a steep rock into the chasm near an old mill, and rushes away down the glen to join the Crimera. The craggy hill-side is covered with luxuriant foliage, and snow-drifted with laurestinus-bloom in spring; the ground is carpeted with violets and blue and white wood-anemonies. Beyond the mill, where we cross the brook upon stepping-stones, a small gateway of mediæval times, opening upon a green lawn overhanging the chasm, with the castle of Isola crowning the opposite cliff, forms a subject dear to artists, and many are the picnics which meet on the turfy slope under the shade of the old cork-trees.

From hence we may begin our explorations of the ancient city, and if we are to visit all its principal remains, it is no short or easy excursion which we are going to undertake. The ruins are widely scattered, and the labyrinthine ravines formed by the windings of the Crimera and the Fosso de' due Fossi, which almost surround the city and meet beneath it, are so bewildering, that a guide is necessary. At first it seems quite impossible that these woody valleys, which only echo now to the song of a thousand nightingales, can really have been Veii, the city which Dionysius underrates when he describes it as being as large as Athens,* which Eutropius (i. 20) writes of as "civitas antiquissima Italiæ atque ditissima," which was a flourishing State at the time of the foundation of Rome, and which once possessed so many attractions that it became a question whether Rome itself should not be abandoned for its sake.

"The city of Veii was not inferior to Rome itself in buildings, and possessed a large and fruitful territory, partly mountainous, and partly in the plain. The air was pure and healthy, the country being free from the vicinity of marshes, which produce a heavy atmosphere, and without any river which might render the morning air too rigid. Nevertheless there was abundance of water, not artificially conducted, but rising from natural springs, and good to drink."—*Dion.* xii. *frag.* 21.

Gradually, as we push through the brushwood, traces of the old walls may be discovered here and there, and of the nine gates to which from local circumstances topographers have assigned the imaginary names of Porta de' Sette Pagi, Porta dell' Arce, Porta Campana, Porta Fidenate, Porta di Pietra Pertusa, Porta dell' Are Muzie, Porta Capenate, Porta del Columbario, and Porta Sutrina.

A long walk through the woods leads to the *Porta Capenate*, which might easily pass unobserved, so slight are its remains. But beneath it is the most interesting spot in the whole circuit of the city, the *Ponte Sodo*, where the Crimera or Fosso di Formello, as it is called here, forces its way for 240 yards through a natural(?) tunnel over-grown with luxuriant bay and ilex. It is necessary to climb down

---

* The circuit of Veii was 43 stadia, that of Athens only 35.

to the level of the stream to enjoy the view through the dark recesses to the light beyond.

"It would be easy to pass the Ponte Sodo without observing it. It is called a bridge; but is a mere mass of rock bored for the passage of the stream. Whether wholly or but partly artificial may admit of dispute. It is, however, in all probability, an Etruscan excavation—a tunnel in the rock, two hundred and forty feet long, twelve or fifteen wide, and nearly twenty high. From above it is scarcely visible. You must view it from the banks of the stream. You at first suspect it to be of natural formation, yet there is a squareness and regularity about it which prove it artificial. The steep cliffs of tufa, yellow, grey, or white, overhung by ilex, ivy, and brushwood—the deep, dark-mouthed tunnel with a ray of sunshine, it may be, gleaming beyond—the masses of lichenclad rock, which choke the stream, give it a charm apart from its antiquity."—*Dennis' Cities of Etruria.*

Near the Ponte Sodo are remains of an aqueduct of imperial times, confirming the opinion that Veii had a temporary revival during the reign of Tiberius, whose statue, with several inscriptions of his time, has been found here.

About a mile up the stream from this, passing the Roman

Ponte dell' Isola, Veii.

bridge called *Ponte Formello*, we reach the tall Etruscan bridge *Ponte dell' Isola*, which crosses the river with an arch twenty-two feet wide. About the same distance in the opposite direction, descending the river, the remains of a ruined *Columbarium* are seen in the grey rock on the opposite bank, and a little further, on the slope of the hill-side called Poggio Reale, is the *Painted Tomb*.

Before the entrance of the tomb, which is sometimes known as the *Grotta Campana*, are the almost shapeless remains of the stone lions which once guarded it. The custode opens a door in the rock and admits one with lights to the interior of two low vaulted chambers hewn out of the tufa, and they are well worth seeing. On either side of the outer room are stone benches, on which, when the tomb was first opened, skeletons were seen lying, but crumbled away in a few minutes. With one of these, who had been a warrior, lay his breast-plate, helmet, and spear's-head, which still remain, and all around were the large earthen jars and vases which yet stand here. The walls are covered with fantastic paintings of figures, with horses, dogs, leopards, and other animals, all of rude execution, but still fresh in form and colour. The inner-chamber is surrounded by a shelf still laden with vases and curious little cinerary sarcophagi, and in its centre stood the brazier in which perfumes were burnt to purify the air.

These are the sights usually seen at Veii; but if possible another two hours should be devoted to ascending the hill of the *Arx*, called by the natives *Piazza d'Armi*, which may be reached by a little path winding through the brushwood above the Columbarium. Of late years this has been decided to be the citadel of Veii, formerly supposed to have occupied the rock of Isola Farnese, which was separated from the rest of the city by a deep glen, so that, had it been the citadel, Camillus by its capture would not, as Livy tells us, have obtained immediate possession of the town.

These desolate heights, now overgrown with thorns and

thistles, amongst which fragments of precious marbles and alabasters may still be found in abundance, formed the citadel whose fourteen wars are matters of history, and which, having been successfully able to resist the whole forces of Rome during an eight years' siege, was at last only taken (A.C. 393) by a stratagem.

"It was a time of truce round the walls of Veii; and many who from living so near had known each other before the war, would often fall into discourse. In this manner the inhabitants heard of the prodigy of the (Alban) lake: and a soothsayer was impelled by destiny to scoff at the efforts of the Romans, the futility of which was foretold in the prophetic books. Some days after, a Roman centurion invited the soothsayer to come into the plain between the walls and the Roman trenches, to hear an account of a portent that had fallen out at his house, and to teach him in what way to appease the gods: the aruspex was seduced by the reward promised him, and incautiously let himself be led near the Roman lines. On a sudden the stout centurion seized the old man, and dragged him, an easy prey, into the camp. From hence he was carried to Rome before the senate; where he was forced by threats to speak the truth, and, loudly bewailing the destiny that had infatuated him to betray the secret of his nation, confessed that the Veientine books of fate announced that, so long as the lake kept on overflowing, Veii could not be taken, and that if the waters were to reach the sea, Rome would perish. Not long afterwards the ambassadors returned from Delphi, and brought an answer to a like effect: whereupon the tunnel was begun, in order that the lake might cease to overflow, and that the water drawn from it might be spread through the fields in ditches. This work was carried on unremittingly; and the Veientines learnt that the fatal consummation, on which their ruin hung, was at hand. They sent an embassy to implore forbearance; but they found no compassion. The chief of the envoys, before they quitted the senate-house with the unrelenting answer, warned the Romans once more of the penalty that would inevitably await them: for, as certainly as Veii was now doomed to fall, so surely did the same oracles foretell, that, soon after the fall of Veii, Rome would be taken by the Gauls. Nobody listened to him.

"Camillus was already commanding as dictator before the city, and was unsuspectedly executing the work which opened the way for its destruction. The Romans seemed to be standing quietly at their posts, as if they were waiting the slow issue of a blockade which could not be forced. But the army was divided into six bands; and these, relieving one another every six hours, were labouring incessantly in digging a mine, which was to lead into the citadel of Veii, and there to open into the temple of Juno.

"Before the assault was made, the dictator inquired of the senate, what was to be done with the spoil. Appius Claudius, the grandson of the decemvir, advised selling it for the benefit of the treasury, that it might supply pay for the army without need of a property-tax. This was opposed by P. Licinius, the most eminent among the plebeian military tribunes: he even declared it would be unfair if none but the soldiers then on the spot were to have a share in the booty, for which every citizen had made some sacrifice or other. Notice, he said, ought to be given, for all who wished to partake in it to proceed to the camp. This was decreed; and old and young flocked toward the devoted city. Hereupon, as soon as the water was dispersed over the fields, and the passage into the citadel finished, Camillus made a vow to Matuta, a goddess highly revered on the adjacent Tyrrhenian coast, and addressed prayers to Juno, whose temple covered the way destined to lead the Romans into the city, with promises that she should receive higher honours than ever. Nor were his adjurations fruitless. To the Pythian Apollo, whose oracle, when it encouraged the Romans to put faith in the words of the aruspex, demanded an offering for Delphi, he vowed a tenth of the spoil. Then, at the appointed hour, the passage was filled with cohorts: Camillus himself led the way. Meanwhile the horns blew the signal for the assault; and the countless host brought scaling ladders, as if they meant to mount the walls from every side. Here the citizens stood expecting the enemy, while their king was sacrificing in the temple of Juno. The aruspex, when he saw the victim, declared that whoever brought the goddess her share of the slaughtered animal would conquer. This was heard by the Romans underground. They burst forth and seized the flesh; and Camillus offered it up. From the citadel they rushed irresistibly through the city, and opened the nearest gates to the assailants.

"The incredible amount of the spoil even surpassed the expectations of the conquerors. The whole was given to the army, except the captives who had been spared in the massacre, before the unarmed had their lives granted to them, and who were sold on account of the state. All objects of human property had already been removed from the empty walls: the ornaments and statues of the gods alone were yet untouched. Juno had accepted the vow of a temple on the Aventine. But every one trembled to touch her image; for, according to the Etruscan religion, none but a priest of a certain house might do so without fear of death. A body of chosen knights, who took courage to venture upon removing it from its place, proceeded to the temple in white robes, and asked the goddess whether she consented to go to Rome. They heard her voice pronounce her assent; and the statue of its own accord followed those who were leading it forth.

"While Camillus was looking down from this temple on the magnificence of the captured city, the immense wealth of which the spoilers were amassing, he called to mind the threats of the Veientines, and that the gods were wont to regard excessive prosperity with displeasure; and he prayed to the mighty queen of heaven to let the calamity that was to expiate it be such as the republic and he himself could support. When after ending his prayer he turned round to the right, with his head veiled according to custom, his foot stumbled, and he fell. It seemed as if the goddess had graciously appeased destiny with this mishap: and Camillus, forgetting the foreboding which had warned him, provoked the angry powers by the unexampled pomp and pride of his triumph. Jupiter and Sol saw him drive up with their own team of white horses to the Capitol. For this arrogance he atoned by a sentence of condemnation, Rome by her destruction."—*Niebuhr's Hist. of Rome*, ii. 476.

From this time, with the exception of a brief revival under the Empire, the site of Veii has been utterly desolate. In 117 Florus (in allusion to the Etruscan city) wrote, " Who knows the situation of Veii ' It is only to be found in our annals."

> ... "Tarpeia sede perusta
> Gallorum facibus, Veiosque habitante Camillo,
> Illic Roma fuit."
>
> *Lucan.* v. 27.
>
> ... "Tunc omne Latinum
> Fabula nomen erit; Gabios, Veiosque, Coramque
> Pulvere vix tectæ poterunt monstrare ruinæ."
>
> *Id.* vii. 392.

There are many other points which may be visited in or near the circle of the ancient city. Such is the *Scaletta*, a staircase of uncemented blocks of masonry near the Porta Fidenate, which attracted much attention twenty years ago, but is now greatly mutilated; and most especially the *Arco di Pino*, a very picturesque arch in the tufa, whether natural or artificial is unknown, on the east of the city near the large tumulus called *La Vaccareccia*.* Many other remains are doubtless still waiting to be discovered, but the place has never been fully investigated. None of the dangers now await travellers which are described by Mrs Hamilton Gray.

"Isola is a sweet quiet-looking hamlet, but about three weeks after our visit forty of the inhabitants were taken up as leagued banditti, and brought to Rome. The master of the inn was one of their leaders, and said at times to have given his guests human flesh to eat—detected by a young surgeon, who found a finger in his plate."—*Sepulchres of Etruria.*

The rock of Isola itself is perforated with tombs, and was probably the necropolis of the city.

"Such, then, is Veii—once the most powerful, the most wealthy city of Etruria, renowned for its beauty, its arts, and refinement, which in size equalled Athens and Rome, in military force was not inferior to the latter, and which for its size, strong by nature and almost impregnable by art, and for the magnificence of its buildings and the superior extent and fertility of its territory, was preferred by the Romans to the Eternal City itself, even before the destruction of the latter by the Gauls,—now void and desolate, without one house or inhabitant, its temples and palaces level with the dust, and nothing beyond a few fragments of walls, and some empty sepulchres, remaining to tell the traveller that here Veii was. The plough passes over its bosom, and the shepherd pastures his flock on the waste within it. Such must it have been in the earlier years of Augustus, for Propertius pictures a similar scene of decay and desolation.

' Et Veii veteres, et vos tum regna fuistis ;
   Et vestro posita est aurea sella foro ;
   Nunc intra muros pastoris buccina lenti
     Cantat, et in vestris ossibus arva metunt.'

* Those who ride may visit this on the way to or from Rome.

"Veii, thou hadst a royal crown of old,
And in thy forum stood a throne of gold !—
Thy walls now echo but the shepherd's horn,
And o'er thine ashes waves the summer corn.'

How are we to account for this neglect? The city was certainly not destroyed by Camillus, for the superior magnificence of its public and private buildings were temptations to the Romans to desert the Seven Hills. But after the destruction of Rome by the Gauls Veii was abandoned, in consequence of the decree of the senate threatening with the severest punishment the Roman citizens who should remain within its walls; and Niebuhr's conjecture is not perhaps incorrect, that it was demolished to supply materials for the rebuilding of Rome, though the distance would preclude the transport of more than the architectural ornaments. Its desolation must have been owing either to the policy of Rome which proscribed its habitation, or to *malaria*; otherwise a city which presented so many advantages as almost to have tempted the Romans to desert the hearths and the sepulchres of their fathers would scarcely have been suffered to fall into utter decay, and remain so for nearly four centuries."—*Dennis*.

A leading feature in all the views from Veii, is the conical hill called *Monte Musino*, six miles distant. This curious place may be reached by following the Via Cassia as far as the posthouse of *Baccano*, the ancient "Ad Baccanas," 18 miles from Rome. It is situated in the crater of a volcano, afterwards a lake, which was drained in very early times. Two miles further north lies *Campagnano*, a village with a few insignificant Etruscan and Roman remains. Hence a path runs eastward for five miles to *Scrofano*, which has many Etruscan tombs and lies at the foot of Monte Musino, which is most easily ascended from thence. The hill is conical, and is cut into a series of artificial terraces whose origin cannot be satisfactorily explained, unless this is the "Oscum" mentioned by Festus, the sacred country retreat of the Roman augurs. Near the summit is a cave. The whole is crested by a wood which has been preserved intact by the superstition of the inhabitants of Scrofano, who believe that the felling of the trees would be followed by the death of the head of each family. On the top of the hill a treasure is supposed to be buried, and protected by demons, who would arouse a tempest, were any attempt made to discover it. The view is very striking.

Twenty-two miles from Rome on the Via Cassia is the large inn of *Le Sette Vene*, near which there is a small Etruscan bridge in good preservation.

CHAPTER VII.

GALERA AND BRACCIANO.

(There is a public conveyance daily from Rome to Bracciano, which toils along the road in five hours. Two good horses will take a light carriage containing four persons thither in three hours. Though it is *said* to be 26 miles distant, Bracciano is within an easy day's excursion from Rome. There are two tolerably decent inns at Bracciano, which has a population of above 2000.)

STORMS were sweeping over the Janiculan, and occasionally shrouding S. Peter's in a white mist, while the Campagna beyond the Aventine seemed blotted with ink, but as we had settled to go to Bracciano, and an excursion of more than 20 miles is very difficult to re-arrange, we determined not to be deterred by weather, and, as usual in such cases, things turned out better than we anticipated.

It was again the Via Cassia, which had led us to Veii; but, beyond La Storta, the road to Bracciano turns to the left, over a most·dreary thistle-grown part of the Campagna, with here and there a deep cutting in the tufa, and banks covered with violets and crowned with golden genista. A bridle road, turning off on the right, one mile from La Storta, leads to the picturesque and lonely convent of *La Madonna del Sorbo* (about seven or eight miles distant), founded in 1400 by the Orsini.

On the main road there is little interest, till the tiny rivulet Arrone, an outlet of the lake of Bracciano, crosses the road, and tumbles in a waterfall over a cliff into one of those deep glens which suggest the sites of so many Etruscan cities, and which here encircles that of the forgotten Etruscan fortress of Galeria, afterwards occupied by the mediæval town of *Galera.* Those who pass along the high road catch glimpses of its tall tower and ivy-grown walls, but they must cross the fields, and descend into its ravine (leaving their carriage at the farm-house called Santa Maria di Galera) to realize that the whole place is absolutely deserted except by bats and serpents, and that it is one of the most striking of " the lost cities of the Campagna."

The situation is wonderfully picturesque, the walls rising from the very edge of a steep lava precipice, round which

Galera.

the beautiful Arrone circles and sparkles through the trees, and unites itself to another little stream, the Fosso, just below the citadel. In the eleventh century Galera belonged to the Counts Tosco, troublesome barons of the Campagna, against whom in 1058 Pope Benedict X. called in the assistance of the Normans, who were only too happy to ravage and plunder the town. In the thirteenth and fourteenth centuries the place became an important stronghold of the Orsini, who held it by tenure of an annual payment of three pounds of wax to the Pope. Their arms are over the gateway, and they built the tall handsome tower of the church, which was dedicated to S. Nicholas; but they were unable to defend the town against their deadly enemies the Colonnas, who took it and utterly sacked it in July, 1485. The last historical association of the place is that Charles V. slept there, the day he left Rome, April 18, 1536.

Only a short time ago Galera had ninety inhabitants. Now

Castle of Galera.

it has none. There is no one to live in the houses, no one to pray in the church. Malaria reigns triumphant here, and keeps all human creatures at bay. Even the shepherd who comes down in the day to watch the goats who are scrambling about the broken walls, would pay with his life for passing the night here. It is a bewitched solitude, with the ghosts of the past in full possession. All is fast decaying: the town walls, some of which date from the eleventh century, are sliding over into the thickets of brambles. Above them rise the remains of the fine old Orsini castle, from which there is an unspeakably desolate view, the effect of the scene being enhanced by the knowledge that the strength of Galera has fallen beneath no human foe, but that a more powerful and invincible enemy has been found in the mysterious "scourge of the Campagna." The only bright point about the ruins is the old washing-place of the town in the glen, where the waters of the Arrone, ever bright and sparkling, are drawn off into stone basons overhung with fern and creepers.

Beyond Galera, leaving the Convent of Santa Maria in Celsano to the east, the road to Bracciano enters a more fertile district. On the left is passed a marsh, once a lake, called the *Lago Morto*. Green corn now covers the hill-sides, and here and there is an olive garden. Soon, upon the right, the beautiful *Lake of Bracciano*, 20 miles in circumference, and six miles across in its widest part, is seen sleeping in its still bason surrounded by green wooded hills. Then the huge Castle of the Odescalchi, built of black lava, and fringed by deeply-machicolated towers, rises before us, crowning the yellow lichen-gilded roofs of the town. We rattle into the ill-paved street, and, between the dull white-washed houses, we see the huge towers frowning down upon us. At last the carriage can go no further and stops in a little piazza. The steep ascent to the fortress can only be surmounted on mule-back or on foot, and is cut out of the solid rock. On and in this rock the castle was built by the Orsini in the fifteenth century, just after their normal enemies, the Colonnas, had destroyed a former fortress of theirs. So they were determined to make it strong enough. As we enter beneath the gateway surmounted by the arms of the Orsini, we see that the rock still forms the pavement, and reaches half-way up the walls around us. The rest of these grim walls is of black lava, plundered, it is said, from the paving-blocks of the Via Cassia. Gloomy passages, also cut out of the solid rocks, lead into profundities suggestive

Bracciano.

of the most romantic adventures and escapes. One does not wonder that Sir Walter Scott was more anxious to see Bracciano than anything else in Italy, and set off thither almost immediately after his arrival in Rome.

The inner court of the castle is much more cheerful. It

has a gothic loggia and a curious outside staircase, at once descending and ascending, and adorned with frescoes. As we were sitting here to draw, the old housekeeper came out to welcome us. She had been the German nurse of the young Prince Odescalchi, to whom the castle now belongs; we brought her a letter from the Princess-mother, and she was delighted to have the break in the monotony of her life. She had "told the Princess she wished for repose — she wished to have time to think in her old age—and here she found it, but sometimes the repose was almost too much. The wind whistled through the long galleries louder than was pleasant, when there was no voice to enliven it; and last week in the earthquake—when the castle went crick-crack, and the plaster fell from the walls, and the tiles rattled upon the roof—oh, then it was roba da spaventare."

Castle Court. Bracciano.

Of the few mediæval castles in Italy which are still inhabited Bracciano is one of the largest. The Odescalchi family still occasionally come here in summer, when the vast chambers must be delightfully cool, and the views over lake and town and mountains most enjoyable. On the upper floor is the Hall of Justice, where the Orsini barons, who had the right of appointing magistrates, and being judges in their own persons, used for several centuries to sit in judgment upon their dependants. The Great Hall on the ground floor has some rapidly-vanishing frescoes of Zucchero, and looks like a place where ten thousand ghosts might hold carnival, only perhaps their revels would be hindered by the tiny chapel which opens out of it. In the living apartments are some fine old chairs and carved modern furniture, splendid beds and wardrobes, and infinitesimal washing-apparatus. One room has family portraits from old times down to the present possessors. These are very proud of their home, though they are not often here. Some years ago, poverty obliged them to sell their castle, but they did so with aching hearts, and when it was bought by Prince Torlonia, a reservation was made, that if the wheel of their fortunes should revolve within a limited space of years, they should be allowed to buy it back again at the same price which he had given. Torlonia felt secure, spent much time and money at Bracciano, and was devoted to his new purchase. As the time was drawing to a conclusion, all doubt as to the future vanished from his mind, but, just in time, the fortune of the Princess-mother Odescalchi enabled the family to redeem their pledge, and the former possessors returned, to their own triumph and the delight of the inhabitants. The Princess Odescalchi, whose fortune redeemed Bracciano, is almost a historical character in Rome. She has been one of the strongest supporters of the Pope, which is not unnatural, for in a great illness, the physicians had given up her case as hopeless, and declared that nothing short of a miracle could save her. At this juncture, when all her family were assembled to see her die, the Pope, from the Vatican, sent her his absolution and blessing, and with it a very tiny loaf of bread—"panetella,"* which he desired her to swallow, — he had prayed over it and blessed it, and perhaps it would save her life. She *did* swallow it, recovered, and the next day went in person to the Vatican to return thanks to the Holy Father!

But it was only in the last century that the Odescalchi purchased Bracciano from the Orsini, who were then beginning to fall into decadence, after a splendid historical career of more than six hundred years. Pope Celestin III. (1191—98) was an Orsini, and Pope Nicholas III. (1277—81), whom Dante sees in hell, among the Simonists.

> "Sappi ch'io fui vestito del gran manto.
> E veramente fui figliuol dell' Orsa
> Cupido sì per avanzar gli Orsatti,
> Che su l'avere, e qui me misi in borsa."
>
> *Inferno,* xix.

But having bestowed two popes upon the Church is the least of the glories of the Orsini, and it is their ceaseless contests with the Colonnas, in which they were alternately victorious and defeated, which gives them their chief historical consequence.

> "*Orsi,* lupi, leone, aquile e serpi
> Ad una gran marmorea *Colonna*
> Fanno noja sovente e à se danno."
>
> *Petrarca, Canz.* vi.

---

* "Panetelle di San Nicolo" are still eaten by the lower classes in and near Rome on the festival of that popular saint—the Bishop of Myra—"per divozione," in remembrance of the little loaves of this kind which he used to distribute to the poor.

THE ORSINI.

"The Ursini migrated from Spoleto: the sons of Ursus, as they are styled in the twelfth century, from some eminent person, who is only known as the father of their race. But they were soon distinguished among the nobles of Rome, by the number and bravery of their kinsmen, the strength of their towers, the honours of the senate and sacred college, and the elevation of two popes, Celestin III. and Nicholas III., of their name and lineage. Their riches may be accused as an early abuse of nepotism; the estates of S. Peter were alienated in their favour by the liberal Celestin; and Nicholas was ambitious for their sakes to solicit the alliance of monarchs; to found new kingdoms in Lombardy and Tuscany; and to invest them with the perpetual office of senators of Rome. All that has been observed of the greatness of the Colonna, will likewise redound to the glory of the Ursini, their constant and equal antagonists in the long hereditary feud, which distracted above two hundred and fifty years the ecclesiastical state. The jealousy of pre-eminence and power was the true ground of their quarrel; but as a specious badge of distinction, the Colonna embraced the name of Ghibellines and the party of the Empire; the Ursini espoused the title of Guelphs and the cause of the Church. The eagle and the keys were displayed in their adverse banners; and the two factions of Italy most furiously raged when the origin and nature of the dispute were long since forgotten. After the retreat of the popes to Avignon, they disputed in arms the vacant republic; and the mischiefs of discord were perpetuated by the wretched compromise of electing each year two rival senators. By their private hostilities, the city and country were desolated, and the fluctuating balance inclined with their alternate success. But none of either family had fallen by the sword, till the most renowned champion of the Ursini was surprised and slain by the younger Stephen Colonna. His triumph is stained with the reproach of violating the truce; their defeat was basely avenged by the assassination, before the church door, of an innocent boy and his two servants. Yet the victorious Colonna, with an annual colleague, was declared senator of Rome during the term of five years. And the muse of Petrarch inspired a wish, a hope, a prediction, that the generous youth, the son of his venerable hero, would restore Rome and Italy to their pristine glory; that his justice would extirpate the wolves and lions, the serpents and *bears*, who laboured to subvert the eternal basis of the marble *Column*."—*Gibbon's Roman Empire*, ch. lxix.

——"genuit quem nobilis Ursæ
Progenies, Romana domus, veterataque magnis
Fascibus in clero, pompasque experta senatûs,
Bellorumque manu grandi stipata parentum

>   Cardineos apices, necnon fastigia dudum
>   Papatûs *iterata* tenens."
>   *Cardinal St. George on Celestin V.*

The broad terrace immediately under the castle looks down upon the great Lake of Bracciano, which in ancient times was called the Lacus Sabatinus, and is mentioned by Festus. Near the site of Bracciano, says tradition, stood the city of Sabate, which was overwhelmed by the lake long ago, though its houses, its temples, and statues, may still be seen, on a clear day, standing intact beneath the glassy waters. The silvery expanse is backed by distant snow mountains, and here and there a little feudal town crowns the hill-sides or stands on the shore and is reflected in the lake. *Oriolo* has a villa of the Altieri, and its church-porch bears an inscription, which shows that it occupies the site of Pausilypon, built by Metia, wife of Titus Metius Herdonius. *Vicarello* (from Vicus Aureliæ) has the ruins of a Roman villa, and is still celebrated for the baths so useful in cutaneous disorders, which were well known in old times as Aquæ Aureliæ. Many curious Roman coins and vases have been found there. Beyond Vicarello is *Trevignano*, another Orsini stronghold, picturesquely crowned by their old castle. Lastly we must notice *Anguillara*, with a fine machicolated castle, bearing the celebrated 'crossed eels' of the famous Counts of Anguillara, of whom were Pandolfo d'Anguillara who built the church of S. Francesco a Ripa at Rome, Everso d'Anguillara, celebrated as a robber chief of the fifteenth century, and Orso d'Anguillara, the senator who crowned Petrarch upon the Capitol, and lived in the old palace which still remains in the Trastevere. Their country castle, which successfully withstood a siege from the Duke of Calabria in

1486, overhangs the quiet lake, which indeed at one time bore its name, and the town, which is 20 miles from Rome, is well worth visiting, by a road which turns off on the right not far from Galera.

As we stood on the terrace, looking down upon all these historical scenes, the violet sky suddenly opened, a rainbow arched across the expanse of waters, and rays of light flitting along the green encircling slopes, lit up one old fortress after another, as with a golden glory, which lasted for an instant, and faded again into the purple mist. It was a beautiful effort of Nature, cheering the monotony of a cloudy, misty day.

CHAPTER VIII.

GABII AND ZAGAROLO.

(Gabii, 11 miles from Rome, is a pleasant short-day's excursion in a carriage (which, with two horses, ought not to cost more than 15 francs). On horseback Gabii, Collatia, and Lunghezza, may be visited in the same day.)

THE road which leads to Gabii is the *Via Prænestina*, sometimes called *Via Gabina*, which emerges from the Porta Maggiore, and turns to the left (the central road of three). On the left, about half a mile from the walls, we pass a tomb said to be that of T. Quintus Atta, A.U.C. 678. Then, crossing a small streamlet in a hollow, believed to be the *Aqua Bollicante*, which marked the limits of ancient Rome, where the Arvales sang their hymn, we reach the ruins of the *Torre degli Schiavi*, the villa and temple of the Gordian Emperors (see *Walks in Rome*, ii. 133), which, in their richness of colour, backed by the lovely mountains of the Sabina, present one of the most beautiful scenes in the whole Campagna.

At the foot of the little hill upon which the ruins stand, the road to Lunghezza turns off on the left. The Campagna now becomes excessively wild and open. Here and there a tomb or a tower breaks the wide expanse. Far on the left is the great castle of Cervaretto, and beyond it Cervara and

Rustica; further still is the Tor dei Pazzi. To the left the valley is seen opening towards the Hernican and Volscian hills, between the great historic sites of Præneste and Colonna. All is most beautiful, yet unutterably desolate: —

> "The very sepulchres lie tenantless
> Of their heroic dwellers."

Now, on the left, rises, on a broad square basement, the fine tower called *Tor Tre Teste*, from the three heads (from a tomb) built into its walls. Beyond, also on the left, is the *Tor Sapienza*.

The eighth mile from Rome is interesting as the spot where Roman legend, as narrated by Livy (v. 49), tells that Camillus overtook the army of the Gauls laden with the spoils of Rome, and defeated them so totally, that he left not a single man alive to carry the news home to their countrymen.

"Among the fictions attached to Roman history, this was one of the first to be rejected."—*Niebuhr.*

"Such a falsification, scarcely to be paralleled in the annals of any other people, justifies the strongest suspicion of all those accounts of victories and triumphs which appears to rest in any degree on the authority of the family memorials of the Roman aristocracy."—*Arnold.*

At the ninth mile the road passes over the magnificent viaduct called *Pontenona*, consisting of seven arches, built of the gloomy stone called "lapis gabinus." The pavement of the bridge, and even part of the parapet, exist, showing what it was when entire.

"C'est certainement à la plus belle époque de l'architecture republicaine qu'appartient le pont de Nona, sur la voie Prenestine, probablement à l'époque du Tabularium, c'est à dire au temps de Sylla. Il est bati en peperin dont les blocs ont quelquefois dix ou douze pieds de longueur : au-dessous des arches, qui ont de dix-huit à vingt-quatre pieds de hauteur, est un pont beaucoup plus petit, qui a précédé l'autre. Ce petit pont primitif était sans doute l'œuvre des habitants du lieu et leur suffisait ; mais Rome est venue ; elle a élevé le niveau du pont jusqu'au niveau de la voute, à laquelle il était lié, et a laissé subsister à ses pieds son humble prédécesseur comme pour servir à mesurer sa grandeur par le contraste."—*Ampère*, iv. 71.

More and more desolate becomes the country, till at the Osteria del Osa, 11 miles from Rome, the road to Gabii, now exceedingly rough for carriages, leaves the Via Prænestina to the right, and, skirting the edge of the crater-lake of Gabii, now almost dried up, reaches the few huts which mark the site of the town, and a low massive ruin, which might easily pass overlooked, but which is no less than a fragment—the *cella*—of the famous *Temple of Juno*, celebrated by Virgil:—

". . . . . quique arva Gabinæ
Junonis, gelidumque Anienem, et roscida rivis
Hernica saxa colunt."
Æn. vii. 682.

and by Silius Italicus ;

". . . . nec amœna retentant
Algida, nec juxta Junonis tecta Gabinæ."
xii. 5, 36.

"The temple (the cell of which remains almost entire, but rent in certain parts apparently by lightning) is built of rectangular blocks of peperino. It has the same aspect as that of Diana at Aricia; that is, the wall of the posticum is prolonged beyond the cella, to the width of the portico on each side :

'Columnis adjectis dextrâ et sinistrâ ad humeros pronäi.'
Vitruvius.

The number of columns could scarcely be less than six in front; those of the flanks have not been decided. The columns were fluted, and of peperino, like the rest of the building; but it might perhaps be hazardous to assign them to a very remote period. The pavement is a mosaic of large white tesseræ."—*Sir W. Gell.*

"The form of this temple was almost identical with that at Aricia. The interior of the cella was twenty-seven feet wide, and forty-five feet long. It had columns of the Doric order in front and at the sides, but none at the back. The surrounding area was about fifty-four feet at the sides, but in front a space of only eight feet was left open, in consequence of the position of the theatre, which abutted closely upon the temple. On the eastern side of the cella are traces of the rooms in which the priests in charge of the temple lived."—*Burn, The Roman Campagna.*

From the temple we look across the grey-green crater of the lake—which has lately been drained by Prince Torlonia, to whom it belongs, to the great destruction of its beauty, and the improvement of his property—to the mediæval tower of *Castiglione* (which is mentioned in a deed of 1225) occupying the highest part of the ridge, and marking the site of the citadel of Gabii. Slight remains of wall exist near the tower, and small fragments of ruins with scattered pieces of marble may be found all along the ridge. Near the temple remains of semi-circular seats, perhaps indicating a *Theatre*, have been discovered, and nearer the high-road it has become possible to trace the plan of the *Forum*, a work of imperial times, surrounded on three sides by porticoes, and adorned with statues.

These fragments, ill-defined and scattered at long intervals in the corn or rank weeds with which the Campagna is overgrown, are all that remains of Gabii.

Virgil and Dionysius say that Gabii was a Latin colony of Alba. Solinus asserts that it was founded by two Siculian brothers Galatios and Bios, from whose united names that of the city was formed. Dionysius says that it was one of the largest and most populous of Latin cities. It seems to have been the university of Latium, and Plutarch and Strabo narrate that Romulus and Remus were sent there to learn Greek and the use of arms. In the reign of Tarquinius Superbus, Gabii gave refuge to exiles from Rome and other cities of Latium, and so aroused the hostility of the King.

> "Ultima Tarquinius Romanæ gentis habebat
> Regna; vir injustus, fortis ad arma tamen.
> Ceperat hic alias, alias everterat urbes;
> Et Gabios turpi fecerat arte suos."
>
> *Ovid. Fast.* ii. 687.

"The primeval greatness of Gabii is still apparent in the walls of the cell of the temple of Juno. Dionysius saw it yet more conspicuous in the ruins of the extensive walls, by which the city, standing in the plain, had been surrounded, and which had been demolished by a destroying conqueror, as well as in those of several buildings. It was one of the thirty Latin cities: but it scorned the determination of the confederacy—in which cities far from equal in power were equal in votes—to degrade themselves. Hence it began an obstinate war with Rome. The contending cities were only twelve miles apart; and the country betwixt them endured all the evils of military ravages for years, no end of which was to be foreseen: for within their walls they were invincible.

"But Sextus, the son of Tarquinius Superbus, pretended to rebel. The king, whose anger appeared to have been provoked by his wanton insolence, condemned him to a disgraceful punishment, as if he had been the meanest of his subjects. He came to the Gabines under the mask of a fugitive. The bloody marks of his stripes, and still more the infatuation which comes over men doomed to perish, gained him belief and goodwill. At first he led a body of volunteers: then troops were trusted to his charge. Every enterprise succeeded; for booty and soldiers were thrown in his way at certain appointed places; and the deluded citizens raised the man, under whose command they promised themselves the pleasures of a successful war, to the dictatorship. The last step of his treachery was yet to come. None of the troops being hirelings, it was a hazardous venture to open a gate. Sextus sent to ask his father in what way he should deliver Gabii into his hands. Tarquinius was in his garden when he received the messenger: he walked along in silence, striking off the heads of the tallest poppies with his stick, and dismissed the man without an answer. On this hint, Sextus put to death, or by means of false charges banished, such of the Gabines as were able to oppose him. By distributing their fortunes he purchased partisans among the lowest class; and, acquiring the uncontested rule, brought the city to submit to his father."—*Niebuhr's Hist. of Rome,* i. 491.

The treaty concluded at this time between Rome and Gabii was preserved on a wooden shield in the temple of Jupiter Fidius at Rome. It is evidently one of those alluded to by Horace as the :—

"foedera regum
Cum Gabiis aut cum rigidis æquata Sabinis."*

After the expulsion of the kings, Sextus Tarquinius took refuge at Gabii, where, according to Livy, he was murdered. But Gabii was one of the cities which combined in behalf of the Tarquins at the Lake Regillus. After that battle it became subject to Rome, and almost disappears from history for several centuries, and was so reduced that :—

". . . Gabios, Veiosque, Coramque
Pulvere vix tectæ poterunt monstrare ruinæ."
Lucan. vii. 392.

"Scis Lebedus quam sit Gabiis desertior atque
Fidenis vicus."
Hor. i. *Ep.* 11.

"Quippe suburbanæ parva minus urbe Bovillæ ;
Et, qui nunc nulli, maxima turba Gabi."
Propert. iv. *El.* 1.

"Hujus qui trahitur prætextam sumere mavis ;
An Fidenarum, Gabiorumque esse potestas ?"
Juvenal. Sat. x. 100.

"Quis timet, aut timuit gelida Præneste ruinam ;
Aut positis nemorosa inter juga Volsiniis ; aut
Simplicibus Gabiis."
Juvenal. Sat. iii. 189.

". . . . . . cum jam celebres notique poëtæ
Balneolum Gabiis, Romæ conducere furnos
Tentarent."
Juvenal. Sat. vii. 4.

The Gabini had a peculiar mode of girding the toga,

* See Smith's Dict. of Greek and Roman Geography.

which gave more freedom to the limbs, and which was found useful when hurrying to battle from a sacrifice. Virgil alludes to it :—

> "Ipse, Quirinali trabea cinctuque Gabino
> Insignis, reserat stridentia limina consul."
> *Æn.* vii. 612.

Under Tiberius the town had a slight revival, which was increased under Hadrian, who adorned it with handsome public buildings, colleges, and an aqueduct. In the first ages of Christianity it became the seat of a bishopric (a list of its bishops from A.D. 465 to 879 is given in Ughelli's *It alia Sera*), but it was finally ruined when Astolphus ravaged the Campagna, at the head of 6000 Lombards. It is only a mile's walk or ride from the Osteria del Osa (turning left) to the Castello del Osa or Collatia, for which see chapter ix.

Continuing along the Via Præenestina, much of the old pavement is visible. This is most perfect at *Cavamonte* (seven miles beyond Gabii), where the road passes through a deep cutting in the rocks which guard the valley of Gallicano. The cliffs on either side of the road reach a height of 70 feet, and are most picturesquely overhung with shrubs and ivy. The road, which is generally only 14 feet wide, here has a width of 27 feet. After passing through Cavamonte, the Via Præenestina ascends towards Præneste by the Convent of the Buon Pastore.

On the left of the road (19 miles from Rome) is the village of *Gallicano*, supposed to occupy the site of the ancient Pedum, whose name is familiar to readers of Horace, from the epistle to Albius Tibullus.

"Albi, nostrorum sermonum candide judex,
Quid nunc te dicam facere in regione Pedana?"

i. *Ep.* iv.

The present name is derived from Ovinius Gallicanus, Prefect of Rome in the time of Constantine, who was afterwards canonized for his charities, and in whose honour the Hospital in the Trastevere was dedicated. The place was formerly a fief of the Colonnas, and now gives a title to the Rospigliosi.

"The towns of Scaptia, Ortona, and Querquetula lay somewhere in this neighbourhood. Scaptia was one of the cities which conspired to restore the Tarquins to the Roman throne. It gave a name to one of the tribes at Rome, but in Pliny's time had fallen entirely into ruins. The site of Passerano has been fixed upon as the representative of Scaptia by most modern topographers. But this opinion rests upon a false reading in Festus, and must be rejected. Ortona lay on the frontier, between the Latins and Æquians, but belonged to the Latins. It seems to have been near Corbio, and on the further side of Mount Algidus. The site of Querquetula is entirely unknown. Gell and Nibby place it at Corcolo, arguing from the similarity of the name. Corcolo is four miles from Gallicano, and six from Zagarolo, at a point where there is an artificial dyke separating a small hill from the neighbouring plateau. There are traces of ancient roads converging to this spot from Præneste, Castellaccio, and Gallicano."—*Burn, The Roman Campagna.*

Zagarola, 21 miles from Rome, will scarcely be made the object of an especial excursion, but may be visited by those who drive to Palestrina. It is a curious old mediæval town chiefly built by the Colonnas, in whose wars it was twice sacked, first by Boniface VIII., and afterwards by Cardinal Vitelleschi in the reign of Eugenius IV. It now gives a ducal title to the Rospigliosi. Many Roman antiquities found in the neighbourhood are built up into the walls and houses, and over the Roman gate is a seated statue of Jupiter. The commission for the revision of the Vulgate under Gregory XIV. met in the palace of Zagarolo.

CHAPTER IX.

CERVARA, LUNGHEZZA, AND COLLATIA.

(It is a short and pleasant afternoon's drive to Cervara, but a day must be given to Lunghezza and Collatia, though, if visited on horseback, they may be combined with the ruins of Gabii.)

AFTER passing the Torre degli Schiavi, the road to Lunghezza turns off to the left. On the right is the Tor Tre Teste, on the left we pass close to a fountain of the Acqua Vergine. On the left is now seen the great castellated farm of the Borgheses called *Cervaretto*, rising above the low marshy ground. The field-road which passes in front of the further side of this castle, leads on a mile further to another Campagna castle, *Cervara*, a most picturesque red-brick tower with some farm buildings attached to it.

Close to this, are the famous *Caves of Cervara*, which are said to have been formed when excavating the materials for the Coliseum. It is a strange place. You are quite unconscious of any break in the wide grassy Campagna, till you suddenly find yourself on the edge of a precipice, with deep, narrow, miniature ravines yawning beneath you and winding in all directions till they emerge on a meadow near the Anio. And when you descend into these, openings in the rocks beneath lead into vast chambers opening one upon another, their roof supported by huge pillars of natural rock, while the floor is deep in sand, and long tresses of ivy, and branches of flowering laurestinus, wave in upon the gloom, whenever the light streams in through a rift overhead. One point is especially charming, where the Anio and the hills beyond it are seen through a great arch of natural rock.

In May these solitudes are enlivened by the revels of the *Festa degli Artisti*, which is well worth seeing. Some historical scene, such as the triumph of Vitellius (as in 1870), is taken as the groundwork of a costumed procession,—tournaments are held in the meadow near the Anio, wonderful cavalcades of Arabs in rich dresses ride waving their long spears through the Petra-like ravines, and a bellowing Dragon vomiting forth fire and smoke emerges from the caves, and is slain by an imaginary S. George in the rock-girt hollow.

Cervara.

About two miles beyond Cervara, the tall tower of *Rustica* rises above the swellings of the Campagna. It stands on the very edge of the Anio in a beautiful situation, and is well worth visiting. It was once the property of Elius. father of the Emperor Lucius Verus, who was adopted by Hadrian as his successor. Rustica is most easily seen from the opposite side of the river, reached by the road to Tivoli, turning off to the right beyond Ponte Mammolo. Returning to the Via Collatina, a tolerable road leads us over an uninhabited part of the Campagna for about five miles further. Then it descends into the valley of the Anio, which is here bordered with willows. The great castle or rather fortified farm of *Lunghezza* is seen on the opposite slope, backed by the purple peaks of the Sabina. This was an ancient possession of the Strozzi family, but has lately been sold to the Duke of Grazioli, one of the richest of the modern Roman nobles.

"C'est le bon plaisir des souverains pontifes qui a fait entrer quelques riches parvenus dans l'aristocratie romaine.

"Un boulanger du nom de Grazioli fait une grande fortune, et le pape ordonne qu'il soit inscrit sur la liste du patriciat romain. Il achète une baronnie et le pape le fait baron. Il achète un duché et le voilà duc Grazioli. Son fils épouse une Lante de la Rovere."—*About.*

There is little remarkable about Lunghezza, except its situation, but some hours may be pleasantly spent in sketching on the river-bank lower down the valley.

A pleasant walk of about two miles up the stream of the Osa (turning to the left in descending from the Castle) leads along fields and through a wood, filled in spring with the snow-drops which are sold in Rome in such abundance, to the ruined castle called *Castellaccio* or *Castello dell' Osa*, which occupies a declivity of lava on the left of the stream.

It is disputed whether Castel dell' Osa or Lunghezza is the site of the famous Collatia. Beneath the ruined castle near the Osa some fragments of ancient wall, in regular blocks, may be observed, but this is the only fact in favour of its being the site of the home of Lucretia, while Sir W. Gell, in favour of Lunghezza, draws attention to the existence of the Via Collatina (apparently leading direct to Lunghezza),

Castello dell' Osa.

which would have been unnecessary had Collatia occupied a site such as Castel dell' Osa, which is only two miles from Gabii, as a slight turning from the Via Gabina would have led to it. Lunghezza accords much better than Castel dell' Osa with the description of Virgil:—

"Collatinas imponent montibus arces."
Æn. vi. 774.

Virgil and Dionysius notice Collatia as a colony of Alba-Longa. It was reduced into subjection to Rome in the reign of Tarquinius Priscus, who established a garrison there, and appointed his nephew Egerius as its governor, who forthwith took, and transmitted to his descendants, the name of Collatinus. His daughter-in-law, Lucretia, was residing here during the siege of Ardea, and thus Collatia became the scene of the events which led to the overthrow of the Roman monarchy.

"As the king's sons and their cousin L. Tarquinius were sitting over their cups at Ardea, a dispute arose about the virtue of their wives. This cousin, surnamed Collatinus, from Collatia, where he dwelt as an independent prince, was the grandson of Aruns, the elder brother of the first Tarquinius, after whose death Lucumo removed to Rome. Nothing was doing in the field: so they straightway mounted their horses to visit their homes by surprise. At Rome, the princesses were revelling at a banquet, surrounded by flowers and wine. From thence the youths hastened to Collatia, where at the late hour of the night Lucretia the wife of Collatinus was spinning amid the circle of her handmaids.

". . . The next day Sextus, the eldest of the king's sons, returned to Collatia, and, according to the rights of gentle hospitality, was lodged in his kinsman's house. At the dead of night he entered sword-in-hand into the matron's chamber, and by threatening that he would lay a slave with his throat cut beside her body, would pretend to have avenged her husband's honour, and would make her memory for ever loathsome to the object of her love, wrung from her what the fear of death could not obtain.

"Who, after Livy, can tell of Lucretia's despair? She besought her father and her husband to come to her, for that horrible things had taken place. Lucretius came, accompanied by P. Valerius, who afterwards gained the name of Publicola; Collatinus with the outcast Brutus. They found the disconsolate wife in the garb of mourning, sitting in a trance of sorrow. They heard the tale of the crime, and swore to avenge her. (Saying, 'I am not guilty, yet must I too share the punishment, lest any should think that they may be false to their husbands and live,' Lucretia drew a knife from her bosom, and stabbed herself to the heart.) Over the body of Lucretia, as over a victim, the vows of vengeance were renewed. Her avengers carried the corpse into the market-place of Collatia. The citizens renounced Tarquinius, and promised obedience to the deliverers. Their young men attended the funeral procession to Rome. Here with one voice the decree of the citizens deposed the last king from his throne, and pronounced sentence of banishment against him and his family."—*Niebuhr's Hist. of Rome.*

Silius Italicus notices Collatia as the birth-place of the elder Brutus:—

". . . altrix casti Collatia Bruti."

viii. 363.

In the time of Strabo (v. 229) Collatia was little more than a village. It is only two miles from the ruins to Gabii, up the valley of the Osa.

CHAPTER X.

ANTEMNÆ AND FIDENÆ.

(This is a pleasant afternoon's drive. Pedestrians may vary the way by going first to the Acqua Acetosa (see *Walks in Rome*, ii. 420), and turning to the right across the hill of Antemnæ to the Ponte Salara.)

LEAVING the Porta Salara, by which Alaric entered Rome (August 24, 410), the Via Salara runs between the walls of half-deserted villas till it reaches the brow of the hill above the Anio. Here, on the left, about two miles from the city, is the green hill-side, which was once the site of the "Turrigeræ Antemnæ"* of Virgil, one of the most ancient cities of Italy.

"Antemnaque prisco
Crustumio prior."
Silius Ital. viii. 367.

"Not a tree—not a shrub on its turf-grown surface—not a house—not a ruin—not one stone upon another, to tell you the site had been inhabited. Yet here once stood Antemnæ, the city of many towers. Not a trace remains above-ground. Even the broken pottery, that infallible indicator of bygone civilization, which marks the site and determines the limits of habitation on many a now desolate spot of classic ground, is here so overgrown with herbage that the eye of an antiquary would alone detect it. It is a site strong by nature, and well adapted for a city, as cities then were; for it is scarcely larger than the Palatine Hill, which, though at first it embraced the whole of Rome, was afterwards too small for a single palace. It has a peculiar interest as the site of one of the three cities of Sabina, whose daughters, ravished

* *Æn.* vii. 630.

by the followers of Romulus, became the mothers of the Roman race."*—*Dennis.*

"It would seem that the high point nearest the road was the citadel; and the descent of two roads, now scarcely perceptible, one toward Fidenæ and the bridge, and the other toward Rome, marks the site of a gate. On the other side of the knoll of the citadel is a cave, with signs of artificial cutting in the rock, being a sepulchre under the walls. There was evidently a gate also in the hollow which runs from the platform of the city to the junction of the Aniene and the Tiber, where there is now a little islet. Probably there was another gate toward the meadows, on the side of the Acqua Acetosa, and another opposite; and from these two gates, which the nature of the soil points out, one road must have run up a valley, tending in the direction of the original Palatium of Rome; and the other must have passed by a ferry toward Veii, up the valley near the present Torre di Quinto. It is not uninteresting to observe how a city, destroyed at a period previous to what is now called that of authentic history, should, without even one stone remaining, preserve indications of its former existence. From the height of Antemnæ, is a fine view of the field of battle between the Romans and the Fidenates, whence Tullus Hostilius despatched M. Horatius to destroy the city of Alba Longa. The isthmus, where the two roads from Palatium and Veii met, unites with the city a higher eminence, which may have been another citadel. The beauty of the situation is such, that it is impossible it should not have been selected as the site of a villa in the flourishing times of Rome.

"The spot is frequently adverted to in the early periods of history. Servius, Varro, and Festus, agree that Antemnæ was so called, '*quasi ante amnem posita.*'"—*Gell.*

Just below the site of Antemnæ the Via Salara crossed the Anio by a fine old bridge built by Narses in the sixth century upon the site of the famous *Ponte Salara*, where Manlius fought with the Gaul. The bridge was blown up during the panic caused by the approach of Garibaldi and the insurgents in 1867 (see *Walks in Rome*, ii. 19), and the ruins, which were of the greatest interest, were destroyed by the Government in 1874. Beyond the ugly modern bridge

---

* The other two were Cæcina and Crustumium.

is a great mediæval tower, *Torre Salara*, built upon a Roman tomb, which is itself used as an Osteria.

The road now runs for several miles through a plain called the Prato Rotondo, the scene of the battle which led to the destruction of Alba.

<small>When the combat between the Horatii and Curiatii was agreed upon, "the compact had been, that the nation whose champions should be victorious, was to command the obedience and service of the other: and the Albans fulfilled it. When Fidenæ, however, having driven out or overpowered the Roman colonists, was defending itself with the help of the Veientines against Tullus and the Romans, in the battle that ensued, the Romans stood against the Veientines: on the right, over against the Fidenates, were the Albans under their dictator Mettius Fuffetius. Faithless, and yet irresolute, he drew them off from the conflict to the hills. The Etruscans, seeing that he did not keep his engagement, and suspecting that he meant to attack their flank, gave way, and fled along his line; when the twofold traitor fell upon them in their disorder, in the hope of cloaking his treachery. The Roman King feigned himself deceived. On the following day the two armies were summoned to receive their praises and rewards. The Albans came without their arms, were surrounded by the Roman troops, and heard the sentence of the inexorable King; that, as their dictator had broken his faith both to Rome and to the Etruscans, he should in like manner be torn in pieces by horses driven in opposite directions, while, as for themselves and their city, they should be removed to Rome, and Alba should be destroyed."—*Niebuhr*, i. 349.

"On the same field was fought many a bloody fight between the Romans and Etruscans. Here, in the year of Rome 317, the Fidenates, with their allies of Veii and Falerii, were again defeated, and Lars Tolumnius, chief of the Veientines, was slain. And a few years later, Mamilius Æmilius and Cornelius Cossus, the heroes of the former fight, routed the same foes in the same plain, and captured the city of Fidenæ. Here, too, Annibal seems to have pitched his camp when he marched from Capua to surprise the City."—*Dennis*.</small>

A low range of hills now skirts the road on the right, and a few crumbling bits of wall near some old bay-trees are pointed out as fragments of the *Villa of Phaon*, the freedman of Nero, where the emperor died.

"The Hundred Days of Nero were drawing rapidly to a close. He was no longer safe in the city... He would have thrown himself into the Tiber, but his courage failed him. He must have time, he said, and repose to collect his spirits for suicide, and his freedman Phaon at last offered him his villa in the suburbs, four miles from the city. In undress and bare-footed, throwing a rough cloak over his shoulders, and a kerchief across his face, he glided through the doors, mounted a horse, and, attended by Sporus and three others, passed the city gates with the dawn of the summer morning. The Nomentane road led him beneath the wall of the prætorians, whom he might hear uttering curses against him, and pledging vows to Galba; and the early travellers from the country asked him as they met, *What news of Nero?* or remarked to one another, *These men are pursuing the tyrant.* Thunder and lightning, and a shock of earthquake, added horror to the moment. Nero's horse started at a dead body on the road-side, the kerchief fell from his face, and a prætorian passing by recognized and saluted him. At the fourth milestone the party quitted the highway, alighted from their horses, and scrambled on foot through a corn-brake, laying their own cloaks to tread on, to the rear of the promised villa. Phaon now desired Nero to crouch in a sand-pit hard by, while he contrived to open the drain from the bath-room, and so admit him unperceived; but he vowed he would not go *alive*, as he said, *under-ground*, and remained trembling beneath the wall. Taking water in his hand from a puddle, *This*, he said, *is the famous drink of Nero.* At last a hole was made, through which he crept on all fours into a narrow chamber of the house, and there threw himself on a pallet. The coarse bread that was offered him he could not eat, but swallowed a little tepid water. Still he lingered, his companions urging him to seek refuge, without delay, from the insults about to be heaped on him. He ordered them to dig a grave, and himself lay down to give the measure; he desired them to collect bits of marble to decorate his sepulchre, and prepare water to cleanse and wood to burn his corpse, sighing meanwhile, and muttering, *What an artist to perish!* Presently a slave of Phaon's brought papers from Rome, which Nero snatched from him, and read that the senate had proclaimed him an enemy, and decreed his death, *in the ancient fashion.* He asked what that was? and was informed that the culprit was stripped, his head placed in a fork, and his body smitten with a stick till death. Terrified at this announcement, he took two daggers from his bosom, tried their edge one after the other, and again laid them down, alleging that *the moment was not yet arrived.* Then he called on Sporus to commence his funeral lamentations; then he implored some of the party to set him the example; once and again he reproached himself with his own timidity. *Fie! Nero, fie!* he muttered in Greek, *Courage, man! come, rouse thee!* Suddenly was heard the trampling of horsemen, sent to seize the culprit alive. Then at last, with a verse of Homer hastily ejaculated, *Sound of swift-footed steeds strikes on my ears*, he placed a weapon to his breast, and the slave Epaphroditus drove it home. The blow was scarcely struck, when the centurion rushed in, and thrusting his cloak against the wound, pretended he was come to help him. The dying wretch could only murmur, *Too late*, and, *Is this your fidelity?* and expired with a horrid stare on his countenance. He had adjured his attendants to burn his body, and not let the foe bear off his head; and this was now allowed him : the corpse was consumed with haste and imperfectly, but at least without mutilation."—*Merivale's Hist. of Romans under the Empire*, vii. 45.

"Néron vit que tout était perdu. Son esprit faux ne lui suggérait que des idées grotesques : se revêtir d'habits de deuil, aller haranguer le peuple en cet accoutrement, employer toute sa puissance scénique pour exciter la compassion, et obtenir ainsi le pardon du passé, ou, faute de mieux, la préfecture de l'Egypte. Il écrivit son discours; on lui fit remarquer qu'avant d'arriver au forum, il serait mis en pièces. Il se coucha : se réveillant au milieu de la nuit, il se trouva sans gardes ; on pillait déjà sa chambre. Il sort, frappe à diverses portes, personne ne répond. Il rentre, veut mourir, demande le mirmillon Spiculus, brillant tueur, une des célébrités de l'amphithéâtre. Tout le monde s'écarte. Il sort de nouveau, erre seul dans les rues, va pour se jeter dans le Tibre, revient sur ses pas. Le monde semblait faire le vide autour de lui. Phaon, son affranchi, lui offrit alors pour asile sa villa située entre la voie Salaria et la voie Nomentane, vers la quatrième borne milliare. Le malheureux, à peine vetu, couvert d'un méchant manteau, monté sur un cheval misérable, le visage enveloppé pour n'être pas reconnu, partit accompagné de trois ou quatre de ses affranchis, parmi lesquels étaient Phaon, Sporus, Epaphrodite, son secrétaire. Il ne faisait pas encore jour ; en sortant par la porte Colline, il entendit au camp des prétoriens, près duquel il passait, les cris des soldats qui le maudissaient et proclamaient Galba. Un écart de son cheval, amené par la puanteur d'un cadavre jeté sur le chemin, le fit reconnaître. Il put cependant atteindre la villa de Phaon, en se glissant à plat ventre sous les broussailles et en se cachant derrière les roseaux.

" Son esprit drolatique, son argot de gamin ne l'abandonnèrent pas. On voulut le blottir dans un trou à Pouzzolane comme on en voit beaucoup en ces parages. Ce fut pour lui l'occasion d'un mot à effet !

'Quelle destinée,' dit-il ; 'aller vivant sous terre !' Ses réflexions étaient comme un feu roulant de citations classiques, entremêlées des lourdes plaisanteries d'un bobèche aux abois. Il avait sur chaque circonstance une réminiscence littéraire, une froide antithèse : 'Celui qui autrefois était fier de sa suite nombreuse n'a plus maintenant que trois affranchis ?' Par moments, le souvenir de ses victimes lui revenait, mais n'aboutissait qu'à des figures de rhétorique, jamais à un acte moral de repentir. Le comédien survivait à tout. Sa situation n'était pour lui qu'un drame de plus, un drame qu'il avait répété. Se rappelant les rôles où il avait figuré des parricides, des princes réduits à l'état de mendiants, il remarquit que maintenant il jouait tout cela pour son compte, et chantonnait ce vers qu'un tragique avait mit dans la bouche d'Œdipe :

> Ma femme, ma mère, mon père
> Prononcent mon arrêt de mort.

Incapable d'une pensée serieuse, il voulut qu'on creusât sa fosse à la taille de son corps, fit apporter des morceaux de marbre, de l'eau, du bois pour ses funérailles ; tout cela, pleurant et disant : ' Quel artiste va mourir ?'

"'Le courrier de Phaon, cependant, apporte une dépêche ; Néron la lui arrache. Il lit que le sénat l'a déclaré ennemi public et l'a condamné à être puni 'selon la vieille coutume.'—'Quelle est cette coutume ?' demande-t-il. On lui répond que la tête du patient tout nue est engagée dans une fourche, qu'alors on le frappe de verges jusqu'à ce que mort s'ensuive, puis que le corps est traîné par un croc et jeté dans le Tibre. Il frémit, prend deux poignards qu'il avait sur lui, en essaye la pointe, les resserre, disant que l'heure fatale n'était pas encore venu ? Il engageait Sporus à commencer sa nénie funèbre, essayait de nouveau de se tuer, ne pouvait. Sa gaucherie, cette espèce de talent qu'il avait pour faire vibrer faux toutes les fibres de l'âme, ce rire à la fois bête et infernal, cette balourdise prétentieuse qui fait ressembler sa vie entière aux miaulements d'un sabbat grotesque, atteignaient au sublime de la fadeur. Il ne pouvait réussir à se tuer. 'N'y aura-t-il donc personne ici, demanda-t-il, pour me donner l'exemple ?' Il redoublait de citations, se parlait en grec, faisait des bouts de vers. Tout-à-coup on entend le bruit du détachement de cavalerie qui vient pour le saisir vivant.

"'Le pas des lourds chevaux me frappe les oreilles,' dit-il. Epaphrodite alors pesa sur le poignard et le lui fit entrer dans la gorge. Le centurion arrive presque au même moment, veut arrêter le sang, cherche à faire croire qu'il vient le sauver. 'Trop tard !' dit le mourant, dont les yeux sortaient de la tête et glaçaient d'horreur. 'Voila où en est la fidélité!' ajouta-t-il en expirant. Ce fut son meilleur trait comique. Néron laissant tomber une plainte mélancholique sur la méchanceté de son siècle, sur la disposition de la bonne foi et de la vertu! . . . . Applaudissons. La drame est complet. Une seule fois, nature aux mille visages, tu as su trouver un acteur digne d'un pareil rôle."—*Ernest Renan*, '*L'Antechrist*.'

Castel Giubeleo.

On the left of the road now rises an almost isolated hill, overlooking the valley of the Tiber, called *Castel Giubeleo*, from the farm-buildings upon it, which were erected by Boniface VIII. in the year of Jubilee. This hill is believed to have been the arx of ancient Fidenæ. Towards the river it is very steep, but it is united by a kind of isthmus to the high table-land, where the rest of the city is supposed to have stood.

"Dionysius, who is generally an excellent antiquary, says that Fidenæ was an Alban colony, founded at the same time with Nomentum and Crustumerium, the eldest of three emigrant brothers building Fidenæ. But it is evident that the great mass of the original inhabitants were Etruscans, for it appears, from Livy (lib. i. 27), that only a portion of the inhabitants '(ut qui coloni additi Romanis essent) Latinè sciebant.' The same author elsewhere relates, that when the Romans wanted a spy upon the Fidenates, they were obliged to employ a person who had been educated at Cære, and had learned the language and writing of Etruria : and in another place (lib. i. 15) he expressly says, 'Fidenates quoque Etrusci fuerunt.' The Fidenates were the constant allies of the Veientes, with whom they were probably connected by race.

"'The city,' says Dionysius, 'was in its glory in the time of Romulus, by whom it was taken and colonized; the Fidenates having seized certain boats laden with corn by the Crustumerini for the use of the Romans, as they passed down the Tiber under the walls of Fidenæ.' Livy (lib. iv. 22) calls Fidenæ 'urbs alta et munita;' and says, 'neque scalis capi poterat, neque in obsidione vis ulla erat.'"—*Gell.*

"Making the circuit of Castel Giubeleo, you are led round till you meet the road, where it issues from the hollow at the northern angle of the city. Besides the tombs which are found on both sides of the southern promontory of the city, there is a cave, running far into the rock, and branching off into several chambers and passages. Fidenæ, like Veii, is said to have been taken by a mine; and this cave might be supposed to indicate the spot, being subsequently enlarged into its present form, had not Livy stated that the *cuniculus* was on the opposite side of Fidenæ, where the cliffs were loftiest, and that it was carried into the Arx.

"The ruin of Fidenæ is as complete as that of Antemnæ. The hills on which it stood are now bare and desolate: the shepherd tends his flock on its slopes, or the plough furrows its bosom. Its walls have utterly disappeared; not one stone remains on another, and the broken pottery and the tombs around are the sole evidences of its existence. Yet, as Nibby observes, 'few ancient cities, of which few or no vestiges remain, have had the good fortune to have their sites so well determined as Fidenæ.' Its distance of forty stadia, or five miles, from Rome, mentioned by Dionysius, and its position relative to Veii, to the Tiber, and to the confluence of the Anio with that stream, as set forth by Livy, leave not a doubt of its true site."—*Dennis.*

"When we climb the promontory of Castel Giubeleo, and look around, standing in the shelter of the old house, what a strange prospect opens before us! Once how full of life and conflict!—now, how entirely a prey to decay and solitude! At our feet the lordly Tiber winds, with many a sweeping curve, away to Rome, which bristles in the horizon with its domes and towers. It is hardly possible to imagine that two hundred thousand human beings are living and moving two leagues off. As we turn the eye northwards not a creature is seen, not a single habitation of man. Still, how memory peoples the waste! That stream, which, marking its devious valley with a line of bare wintry trees, enters the Tiber opposite to the marshy meadow under our feet, is the Crimera—name of fatal omen, and yet eloquent of heroic daring. On that stream the race of the Fabii, who had undertaken on their own account the war with the people of Veii, perished, all, to the number of 306, being cut off by an ambush of the enemy.

"Further to the right, another stream, more faintly marked, comes into the Tiber on the other side. That is the Allia, a name of even more fatal sound; for on its banks took place that great defeat by the Gauls which issued in the taking of Rome.

"This scene surveyed, we descend again into the valley, and climb the lower opposite hill, which was evidently the site of Fidenæ. Here, as in several other places in the Campagna, we find mysterious ranges of rock-caverns communicating with one another, and opening into vast halls, now the stalls of cattle. It would seem that this was Fidenæ. Yet, how should these holes represent a city? Whence issued the legions that met the legions of Rome? Where are the walls—where the materials of the houses? One ruin only appears containing anything like masonry, and that apparently of the Middle Ages. Were these caves, hewn in the tufa, the ancient city? Then were the inhabitants little more than savages; then were the narratives of the historians impossible and self-contradicting. The whole matter is wrapped in impenetrable darkness."—*Dean Alford.*

Horace speaks of Fidenæ as if it was almost deserted in his time :—

"Scis Lebedus quam sit Gabiis desertior atque
Fidenis vicus—"

1 *Epist.* ii. 7.

but in the reign of Tiberius it appears to have been a municipal town :—

"Hujus qui trahitur prætextam sumere mavis,
An Fidenarum, Gabiorumque esse potestas."

Juvenal, Sat. x. 99.

and that its population was considerable is attested by the greatness of a public calamity which took place there.

"The retirement of Tiberius was followed by a succession of public calamities. . . . A private speculator had undertaken, as a matter of profit, one of the magnificent public works, which in better times it was the privilege of the chief magistrates or candidates for the highest offices to construct for the sake of glory or influence. In erecting a vast wooden amphitheatre in the suburban city of Fidenæ, he had omitted the necessary precaution of securing a solid foundation; and when the populace of Rome, unaccustomed, from the parsimony of Tiberius, to their favourite spectacles at home, were invited to the diversions of the opening day, which they attended in immense numbers, the mighty mass gave way under the pressure, and covered them in its ruins. Fifty thousand persons, or, according to a lower computation, not less than twenty thousand, men and women of all ranks, were killed or injured by this catastrophe."—*Merivale's Hist. of the Romans*, ch. xiv.

CHAPTER XI.

MENTANA AND MONTE ROTONDO.

(This is a delightful day's excursion from Rome, and comprises much of interest. It may be easily made in a carriage with two horses. Monte Rotondo may be visited between two trains on the Ancona line of railway.)

THE ancient road which led from Rome to Nomentum was called the *Via Nomentana*. It issued from the city by the now closed gate of the Porta Collina, and separating from the Via Salaria, proceeded almost in a direct line to its destination. The modern road nearly follows the Roman Way. It was on this side that the Italian troops approached Rome, on the day which so many patriotic spirits regarded as the dawn of freedom for Rome.

> " The blind, and the people in prison,
>   Souls without hope, without home,
> How glad were they all that heard !
> When the winged white flame of the word
> Passed over men's dust, and stirred
>   Death ; for Italia was risen,
>   And risen her light upon Rome.
>
> The light of her sword in the gateway
>   Shone, an unquenchable flame,
> Bloodless, a sword to release,
> A light from the eyes of peace,
> To bid grief utterly cease,
>   And the wrong of the old world straightway
>   Pass from the face of her fame :

> Hers, whom we turn to and cry on,
>   Italy, mother of men :
> From the sight of the face of her glory,
> At the sound of the storm of her story,
> That the sanguine shadows and hoary
> Should flee from the foot of the lion,
>   Lion-like, forth of his den."
>
> *Swinburne*, " *The Halt before Rome.*"

Below the basilica of S. Agnese (see *Walks in Rome*, ii. 26) we cross the Anio by the picturesque Ponte Nomentana or Lomentana, occupying the site of the ancient bridge, but in itself mediæval, with forked battlements. The green slopes beyond the bridge are those of the *Mons Sacer*, where the famous secession and encampment of the plebs, in B.C. 549, extorted from the patricians the concessions of tribunes who were to represent the interests of the people.

"The spot on which this great deliverance had been achieved became to the Romans what Runnymede is to Englishmen : the top of the hill was left for ever unenclosed and consecrated, and an altar was built on it, and sacrifices offered to Jupiter, who strikes men with terror and again delivers them from their fear; because the commons had fled thither in fear, and were now returning in safety. So the hill was known for ever by the name of the Sacred Hill."—*Arnold's Hist. of Rome*, i. 149.

Passing the Casale dei Pazzi, and the tomb known as Torre Nomentana, we reach, on the right, the disinterred Basilica of S. Alessandro (see *Walks in Rome*, ii. 32). A little beyond this, after passing the farm called Cesarini, the road divides. The turn to the right passes under the Montes Corniculani, of which the nearest height is occupied by S. Angelo in Cappoccia, considered by Nibby (quoted by Murray), without any authority, to occupy the site of the Latin city Medullia. It finally leads to *Palombara*, a town of the Sabina, once a fortress of the Savelli, but now belonging to the Borghese, most beautifully situated at the foot of Monte Gennaro.

Following (to the left) the Via Nomentana, where the ancient pavement is now very perfect, we reach Casa Nuova, and, about 11 miles from Rome (on the left) the fine mediæval tower called *Torre Lupara*, built of alternate courses of brick and stone. The next hill is called *Monte Gentile*, and is the supposed site of the Latin city of *Ficulea* or Ficulnea, which is frequently mentioned both by Livy and Dionysius in the early history of Rome. Gell speaks of the ground near Torre Lupara as "strewn with tiles and pottery—perhaps one of the surest indications of an ancient city." It has been supposed, from an inscription found near the farm Cesarini referring to a charitable institution of M. Aurelius for " Pueri et Puellæ Alimentarii Ficolensium," and from the expression " Ficulea vetus " used by Livy (i. 38), and " Ficelias veteres " by Martial (vi. 27), that there may have been a second town called Ficulea, built in later times nearer the capital. Ficulea was the seat of an early bishopric. It is said to derive its name from the wild figs, which are still found in abundance on its supposed site. In the acts of Pope Caius and St. Lawrence the Martyr it is called " Civitas Figlina extra Portam Salariam." The Via Nomentana is sometimes spoken of as Via Ficulea.

Beyond Monte Gentile, the road passes through forests of oaks, a great contrast to the bare Campagna, till, when it first comes in sight of the village of Mentana, it reaches the height which was the site of the battle, in which, Oct. 1867, the Papal troops, assisted by the French, entirely defeated the Italians under Garibaldi.

Some blocks of marble in the village street are the only

remains of the ancient Latin city Nomentum, which is spoken of by Virgil (vi. 773) and Dionysius (ii. 53) as a colony of Alba. It was one of the thirty cities of the Latin league,* and continued to flourish in the times of the Empire, when Seneca had a country house-there,† and also Martial, who frequently speaks of it in his poems, and contrasts its peaceful retirement with the vanities of Baiæ and more fashionable summer *villeggiature*.

> " Me Nomentani confirmant otia ruris,
>   Et casa jugeribus non onerosa suis,
> Hîc mihi Baiani soles, mollisque Lucrinus ;
>   Hîc vestræ mihi sunt, Castrice, divitiæ.
> Quondam laudatas quocunque libebat ad undas
>   Currere, nec longas pertimuisse vias :
> Nunc urbi vicina juvant, facilesque recessus,
>   Et satis est, pigro si licet esse mihi."
> vi. 43.

> " Numæ colles, et Nomentana relinques
> Otia? nec retinent rusque focusque senem."
> x. 44.

> " Cur sæpe sicci parva rura Nomenti,
> Laremque villæ sordidum petam, quæris?
> Nec cogitandi, Sparse, nec quiescendi :
> In urbe locus est pauperi."
> xii. 57.

Martial praises its wine, which is also extolled by Seneca and Pliny.

> " In Nomentanis, Ovidi, quod nascitur agris,
>   Accepit quoties tempora longa merum,
> Exuit annosæ mores nomenque senectæ,
>   Et quidquid voluit, testa vocatur anus."
> i. 106.

In the Middle Ages the place was called Civitas Nomentana, and was the seat of a bishopric. Here, in A.D. 800,

---

* *Niebuhr*, ii. 17.   † *Sen. Ep.* 104.

Leo III. met Charlemagne, when he came to be crowned at Rome, and here the great Consul Crescentius was born. Mentana was granted by Nicholas III. (1277-81) to his own family, the Orsini, by whom it was sold to the Peretti, whose arms still remain upon the walls of its 15th-century castle. The place now belongs to the Borghese.

The Via Nomentana proceeds to join the Via Salara near Correse, passing—three miles beyond Mentana—*Grotta Marozza*, which is believed with much reason to occupy the site of the Sabine Eretum, which, from its position on the frontier between the Latins and Sabines, was constantly the scene of warfare between the two nations. It was never a place of much importance. Valerius Maximus speaks of it as " Vicus Sabinæ regionis."

It is two miles from Mentana to *Monte Rotondo*, also the site of a battle between the Papal troops and the Garibaldians. Here is a fine old castle built by the Barberini, on the site of a fortress of the Orsini: it is now the property of the Buoncompagni. There is a wide and beautiful view from its summit. A road of two miles leads to the railway station in the valley, whence we may return to Rome by the Via Salara.

One and a half mile from hence, near Fonte di Papa, the road crosses an insignificant brook, which is decided to coincide more than any other with the description which Livy (v. 37) gives of the fatal *Allia*, a description so accurate as to show that the place was not necessarily familiar to his readers, viz. :

" Ægre ad undecimum lapidem occursum est, qua flumen Allia Crustuminis montibus præalto defluens alveo, haud multum infra viam Tiberino amni miscetur."

Here, then, and in the upland hollows, which are watered by the same brook, the Romans underwent their famous defeat by the Gauls under Brennus (B.C. 390), which led to the capture of the city, on the 18th of July (A.D. XV. Kal. Sextiles) called thenceforth Dies Alliensis, and regarded as so ill-omened, that no business was transacted upon it.

> " Hæc est in fastis cui dat gravis Allia nomen."
> *Ovid in Ibin.* 221.

> " Quosque secans infaustum interluit Allia nomen."
> *Æn.* vii. 717.

> " Damnata diu Romanis Allia fastis."
> *Lucan.* vii. 408.

At about nine miles from the city, we pass (on the left) beneath the extensive farm-buildings called *Marcigliana Vecchia*, which are usually believed to occupy the site of the city of Crustumerium, though some place it at *Sette Bagni*, the next large farm on the left of the road to Rome, where there are traces of ancient buildings; while others refer it to Monte Rotondo.

Dionysius speaks of Crustumerium as an Alban colony sent out long before the building of Rome. The city was taken by Romulus, again by Tarquinius Priscus, and again during the Roman Republic, B.C. 499, after which it remained subject to Rome. In B.C. 477 occurred the " Crustumerina Secessio," when the army which was being led by the Decemvirs against the Sabines deserted, and retreated to Crustumerium. Virgil * mentions the Crustumian pears, and Servius says that they were red only on one side. It is interesting that wild pears of this kind still grow in abundance

* *Georgics*, ii. 88.

over all these desolate uplands, amongst which Crustumerium must certainly have been situated. Two miles further we reach, on the right, Castel Giubileo, the site of Fidenæ, described in chapter x.

CHAPTER XII.

TIVOLI.

(This, 18 miles distant, is the most attractive of all the places in the immediate neighbourhood of Rome, and *the* one excursion which no one should omit, even if they are only at Rome for a week. A carriage with two horses ought not to cost more than 25 francs for the day. The Villa Adriana may be visited on the way: then the Temple of the Sibyl, the Cascades, the view of the Cascatelle from the opposite side of the valley, and last of all the Villa d'Este. Those who are not strong enough for the whole should see the view of the Cascatelle and the Villa d'Este. The round which Tivoli guides and donkey-men take strangers, through the woods and underneath the waterfalls, is very long and fatiguing. There are two hotels at Tivoli, la Regina (in the town), which is comfortable, clean, and well-furnished, but where it is necessary to come to a very strict agreement as to prices on arriving, and La Sibylla, far humbler, but not uncomfortable, and in the most glorious situation. In the former, guests are received *en pension* at 8 francs; at the latter, at 6 francs a day. Those who stay long will find endless points of interest both in the place itself and the excursions which may be made from it. Visitors who are pressed for time may omit the Villa Adriana, but on no account the Villa d'Este.)

THE road to Tivoli follows the ancient Via Tiburtina for the greater part of its course, and leads through one of the most desolate and least interesting parts of the Campagna. Issuing from the Porta S. Lorenzo, we pass the great basilica of the same name, and descending into the valley of the Anio, cross the river by a modern bridge, near the ancient *Ponte Mammolo*, which took its name (Pons Mammæus) from Mammæa, mother of Alexander Severus.

The little river Teverone, or Anio, in which Silvia, the mother of Romulus and Remus, exchanged her earthly life for that of a goddess, adds greatly to the charm of the Campagna.—It rises near Treba in the Simbrivian hills, and flows through the gorges of Subiaco and the country of the Æquians till it forms the glorious falls of Tivoli. After this stormy beginning it assumes a most peaceful character, gliding gently between deep banks, and usually marked along the brown reaches of the burnt-up Campagna by its fringe of green willows. Silius calls it "sulphureus," from the sulphuretted hydrogen which is poured into it by the springs of Albula.

"Sulphureus gelidus qua serpit leniter undis
Ad genitorem Anio labens sine murmure Tybrim."
Sil. Ital. xii. 539.

On its way through the plain a whole succession of historical brooks pour their waters into the Anio. Of these, the most remarkable, as we ascend it, are (on the left) the torrent Le Molette (the Ulmanus), the Magliano, the Tutia, and the Albula; and (on the right) the Marrana, and the Osa which flows beneath the walls of Collatia. Nibby says that "anciently the Anio was navigable from the Ponte Lucano to its mouth." Strabo mentions "that the blocks of travertine from the quarries near Tibur, and of Lapis Gabina from Gabii, were brought to Rome by means of it. But in the dark ages the channel was neglected, and the navigation interrupted and abandoned."

When we reach the dismal farm-buildings, which encircle the Osteria del Fornaccio, the caves of Cervara and the mediæval towers of Rustica and Cervara are visible at no great distance, rising above the Campagna on the opposite bank of the Anio. Nothing more is to be seen, except, here and there, the pavement of the ancient road, till we pass, on the left, the ruins of the mediæval Castel Arcione. Across the Campagna, on the left, near the Sabine mountains, the picturesque little hills called Montes Corniculani may be seen, their three summits occupied by the villages of St. Angelo, Colle Cesi, and Monticelli; on the right we overlook the distant sites of Collatia and Gabii, with many other cities of the plain, whose exact positions are unknown. After crossing the brook Tuzia, the ancient Tutia on whose banks Hannibal encamped,* and leaving to the left the now drained Lago de' Tartari, a terrible smell of sulphur announces the neighbourhood, about a mile distant on the left, of the lakes of the *Solfatara*, the Aquæ Albulæ, from which a canal, cut in 1549 by Cardinal d'Este, to take the place of the ancient Albula, carries their rushing milk-white waters under the road towards the Anio. Here, near "the hoary Albula," was the hallowed grove of the Muses mentioned by Martial:—

"Itur ad Herculei gelidas qua Tiburis arces,
    Canaque sulphureis Albula fumat aquis,
  Rura, nemusque sacrum, dilectaque jugera musis
    Signat vicina quartus ab urbe lapis."
I. Ep. 13.

There are now three lakes. On the largest, the *Lago delle Isole Natanti*, are some floating islands formed by matted weeds. The ruins near it, called Bagni della Regina, are supposed to have been the baths of Queen Zenobia during her semi-captivity at Tibur. The two smaller lakes have the names of *Lago di S. Giovanni* and *Lago delle Colonelle*. There is no reason for supposing the temple of Faunus (Æn. vii.), which is spoken of by Murray as if it were here, to

* *Livy*, xxvi. 10.

have been in this neighbourhood. It was more probably at La Solfatara in the great Laurentine wood sacred to Picus and Faunus. Thither, and not hither, the king of Laurentum would naturally go to consult the oracle.*

"Sir Humphrey Davy made some curious experiments on the process by which the water in these lakes continually adds to the rocks around, by petrifaction or incrustation. He says, that the water taken from the most tranquil part of the lake, even after being agitated and exposed to the air, contained in solution more than its own volume of carbonic acid gas, with a very small quantity of sulphuretted hydrogen. The temperature is 80 degrees of Fahrenheit. It is peculiarly fitted to afford nourishment to vegetable life. Its banks of Travertino are everywhere covered with reeds, lichen, confervæ, and various kinds of aquatic vegetables; and at the same time that the process of vegetable life is going on, crystallizations of the calcareous matter are everywhere formed, in consequence of the escape of the carbonic acid of the water.

"In the line between the bridge and the Solfatara, the rocky crust was broken in on the left near the stream, in the year 1825, and a portion of the water was lost; and another stream, called Acqua Acetosa, falls into a hole on the right: these instances show that the crust is but thin in some places. It probably covers an unfathomable abyss; for a stone thrown into the lake, occasions in its descent so violent a discharge of carbonic acid gas, and for so long a time, as to give the idea of an immense depth of water. The taste is acid, and the sulphureous smell so strong, that when the wind assists, it has sometimes been perceived in the higher parts of Rome."—*Gell.*

Two miles beyond the canal is the *Ponte Lucano*, well known by engravings from the beautiful picture by G. Poussin in the Doria Palace. Close beyond the bridge rises, embattled into a tower by Pius II., the massive round tomb of the Plautii, built by M. Plautius Silvanus in B.C. 1, and long used by his descendants. At Barco, near this, were the principal quarries for the Travertino used in the buildings of ancient Rome.

* But two inscriptions have been found which show that there was once a temple of Cybele here, and that the waters themselves were honoured as "Aquæ Albulæ Sanctissimæ."

About half a mile beyond the bridge a lane to the left leads to the gates of the *Villa Adriana,* which is said once to have been from 8 to 10 miles in extent. It is believed to have been ruined during the siege of Tibur by Totila. The chief interest of the ruins arises from their vast extent, and from the lovely carpet of the shrubs and flowers, with which Nature has surrounded them. In spring nothing can exceed the beauty of the violets and anemonies here.* Successive generations of antiquaries have occupied themselves with the nomenclature of the different masses of ruin, and they always disagree: most travellers will consider such discussions of little consequence, and, finding them exceedingly fatiguing, will rest satisfied in the knowledge that the so-called villa was once a most stupendous conglomeration of unnecessary buildings, and in the joyful contemplation of its present loveliness.

"I went down to Adrian's villa with exalted ideas of its extent, variety, and magnificence. On approaching it, I saw ruins overgrown with trees and bushes; I saw mixt-reticular walls stretching along the side of a hill, in all the confusion of a demolished town; but I saw no grandeur of elevation, no correspondence in the parts. I went on. The extent and its variety opened before me—baths, academies, porticos, a library, a *palestra,* a *hippodrome,* a menagerie, a *naumachia,* an aqueduct, theatres both Greek and Latin, temples for different rites, and every appurtenance suitable to an imperial seat. But its magnificence is gone: it is removed to the Vatican, it is scattered over Italy, it may be traced in France. Anywhere but at Tivoli you may look for the statues and *caryatides,* the columns, the oriental marbles, and the mosaics, with which the villa was once adorned, or supported, or wainscoted, or floored."—*Forsyth.*

"The drive was less beautiful than most of those which lie round Rome. Thus two hours and a half went by, dully; and I was not sorry when, turning aside from the castellated tomb of the Plautii family,

* Since this account was written (1873) the destroying hand of Signor Rosa has been here, the flowers are all rooted up, the ruins stripped of their creepers, and of the fringes of lovely shrubs which gave them all their charm; and, for the present, the Villa Adriana—a mass of bare walls in a naked country—is little worth visiting—

we passed down a shady lane, and stopped at the gate of Hadrian's Villa. Alighting here, we passed into that wide and wondrous wilderness of ruin, through avenues dark with cypress, and steep banks purple with violets. The air was heavy with perfume. The glades were carpeted with daisies, wild periwinkle, and white and yellow crocus-blooms. We stepped aside into a grassy arena which was once the Greek theatre, and sate upon a fallen cornice. There was the narrow shelf of stage on which the agonies of Œdipus and Prometheus were once rehearsed; there was the tiny altar which stood between the audience and the actors, and consecrated the play; there, row above row, were the seats of the spectators. Now, the very stage was a mere thicket of brambles; and a little thrush lighted on the altar, while we were sitting by, and filled all the silent space with song.

"Passing hence, we came next upon open fields, partly cultivated, and partly cumbered with shapeless mounds of fallen masonry. Here, in the shadow of a gigantic stone pine, we found a sheet of mosaic pavement, glowing with all its marbles in the sun; and close by, half buried in deep grass, a shattered column of the richest porphyry. Then came an olive plantation; another theatre; the fragments of a temple; and a long line of vaulted cells, some of which contained the remains of baths and conduits, and were tapestried within with masses of the delicate maiden-hair fern. Separated from these by a wide space of grass, amid which a herd of goats waded and fed at their pleasure, rose a pile of reticulated wall, with part of a vast hall yet standing, upon the vaulted roof of which, sharp and perfect, as if moulded yesterday, were encrusted delicate bas-reliefs of white stucco, representing groups of Cupids, musical instruments, and figures reclining at table. Near this spot, on a rising ground formed all of ruins, overgrown with grass and underwood, we sate down to rest, and contemplate the view.

"A deep romantic valley opened before us, closed in on either side by hanging woods of olive and ilex, with here and there a group of dusky junipers, or a solitary pine, rising like a dark green parasol above all its neighbours. Interspersed among these, and scattered about the foreground, were mountainous heaps of buttressed wall, arch, vault, and gallery, all more or less shattered out of form, or green with ivy. At the bottom of the valley, forming, as it were, the extreme boundary of the middle distance, rose two steep volcanic hills, each crowned with a little white town, that seemed to wink and glitter in the sun; while beyond these again, undulating, melancholy, stretching mysteriously away for miles and miles in the blue distance, lay the wastes of the Campagna."—*Barbara's History*.

"Autour de moi, à travers les arcades des ruines, s'ouvraient des points de vue sur la campagne romaine : des buissons de sureau remplissaient les salles désertes, où venaient se réfugier quelques merles solitaires ; les fragments de maçonnerie étaient tapissés de feuilles de scolopendre, dont la verdure satinée se dessinait comme un travail en mosaïque sur la blancheur des marbres. Cà et là de hauts cyprès remplaçaient les colonnes tombées dans ces palais de la mort. L'acanthe sauvage rampait à leurs pieds sur des débris, comme si la nature s'était plu à reproduire sur ces chefs d'œuvre inutiles de l'architecture l'ornement de leur beauté passée ; les salles diverses, et les sommités des ruines, ressemblaient à des corbeilles et à des bouquets de verdure ; le vent en agitait les guirlandes humides, et les plantes s'inclinaient sous la pluie du ciel."—*Chateaubriand.* *

The villa formed part of a large estate purchased by Pius VI. It is now the property of his representative, Duke Braschi.

On *Monte Affliano*, which rises behind the Villa Adriana, to the south of Tivoli, most authorities place the site of the Latin city Æsula. The mountain of Tivoli is divided into three positions : Ripoli, towards the town ; Spaccato, in the centre ; and Monte Affliano, at the southern extremity. Porphyrion has accurately described the position of Æsula as on this southern extremity of the centre of Tibur.

"Udum Tibur propter aquarum copiam. . . Æsula, nomen urbis, alterius in latere montis constitutæ."

There are remains of a city having stood here.

"Æsula declive contempleris arvum."
Horace, iii. *Ode* 29.

It was probably deserted on account of its inconvenient situation, and the temple of Bona Dea or Ops was its representative, in later times.†

A winding road, constructed by the Braschi, winds up the

---

* The powerful description of Chateaubriand cannot be realized *now*, but is inserted, in the hope that when the reign of Signor Rosa is over, Nature will be permitted to restore the ruins of the Villa Adriana to their former beauty.

† See Gell's "Topography of Rome and its Vicinity."

hill to Tivoli, through magnificent olive-groves, the silvery trunks of the old trees caverned, loop-holed, and twisted in every possible contortion.

"It is well to have felt and seen the olive-tree; to have loved it for Christ's sake, partly also for the helmed Wisdom's sake which was to the heathen in some sort as that nobler Wisdom which stood at God's right hand, when he founded the earth and established the heavens: to have loved it, even to the hoary dimness of its delicate foliage, subdued and faint of hue, as if the ashes of the Gethsemane agony had been cast upon it for ever; and to have traced, line by line, the gnarled writhing of its intricate branches, and the pointed petals of its light and narrow leaves, inlaid on the blue field of the sky, and the small rosy-white stars of its spring blossoming, and the beads of sable fruit scattered by autumn along its topmost boughs—the right, in Israel, of the stranger, the fatherless, and the widow,—and, more than all, the softness of the mantle, silver grey, and tender like the down on a bird's breast, with which, far away, it veils the undulation of the mountains."—*Ruskin, Stones of Venice*, iii. 176.

As we drive slowly up the ascent it may be pleasant to consider the history of Tibur, which claims to go back much further than that of Rome. Dionysius says that it was a city of the Siculi, and called Siculetum or Sicilis, and that the original inhabitants were expelled by Tiburtus, Corax, and Catillus, the three grandsons of Amphiaraus, the king and prophet of Thebes, who flourished a century before the Trojan war. Tibur was named after the eldest of the brothers.

"Tum gemini fratres Tiburtia mœnia linquunt,
 Fratris Tiburti dictam cognomine gentem,
 Catillusque, acerque Coras, Argiva juventus."
                                             Æn. vii. 670.

"Jam mœnia Tiburis udi
 Stabant, Argolicæ quod posuere manus."
                                             Ovid. Fast. iv. 71.

"Nullam, Vare, sacrâ vite prius severis arborem
 Circa mite solum Tiburis, et mœnia Catili."
                                             Horace, Od. l. xviii. 1.

> "Hic tua Tiburtes Faunos chelys et juvat ipsum
> Alciden dictumque lyra majore Catillum."
> *Statius, Silv.* 1. 3.

The inhabitants of Tibur frequently incurred the anger of Rome by assistance they gave to the Gauls upon their inroads into Latium, and they were completely subdued by Camillus in B.C. 335. Ovid narrates how when they were requested to send back the Roman pipers, "tibicines," who had seceded to Tibur from offence which they had taken at an edict of the censors, they made them drunk, and took them thus in carts to Rome.

> "Exilio mutant urbem, Tiburque recedunt!
> —Exilium quodam tempore Tibur erat!—
> Quæritur in scena cava tibia, quæritur aris,
> Ducit supremos nænia nulla choros.
>   . . . .
> Alliciunt somnos tempus, motusque, merumque,
> Potaque se Tibur turba redire putat.
> Jamque per Esquilias Romanam intraverat urbem;
> Et mane in medio plaustra fuere foro."
> *Fasti*, vi. 665.

The second line of this passage expresses the fact that Tibur was an asylum for Roman fugitives, a result of its never having been admitted to the Roman franchise.

In his Pontic Epistles, also, Ovid says:—

> "Quid referam veteres Romanæ gentis, apud quos
> Exilium tellus ultima Tibur erat?"
> *Pont.* 1. *El.* 3.

Brutus and Cassius are said to have fled thither after the murder of Cæsar. Under the earlier emperors, Tibur was the favourite retreat of the wealthy Romans,—the Richmond of Rome—and, as such, it was celebrated by the poets. It was also the scene of the nominal imprisonment of Zenobia, the brave and accomplished Queen of Palmyra, who lived here like a Roman matron, after having appeared in the triumph of Aurelian. She was presented with a beautiful villa by the Emperor. "Here the Syrian queen insensibly sunk into a Roman matron, her daughters married into noble families, and her race was not yet extinct in the fifth century." * In an earlier age, Syphax, king of Numidia, died here B.C. 201, having been brought from Africa to adorn the triumph of Scipio. The town was surrendered by the Isaurian garrisons, which Belisarius had placed there, to the Goths under Totila, who both burnt and rebuilt it. In the eighth century the name was changed to Tivoli. In the wars of the Guelphs and Ghibellines it bore a prominent part and was generally on the imperial side.

The climate of Tivoli was esteemed remarkably healthy, and was considered to have the property of blanching ivory.

"Quale micat, semperque novum est, quod Tiburis aura
　　Pascit, ebur."
　　　　　　　　　　　　　　　Sil. Ital. xii. 229.

"Lilia tu vincis, nec adhuc delapsa ligustra,
　　Et Tiburtino monte quod albet ebur."
　　　　　　　　　　　　　　　Martial, viii. 28.

But since the existence of malaria, modern poetry has told a different tale:—

"Tivoli di mal conforto,
　　O piove, o tira vento, o suona a morte."

As we ascend the hill, its wonderful beauty becomes more striking at every turn.

"The hill of Tivoli is all over picture. The town, the villas, the ruins, the rocks, the cascades, in the foreground; the Sabine hills, the three Monticelli, Soracte, Frascati, the Campagna, and Rome in the

* Gibbon, ch. xi.

distance; these form a succession of landscapes superior, in the delight produced, to the richest cabinet of Claude's. Tivoli cannot be described: no true portrait of it exists: all views alter and embellish it: they are poetical translations of the matchless original. Indeed, when you come to detail the hill, some defect of harmony will ever be found in the foreground or distance, something in the swell or channelling of its sides, something in the growth or the grouping of its trees, which painters, referring every object to its effect on canvas, will often condemn as bad Nature. In fact, the beauties of the landscape are all accidental. Nature, intent on more important ends, does nothing exclusively to please the eye. No stream flows exactly as the artist would wish it: he wants mountains where he finds only hills: he wants hills where he finds a plain. Nature gives him but scattered elements, the composition is his own."—*Forsyth.*

Close to the gate of the town, on the right, is the picturesque five-towered *Castle*, built by Pius II. (1458-64).

A street, full of mediæval fragments, leads to *the Regina* and on to *the Sibylla*, which all artists will prefer, and which has never merited the description of George Sand:—

"L'affreuse auberge de la Sibylle, un vrai coupe-gorge de l'Opera-Comique."

It stands on the very edge of the precipice:—

"The green steep whence Anio leaps
In floods of snow-white foam."
Macaulay.

This is an almost isolated quarter of the town, occupying a distinct point of rock, called *Castro Vetere*, which is supposed to have been the *arx* or citadel of ancient Tibur —the Sicelion of Dionysius. Here, on the verge of the abyss, with coloured cloths hanging out over its parapet-wall, as we have so often seen it in pictures, stands the beautiful—the most beautiful—little building, which has been known for ages as the *Temple of the Sibyl.* It was once encircled by 18 Corinthian columns, and of these 10 still remain. In its delicate form and its rich orange colour, standing out against the opposite heights of Monte Peschiavatore, it is impossible to conceive anything more picturesque, and the situation is sublime, perched on the very edge of the cliff, overhung with masses of clematis and ivy, through which portions of the ruined arch of a bridge are just visible, while below the river foams and roars. Close behind the circular temple is another little oblong temple of travertine, with Ionic columns, now turned into the Church of S. Giorgio. Those who contend that the circular temple was dedicated to Vesta, or to Hercules Saxonus, call this the Temple of the Sibyl: others * say it is the Temple of Tiburtus, the founder of the city; others, that it was built in honour of Drusilla, sister of Caligula. We know from Varro that the 10th and last of the Sibyls, whose name was Albunea, was worshipped at Tivoli, and her temple seems to be coupled by the poets with the shrine of Tiburtus above the Anio.

"Illis ipse antris Anienus fonte relicto,
Nocte sub arcana glaucos exutus amictus,
Huc illuc fragili prosternit pectora musco :
Aut ingens in stagna cadit, vitreasque natatu
Plaudit aquas : illa recubat Tiburnus in umbra,
Illic sulphureos cupit Albula mergere crines."
Statius, Silv. I. 3.

Close to the temples a gate will admit visitors into the beautiful walks begun by General Miollis, and finished under the Papal government. Those who are not equal to a long round, should not enter upon these, and in taking a local guide it should be recollected that there is scarcely the slightest ground for anything they say, and that the names they give to villas and temples are generally the merest conjecture.

* Nibby. *Dintorni*, iii. 205.

The walks, however, are charming, and lead by a gradual descent to the caves called the *Grottoes of Neptune and the Sirens*, into the chasm beneath which the Anio fell magnificently till 1826,[*] when an inundation which carried away a church and twenty-six houses led the Papal government to divert the course of the river in order to prevent the temples from being carried away also, and to open the new artificial cascade, 320 feet high, in 1834. The Anio at Tivoli, as the Velino at Terni, has extraordinary petrifying properties, and the mass of stalactites and petrified vegetation hanging everywhere from the rocks adds greatly to their wild picturesqueness.

"Puisque vous me dites que vous avez sous les yeux tous les guides et itinéraires de l'Italie pour suivre mon humble pérégrination, je dois vous prévenir que, dans aucun vous ne trouverez une description exacte de ces grottes, par la raison que les éboulements, les tremblements de terre, et les travaux indispensables à la sécurité de la ville, menacée de s'écrouler aussi, ou d'être emportée par l'Anio, ont souvent changé leur aspect. Je vais tâcher de vous donner succinctement une idée exacte ; car, en dépit des nouveaux itinéraires qui prétendent que ces lieux ont perdu leur principal intérêt, ils sont encore une des plus ravissantes merveilles de la terre.

"Je vous ai parlé d'un puits de verdure ; c'est ce bocage, d'environ un mille de tour à son sommet, que l'on a arrangé dans l'entonnoir d'un ancien cratère. L'abime est donc tapissé de plantations vigoureuses, bien libres et bien sauvrages, descendant sur les flancs de montagne presque à pic, au moyen des zig-zags d'un sentier doux aux pieds, tout bordé d'herbes et de fleurs rustiques, soutenu par les terrasses naturelles du roc pittoresque, et se dégageant à chaque instant des bosquets qui l'ombragent pour vous laisser regarder le torrent sous vos pieds, le rocher perpendiculaire à votre droite, et le joli temple de la Sibylle au-dessus de votre tête. C'est à la fois d'une grâce et d'une majesté, d'une âpreté et d'une fraicheur qui résument bien les caractères de la nature italienne. Il me semble qu'il n'y a ici rien d'austère et de terrible qui ne soit tout à coup tempéré ou dissimulé par des voluptés souriantes.

[*] This fall, though natural, was itself the result of an inundation in A.D. 105, which is recorded by Pliny the Younger. (Ep. viii. 17.)

FALLS OF THE ANIO. 197

"Quand on a descendu environ les deux tiers du sentier, il vous conduit à l'entrée d'une grotte latérale complétement inaperçue jusque-là. Cette grotte est un couloir, une galerie naturelle que le torrent a rencontrée dans la roche, et qui semble avoir été une des bouches du cratère dont le puits de verdure tout entier aurait été le foyer principal.

"De quelles scènes effroyables, de quelles dévorantes éjaculations, de quels craquements, de quels rugissements, de quels bouillonnements affreux cette ravissante cavité de Tivoli a dû être le théâtre! Il me semblait qu'elle devait son charme actuel à la pensée, j'allais presque dire au souvenir évoqué en moi, des ténébreuses horreurs de sa formation première. C'est là une ruine du passé autrement imposante que les débris des temples et des aqueducs ; mais les ruines de la nature ont encore sur celles de nos œuvres cette supériorité que le temps bâtit sur elles, comme des monuments nouveaux, les merveilles de la végétation, les frais édifices de la forme et de la couleur, les véritables temples de la vie.

"Par cette caverne, un bras d'Anio se précipite et roule, avec un bruit magnifique, sur des lames de rocher qu'il s'est chargé d'aplanir et de creuser à son usage. A deux cents pieds plus haut, il traverse tranquillement la ville et met en mouvement plusieurs usines ; mais, tout au beau milieu des maisons et des jardins, il rencontre cette coulée volcanique, s'y engouffre, et vient se briser au bas du grand rocher, sur les débris de son couronnement détaché, qui gisent là dans un désordre grandiose."
—*George Sand, La Daniella.*

"Above the cold deep dell into which you dive to see the mysteries of Anio's urn, raised high on a pedestal of sharply-cut rock and seated as on a throne of velvet verdure, towers, like a pinnacle projected on the deep blue sky, the graceful temple of the Sibyl, that most exquisite specimen of art crowning nature, in perfect harmony of beauties."—
Cardinal Wiseman.

The small ruins of two Roman bridges were rendered visible when the course of the river was changed. Ascending again the upper road beyond the falls, guides, on no authority whatever, point out some ruins as those of the Villa of Vopiscus, a poet of the time of Domitian. That he had a property at Tibur, we know from the verses of Statius, who has left a pleasant account of the villa of his friend : his grounds appear to have extended on both sides of the river.

> "Cernere facundi Tibur glaciale Vopisci
> Si quis et inserto geminos Aniene penates,
> Aut potuit sociæ commercia noscere ripæ.
>
> . . . .
>
> Ingenium quam mite solo! quæ forma beatis
> Arte manus concessa locis! Non largius usquam
> Indulsit natura sibi. Nemora alta citatis
> Incubuere vadis; fallax responsat imago
> Frondibus, et longes eadem fugit unda per umbras.
> Ipse Anien—miranda fides—infraque superque
> Saxeus, hic tumidam rabiem spumosaque ponit
> Murmura, ceu placidi veritus turbare Vopisci
> Pieriosque dies et habentes carmina somnos.
> Litus utrumque domi, nec te mitissimus amnis
> Dividit. Alternas servant prætoria ripas
> Non externa sibi, fluviumve obstare queruntur.
>
> . . . .
>
> Hic æterna quies, nullis hic jura procellis,
> Nusquam fervor aquis. Datur hic transmittere visus
> Et voces, et pæne manus."
>
> *Silv.* I. 3.

We now turn round the base of Monte Catillo to that of Monte Peschiavatore and the point opposite the Cascatelle, which is known to have borne the name of Quintiliolo in the 10th century, and where a little church is still called *La Madonna di Quintiliolo*. It is possible this name may be derived from Quintilius Varus, and that his villa, mentioned by Horace (ode 1. 18) as near the town, may have been in this neighbourhood. Remains of a sumptuous villa with inlaid pavements and statues—especially two Fauns now in the Vatican—have certainly been found here.

Nothing can exceed the loveliness of the views from the road which leads from Tivoli by the chapel of S. Antonia to the Madonna di Quintiliolo. On the opposite height rises the town with its temples, its old houses and churches, clinging to the edge of the cliffs, which are overhung with such a wealth of luxuriant vegetation as is almost indescribable; and beyond, beneath the huge piles of building known

Tivoli.

as the Villa of Mæcenas, the thousand noisy cataracts of the Cascatelle leap forth beneath the old masonry, and sparkle and dance and foam through the green—and all this is only the foreground to vast distances of dreamy campagna, seen through the gnarled hoary stems of grand old olive-trees--rainbow-hued with every delicate tint of emerald and amethyst, and melting into sapphire, where the solitary dome of S. Peter's rises, invincible by distance, over the level line of the horizon.

And the beauty is not confined to the views alone. Each turn of the winding road is a picture; deep ravines of solemn dark-green olives which waken into silver light as the wind shakes their leaves,—old convents and chapels buried in shady nooks on the mountain-side,—thickets of laurestinus, roses, genista, and jessamine,—banks of lilies and hyacinths, anemonies and violets,—grand masses of grey rock, up which white-bearded goats are scrambling to nibble the myrtle and rosemary, and knocking down showers of the red tufa on their way;—and a road, with stone seats and parapets, twisting along the edge of the hill through a constant diorama of loveliness, and peopled by groups of peasants in their gay dresses returning from their work, singing in parts wild canzonetti which echo amid the silent hills, or by women washing at the wayside fountains, or returning with brazen *conche*, poised upon their heads, like stately statues of water-goddesses wakened into life.

"The pencil only can describe Tivoli; and though unlike other scenes, the beauty of which is generally exaggerated in pictures, no representation has done justice to it, it is yet impossible that some part of its peculiar charms should not be transferred upon the canvas. It almost seems as if Nature herself had turned painter when she formed this beautiful and perfect composition."—*Eaton's Rome.*

Deep below Quintiliolo, reached by a winding path through grand old olive-woods, is the *Ponte dell' Acquoria*—"the bridge of the golden water," so called from a beautiful spring which rises near it. It is a fine single arch of travertine, crossed by the Via Tiburtina.

Passengers now cross the Anio by a wooden bridge, and ascend the Clivus Tiburtinus on the other side. Much of the ancient pavement remains. On the right of the road is the curious circular-domed building, somewhat resembling the temple of Minerva-Medica at Rome, and called by local antiquaries *Il Tempio della Tosse*, or "The Temple of Cough." The fact being, that it was probably the sepulchre of the Turcia family, one of the members of which, Lucius

Arterius Turcius, is shown by an inscription to have repaired the neighbouring road in the time of Constans. In the interior are some remains of 13th-century frescoes, which indicate that this was then used as a Christian church.

The *Via Constantina*, which leads into the town from the Ponte Lucano, falls into the Via Tiburtina near this.

On the brow of the hill, we may now visit the immense ruins called *The Villa of Mæcenas*, though there is no reason whatever to suppose that it was his villa, or even that he had a villa at Tibur at all.

> "It is an immense quadrilateral edifice, 637½ feet long, and 450 broad, surrounded on three sides by sumptuous porticoes. The fourth side, or that which looks towards Rome, which is one of the long sides, had a theatre in the middle of it, with a hall or saloon on each side. The porticoes are arched, and adorned on the side towards the area with half-columns of the Doric order. Behind is a series of chambers. An oblong tumulus now marks the site of the house, or, according to Nibby, who regards it as the temple of Hercules, of the Cella. The pillars were of travertine, and of a beautiful Ionic order. One of them existed on the ruins as late as 1812. This immense building intercepted the ancient road, for which, as appears from an inscription preserved in the Vatican, a vault or tunnel was constructed, part of which is still extant. Hence it gave name to the *Porta Scura* or *Obscura*, mentioned in the Bull of Benedict, which it continued to bear at least as late as the 15th century."—*Smith's Dict. of Greek and Roman Geography.*

These ruins are the only remains in Tivoli which at all correspond with the allusions in the poets to the famous Heracleum, or Temple of Hercules, which was of such a size as to be quoted, with the waterfall, by Strabo as characteristics of Tivoli, just as the great temple of Fortune was the distinguishing feature of Præneste. It contained a library, and had an oracle, which answered by sortes like that of Præneste. Augustus, when at Tibur, frequently administered justice in the porticoes of the temple of Hercules.

To trace all the poetical allusions to it would be endless: here are a few of them.

> "Curve te in Herculeum deportant esseda Tibur.'
> *Propertius*, 11. 32.
> "Tibur in Herculeum migravit nigra Lycoris."
> *Martial*, iv. 62.
> "Venit in Herculeos colles: quid Tiburis alti
> Aura valet?"
> *Mart.* vii. 12.
> "Nec mihi plus Nemee, priscumve habitabitur Argos,
> Nec Tiburna domus, solisque cubilia Gades."
> *Stat. Silv.* iii. 1. 182.
> "Quosque sub Herculeis taciturno flumine muris
> Pomifera arva creant Anienicolæ Catilli."
> *Sil. Ital.* iv. 224.

We re-enter the town by a gate with Ghibelline battlements, near which are two curious mediæval houses, one with a beautiful outside loggia. Passing through the dirty streets almost to the Porta Santa Croce, by which we entered Tivoli, a narrow alley on the right leads us to a little square, one side of which is occupied by the *Cathedral of S. Francesco*, a picturesque little building, with a good rose-window. Behind the church is a *cella* of the age of Augustus, which some antiquaries have referred to the temple of Hercules.

> "But it would be difficult to regard these vestiges as forming part of a temple 150 feet in circumference, nor was it usual to erect the principal Christian church on the foundations of a heathen temple. It is pretty certain, however, that the Forum of Tibur was near the cathedral, and occupied the site of the present Piazza dell' Ormo and its environs, as appears from a Bull of Pope Benedict VII., in the year 978. The round temple at the cathedral belonged therefore to the Forum, as well as the crypto-porticus, now called *Porto di Ercole* in the street *del Poggio*. The exterior of this presents ten closed arches about 200 feet in length,

which still retain traces of the red plaster with which they were covered. Each arch has three loop-holes to serve as windows. The interior is divided into two apartments or halls, by a row of 28 slender pillars. Traces of arabesque painting on a black ground may still be seen. The mode of building shows it to be of the same period as the circular remains."—*Smith's Dict. of Greek and Roman Geography.*

Close to the Cathedral is the door of the famous *Villa d'Este*, where we are admitted on ringing a bell, and crossing a court-yard, and descending a long vaulted passage, are allowed unaccompanied to enter and wander about in one of the grandest and wildest and most impressive gardens in the world. The villa itself, built in 1549, by Pirro Ligorio, for Cardinal Ippolito d'Este, son of Alfonso II., Duke of Ferrara, is stately and imposing in its vast forms, bold outlines, and deeply-projecting cornices. Beneath it runs a broad terrace (rather too much grown up now), ending in an archway, which none but the most consummate artist would have placed where it stands, in glorious relief against the soft distances of the many-hued Campagna. Beneath the twisted staircases which lead down from this terrace, fountains send up jets of silvery spray on every succeeding level against the dark green of the gigantic cypresses, which line the main avenue of the garden, and which also, interspersed with the richer verdure of Acacias and Judas trees, snowy or crimson with flowers in spring, stand in groups on the hill-side, with the old churches of Tivoli and the heights of Monte Catillo seen between them. The fountains at the sides of the garden are colossal, like everything else here, and overgrown with maiden-hair fern, and water glitters everywhere in stone channels through the dark arcades of thick foliage. Flowers there are few, except the masses of roses, guelder roses, and lilacs, which grow and blossom where they will.

The villa now belongs to the Duke of Modena, the direct descendant of its founder.

(Those who return to Rome the same evening will do well to order their carriages to wait for them at the entrance of the Villa d'Este.)

Outside the Porta Santa Croce are the old Jesuits' College, with its charming terrace called *La Veduta*, and the *Villa Braschi*, in whose cellar the aqueduct of the Anio Novus may be seen. Some disappointment will doubtless be felt at the uncertainty which hangs over the different homes of the poets at Tivoli, especially over that of Horace, which was near the grove of Tiburnus;* but then, though the actual ruins pointed out to us may not have belonged to them, there is so much of which they tell us that remains unchanged, the luxuriant woods, the resounding Anio, the thymy uplands, that the very atmosphere is alive with their verses; and amid such soul-inspiring loveliness, one cannot wonder that Tibur was beloved by them.

"Mihi jam non regia Roma,
Sed vacuum Tibur placet."

Horace, 1 *Ep.* 7.

"Vester, Camœnæ, vester in arduos
Tollor Sabinos: seu mihi frigidum
Præneste, seu Tibur supinum,
Seu liquidæ placuere Baiæ."

iii. *Od.* 4.

". . . Ego, apis Matinæ
More modoque
Grata carpentis thyma per laborem
Plurimum, circa nemus uvidique
Tiburis ripas, operosa parvus
Carmina fingo."

iv. *Od.* 2.

* Suet. *Vit. Hor.*

> "Sed quæ Tibur aquæ fertile præfluunt,
> Et spissæ nemorum comæ,
> Fingent Æolio carmine nobilem."
>
> iv. Od. 3.

"Que de vers charmants dans Horace, consacrés à peindre ce Tibur tant aimé, ce délicieux Tivoli dont il est si doux de goûter après lui, je dirai presque avec lui, les impérissables enchantements! Comment ne pas y murmurer cette ode ravissante dans laquelle, après avoir énuméré les beaux lieux qu'il avait admirés dans son voyage de Grèce, revenant à son cher Tibur, il s'écrie, comme d'autres pourraient le faire aussi : 'Rien ne m'a frappé autant que la demeure retentissante d'Albunée, l'Anio qui tombe, le bois sacré de Tiburnus, et les vergers qu'arrosent les eaux vagabondes !'

> 'Quam domus Albuneæ resonantis,
> Et præceps Anio, ac Tiburni lucus, et uda
> Mobilibus pomaria rivis.'
>
> Carm. i. 7, 12.

Est-il rien de plus gracieux, de plus sonore, et de plus frais ? Malheureusement il ne reste d'Horace à Tivoli que les cascatelles, dont le murmure semble un écho de ses vers. Les ruines qu'on montre au voyageur, comme celles de la maison d'Horace, ne lui ont jamais appartenu, bien que déjà du temps de Suétone à Tibur on fît voir au curieux la maison du poëte."—*Ampère, Emp. Rom.* 1. 360.

Catullus had a villa here on the boundary between the Sabine and Tiburtine territories, but which he chose to consider in the latter, while his friends, if they wished to tease him, said it was Sabine :—

> "O funde noster, seu Sabine, seu Tiburs
> (Nam te esse Tiburtem autumant, quibus non est
> Cordi Catullum lædere : at quibus cordist,
> Quovis Sabinum pignore esse contendunt),
> Sed seu Sabine sive verius Tiburs,
> Fui libenter in tua suburbana
> Villa, malamque pectore expuli tussim."
>
> Carm. 44.

Here also lived "Cynthia," whose real name was Hostia, the beloved of Propertius, who did not hesitate to test his devotion by summoning him to face the dangers of the road from Rome to Tibur at midnight.

> "Nox media, et dominæ mihi venit epistola nostræ,
>   Tibure me missa jussit adesse mora,
> Candida qua geminas ostendunt culmina turres,
>   Et cadit in patulos lympha Aniena lacus."
>
> <div align="right">iii. <i>El.</i> 16.</div>

And here she died and was buried, and her spirit, appearing to her lover, besought him to take care of her grave.

> "Pelle hederam tumulo, mihi quæ pugnante corymbo
>   Mollia contortis alligat ossa comis.
> Pomosis Anio qua spumifer incubat arvis,
>   Et nunquam Herculeo numine pallet ebur.
> Hic carmen media dignum me scribe columna,
>   Sed breve, quod currens vector ab urbe legat,
> Hic Tiburtina jacet aurea Cynthia terra :
>   Accessit ripæ laus, Aniene, tuæ."
>
> v. 7.

Beyond the Porta Santa Croce is the suburb *Carciano*, a corruption from Cassianum, its name in the 10th century from the villa of the gens Cassia, of which there are considerable remains beneath the Greek College. From the excavations made here in the reign of Pius VI. many of the finest statues in the Vatican were obtained, especially those in the Hall of the Muses.

Painters, and all who stay long enough at Tivoli, should not fail to visit the picturesque ruins of the Marcian and Claudian aqueducts beyond the Porta S. Giovanni. Delightful excursions may also be made to Subiaco, to S. Cosimato and Licenza, to Monte Gennaro, and to Montecelli. A pleasant road leads by the old castle of *Passerano* and Zagarolo to Palestrina.

CHAPTER XIII.

LICENZA AND MONTE GENNARO.

(This is one of the most interesting of the excursions from Tivoli. A carriage may be taken from Tivoli to the farm of Horace itself, or good walkers may take the morning diligence to Subiaco as far as S. Cosimato, and walk from thence to Licenza, returning to meet the diligence in the evening. For the excursion to Monte Gennaro, horses must be ordered beforehand.)

SOON after leaving Tivoli some magnificent arches of the Claudian Aqueduct are seen crossing a ravine on the left, through which a road leads to *Ampiglione* (probably the ancient Empulum), where some of the ancient walls remain. Then, also on the left, rises the most picturesque village of *Castel Madama* crowning a ridge of hill. Then the road passes close to some ruins supposed to be those of the tomb of C. Mænius Bassus of the time of Caligula.

Seven miles from Tivoli we reach *Vicovaro*, the Varia of Horace. Some of the ancient walls remain, of huge blocks of travertine. The place now belongs to Count Bolognetti Cenci, who has a dismal palace here. At one end of a piazza facing the principal church in the upper town, is the beautiful *Chapel of S. Giacomo*, built for one of the Orsini, Count of Tagliacozzo, by Simone, a pupil of Brunelleschi, who (says Vasari) died when he was employed upon it. It is octagonal, with a dome crowned by the figure of a saint. The Italian-gothic is very peculiar. The principal door is richly adorned with saints: above are angels floating over the Virgin and Child, their attitude of adoration very beautiful. Santa Severa is buried here, as well as at Anagni! Pope Pius II. in his "Commentaria" (LVI.) speaks of this church as "nobile sacellum ex marmore candidissimo," and as adorned with "statuis egregiis." Of late years it has become important as a place of pilgrimage from " the miraculous picture " which it contains.

"Outside the church was a stall, at which I bought a copy of a hymn addressed by the inhabitants of the town, 'to their miraculous picture of the most Holy Mary our advocate, which on July 22, 1868, began to move its eyes miraculously.' Then follows the hymn, which is poor enough. Inside the church, over the high altar, surrounded with decorations and with lights, is placed the picture, a beautiful one, full of feeling and pathos. The hands are united as in prayer, and the face is turned upwards, the eyes being large and lustrous, and in the very act of beginning to weep. It is a work of the school of Guido, and might be by the master himself.

"Before the altar were kneeling a group of *contadini*, or country people, on their way from the Easter services at Rome. The priest was kneeling at the altar, singing the Litany of the Virgin, in which she is addressed in direct prayer, 'Mother of mercy, have mercy on us:' 'Mother of grace, have mercy upon us,' &c.: the *contadini* repeating the '*Miserere nobis*' after each title of invocation had been given out by the priest. This being ended, the worshippers all bent down and kissed the pavement, and then went backwards out of the church, bowing repeatedly as they passed down the nave.

"Meantime we were invited into the sacristy to see the book of testimonials to the fact of the miracle. The witnesses were many, of all nations. The purport of their testimony was mainly this : that at such a time the deposer had seen the left, or the right eye, or both, move or enlarge, or fill with tears ; or the expression of the face change, or the throat become agitated. Many of the depositions were accompanied with fervent expressions of thankfulness and joy.

" Now as to the account to be given of the phenomena thus deposed to. It is well known that certain arrangements of lines and of colours cause the appearance, when long contemplated, of unsteadiness and of motion in a picture : especially if combined with the representation of an expression of countenance itself emotioned, and, if I may thus use the word, transitional. Now this last is eminently the case at Vicovaro. I am convinced, that were I a devotee kneeling before that picture, I could in ten minutes imagine it to undergo any such change as those recorded in the book. All is engaging, lustrous, suggestive."—*Dean Alford*, 1865.

A short distance beyond Vicovaro, almost opposite the convent of S. Cosimato (see ch. xix.), a road to the left turns up the valley of Licenza. On the right is the castle of the Marchese del Gallo. About two miles up the valley, on the left, the castle of *Rocca Giovane* is seen rising above its little town. Here was a temple of Vacuna, the Victoria of the Sabines.

The scenery is now classical, for :—

> "where yon bar
> Of girdling mountains intercepts the sight
> The Sabine farm was till'd, the weary bard's delight."
> *Childe Harold.*

The village upon the right, *Bardella*, is Mandela. Between us and it flows the brook *Licenza*, the Digentia of Horace; the hill in front, *Monte Libretti*, is the famous Mons Lucretilis.

> "Me quoties reficit gelidus Digentia rivus,
> Quem Mandela bibit, rugosus frigore pagus ;
> Quid sentire putas ? quid credis, amice, precari ?
> Sit mihi quod nunc est."
> i. *Epist.* xviii. 104.

> Velox amœnum sæpe Lucretilem
> Mutat Lycæo Faunus, et igneam
> Defendit æstatem capellis
> Usque meis pluviosque ventos.
> i. *Ode* 17.

"Le véritable pèlerinage à la demeure champêtre d'Horace, c'est celui qu'on peut faire a sa villa de la Sabine, dont l'emplacement a été si bien déterminé, près de Rocca Giovane, par M. Rosa. S'il ne reste de la maison que des briques et des pierres enfouies à l'endroit où une esplanade en fait connaître aujourd'hui l'emplacement, les lieux d'alentour portent des noms dans lesquels on a pu retrouver les anciens noms. Varia (Ep. i. 14, 3) est *Vico Varo ;* la village de *Mandela* (Ep. i. 18, 105), dont Horace était voisin, s'appelle *Bardella :* la Digentia (Ep. i. 18, 104) est devenue la *Licenza.* Il y a aussi la fontaine d'*Oratini,* et, tout près des débris de l'habitation, la colline du poëte, *colle del Poetello.* On a reconnu encore le mont Lucrétile, qui protégeait les chèvres d'Horace contre l'ardeur de l'été et les vents pluvieux (Carm. i. 13, 1—4).

"Cette villa est celle que Mécène avait donnée à Horace. C'était 'ce champ modeste qu'il avait rêvé, avec un jardin, auprès d'une eau toujours vive' (Sat. ii. 6, 2, et Ep. iii. 16, 12)—celle qui s'appelle encore *fonte d'Oratini,*—et un peu de forêts au-dessus.' La végétation a été changée par la culture, mais les grands traits du paysage subsistent. L'on voit toujours la chaîne des montagnes qui est coupée par une vallée profonde, celle où coule la Licenza ; et l'on peut remarquer la justesse de tous les détails de cette description, que le poëte semble s'excuser de faire si longue, *loquaciter,* et qui est renfermée dans quelques vers charmants et précis :

'Continui montes nisi dissocientur opaca
Valle ; sed ut veniens dextrum latus aspiciet sol,
Lævum decedens curru fugiente vaporet.'—Ep. i. 16, 5."
Ampère, Emp. Rom. i. 363.

The Sabine farm was presented to Horace by Mæcenas. c B. C. 33.

"To the munificence of Mæcenas we owe that peculiar charm of the Horatian poetry, that it represents both the town and country life of the Romans of that age ; the country life, not only in the rich and luxurious villa of the wealthy at Tivoli, or at Baiæ ; but in the secluded retreat and among the simple manners of the peasantry. It might seem as if the wholesome air which the poet breathed, during his retirement on his farm, re-invigorated his natural manliness of mind. There, notwithstanding his love of convivial enjoyment in the palace of Mæcenas and other wealthy friends, he delighted to revert to his own sober and frugal way of living."—*Milman.*

The road comes to an end on the margin of the clear

brook Digentia, which is here sometimes swollen into a
broad river by the winter rains. On the further side of the
wide stony bed it has made for itself, rises *Licenza*, cresting

Licenza.

a high hill and approached by a steep rocky path through
the olives. Further up the valley is the " Fonte Blandusino,"
still pointed out as the spring of Horace. Just where the
road ends, a steep bank covered with chestnuts rises on the
left. Passing through the wood (only a few steps from the
road) to a garden, we find a *contadino*, who shovels up the
rich loam with his spade, exposes a bit of tesselated pavement, and says " Ecco la villa d'Orazio."

"The Sabine farm was situated in the valley of Ustica, thirty miles
from Rome, and twelve miles from Tivoli. It possessed the attraction,
no small one to Horace, of being very secluded—Varia (Vico Varo), the
nearest town, being four miles off—yet, at the same time, within an
easy distance of Rome. When his spirits wanted the stimulus of society
or the bustle of the capital, which they often did, his ambling mule
could speedily convey him thither; and when jaded, on the other hand,
by the noise and racket and dissipations of Rome, he could, in the same

homely way, bury himself within a few hours among the hills, and there, under the shadow of his favourite Lucretilis, or by the banks of the clear-flowing and ice-cold Digentia, either stretch himself to dream upon the grass, lulled by the murmurs of the stream, or do a little farming in the way of clearing his fields of stones, or turning over a furrow here and there with the hoe. There was a rough wildness in the scenery and a sharpness in the air, both of which Horace liked, although, as years advanced and his health grew more delicate, he had to leave it in the colder months for Tivoli or Baiæ. He built a villa upon it, or added to one already there, the traces of which still exist. The farm gave employment to five families of free *coloni*, who were under the superintendence of a bailiff; and the poet's domestic establishment was composed of eight slaves. The site of the farm is at the present day a favourite resort of travellers, of Englishmen especially, who visit it in such numbers, and trace its features with such enthusiasm, that the resident peasantry, 'who cannot conceive of any other source of interest in one so long dead and unsainted than that of co-patriotism or consanguinity,' believe Horace to have been an Englishman.* What aspect it presented in Horace's time we gather from one of his Epistles "(i. 16) :—

> "About my farm, dear Quinctius: You would know
> What sort of produce for its lord 'twill grow;
> Plough-land is it, or meadow-land, or soil
> For apples, vine-clad elms, or olive-oil?
> So (but you'll think me garrulous) I'll write
> A full description of its form and site.
> In long continuous lines the mountains run,
> Cleft by a valley, which twice feels the sun—
> Once on the right, when first he lifts his beams;
> Once on the left, when he descends in streams.
> You'd praise the climate well, and what d'ye say
> To sloes and cornels hanging from the spray?
> What to the oak and ilex, that afford
> Fruit to the cattle, shelter to their lord?
> What, but that rich Tarentum must have been
> Transplanted nearer Rome, with all its green?
> Then there's a fountain, of sufficient size
> To name the river that takes thence its rise—
> Not Thracian Hebrus colder or more pure,
> Of power the head's and stomach's ills to cure.

* Letter by Mr Dennis: Milman's "Horace," London, 1849, p. 109.

This sweet retirement—nay, 'tis more than sweet—
Insures my health even in September's heat." (*C.*)

Here is what a recent tourist found it : *—

"Following a path along the brink of the torrent Digentia, we passed a towering rock, on which once stood Vacuna's shrine, and entered a pastoral region of well-watered meadow-lands, enamelled with flowers and studded with chestnut and fruit trees. Beneath their sheltering shade peasants were whiling away the noontide hours. Here sat Daphnis piping sweet witching melodies on a reed to his rustic Phidyle, whilst Lydia and she wove wreaths of wild flowers, and Lyce sped down to the edge of the stream and brought us cooling drink in a bulging conca borne on her head. Its waters were as deliciously refreshing as they could have been when the poet himself gratefully recorded how often they revived his strength; and one longed to think, and hence half believed, that our homely Hebe, like her fellows, was sprung from the coloni who tilled his fields and dwelt in the five homesteads of which he sings. . . . Near the little village of Licenza, standing like its loftier neighbour, Civitella, on a steep hill at the foot of Lucretilis, we turned off the path, crossed a thickly-wooded knoll, and came to an orchard in which two young labourers were at work. We asked where the remains of Horace's farm were. 'A piè tui!' answered the nearest of them in a dialect more like Latin than Italian. So saying, he began with a shovel to uncover a massive floor in very fair preservation; a little farther on was another, crumbling to pieces. Chaupy has luckily saved one all doubt as to the site of the farm, establishing to our minds convincingly that it could scarcely have stood on ground other than that on which at this moment we were. As the shovel was clearing the floors, we thought how applicable to Horace himself were the lines he addressed to Fuscus Aristius,—'Naturam expelles,' etc.

'Drive Nature forth by force, she'll turn and rout
The false refinements that would keep her out,' (*C.*)

for here was just enough of his house left to show how Nature, creeping on step by step, had overwhelmed his handiwork and re-asserted her sway. Again, pure and Augustan in design as was the pavement before us, how little could it vie with the hues and odours of the grasses that bloomed around it!—'Deterius Lybicis,' etc.

'Is springing grass less sweet to nose and eyes
Than Libyan marble's tesselated dyes?' (*C.*)

* "Pall Mall Gazette," August 16, 1869.

"Indeed, so striking were these coincidences that we were as nearly as possible going off on the wrong tack, and singing 'Io Pæan' to Dame Nature herself at the expense of the bard; but we were soon brought back to our allegiance by a sense of the way in which all we saw tallied with the description of him who sang of Nature so surpassingly well, who challenges posterity in charmed accents, and could shape the sternest and most concise of tongues into those melodious cadences, that invest his undying verse with all the magic of music and all the freshness of youth. For this was clearly the 'Angulus iste,' the nook which 'restored him to himself'—this the lovely spot which his steward longed to exchange for the slums of Rome. Below lay the green sward by the river, where it was sweet to recline in slumber. Here grew the vine, still trained, like his own, on the trunks and branches of trees. Yonder the brook which the rain would swell till it overflowed its margin, and his lazy steward and slaves were fain to bank it up; and above, among a wild jumble of hills, lay the woods where, on the Calends of March, Faunus interposed to save him from the attack of the wolf as he strolled along unarmed, singing of the soft voice and sweet smiles of his Lalage! The brook is now nearly dammed up; a wall of close-fitting rough-hewn stones gathers its waters into a still, dark pool; its overflow gushes out in a tiny rill that rushed down beside our path, mingling its murmur with the hum of myriads of insects that swarmed in the air."—*Horace, by Theo. Martin in "Classics for English Readers."*

Visitors to Licenza will be glad further to beguile the long drive with the following extract :—

"Entering the valley which opens to the north. On a height which rises to the right stand two villages, Cantalupo and Bardela; the latter is supposed to be the Mandela, which the poet describes as *rugosus frigore pagus;* and, certes, it stands in an airy position, at the point of junction of the two valleys. You soon come to a small stream, of no remarkable character, but it is the Digentia, the *gelidus rivus*, at which the poet was wont to slake his thirst—*me quoties reficit*—and which flows away through the meadows to the foot of the said hill of Bardela —*quem Mandela bibit*. You are now in the Sabine valley, so fondly loved and highly prized.

'Cur valle permutem Sabinâ
Divitias operosiores?'

"A long lofty ridge forms the left-hand barrier of the valley. It is Lucretilis. It has no striking features to attract the eye—with its easy swells, undulating outline, and slopes covered with wood, it well merits the title of *amœnus*, though that was doubtless due to its grateful shade, rather than to its appearance. Ere long you espy, high up beneath the brow of the mountain, a village pushed on a precipitous grey cliff. It is Rocca Giovane, now occupying the site of the ruined temple of Vacuna.

"On a conical height in this valley stands the town of Licenza; while other loftier heights tower behind, from which the village of Civitella, apparently inaccessible, looks down on the valley like an eagle from its eyrie. In the foreground a knoll crested with chestnuts, rising some eighty or hundred feet above the stream, marks the site of the much-sung farm.

"This knoll stands at a bend of the stream, or rather at the point where several rivulets unite to form the Digentia. Behind the knoll stood the Farm. Its mosaic pavement, still shown, is black and white, in very simple geometrical figures, and, with the other remains, is quite in harmony with an abode where

> 'Non ebur neque aureum
> Meâ renidet in domo lacunar;
> Non trabes Hymettiæ
> Premunt columnas ultimâ recisas
> Africâ.'

"From the poet's description, we learn that his land was little cultivated:

> 'Quid, si rubicunda leniquè
> Corna vepres et pruna ferunt? si quercus et ilex
> Multâ fruge pecus, multâ dominum juvat umbrâ?'

You may remember, too, that he says of the neighbourhood:—

> 'Angulus iste feret piper et thus ocyus uvâ.'

"*Tempora mutantur*, and soils may change also—the cultivation of nineteen centuries has rendered this more fertile; for vines hang in festoons from tree to tree over the site of his abode; the cornels and sloes have in great measure given way to the olive and fig; and the walnut and Spanish chestnut have taken the place of the oak and ilex. Nevertheless the poet's description still holds good of the uncultivated spots in the neighbourhood, which are overrun with brambles and are fragrant with odoriferous herbs; and until late years the ground was covered with wood—with *cere* and *quercie*, different kinds of oak, and with scarlet-holm and Spanish chestnut.

"The Farm is situated on a rising ground, which sinks with a gentle slope to the stream, leaving a level intervening strip, yellow in the harvest. In this I recognized the *pratum apricum* which was in danger of being overflowed. The *aprica rura* were probably then, as now, sown with corn,—*puræ rivus aquæ, et segetis lecta fides meæ.* Here it must have been that the poet was wont to repose after his meal : *prope rivum somnus in herbâ ;* and here his personal efforts, perhaps, to dam out the stream, provoked his neighbours to a smile—

'Rident vicini glebas et saxa moventem.'"
From a Letter by G. Dennis—"*De Villa Horatii,*"—*given in Milman's* "*Works of Quintus Horatius Flaccus.*"

Those who are able to encounter rather a rough walk will not be satisfied without trying to reach the spring, which is supposed to be the Fons Blandusiæ.

"The spring now commonly called the 'Fonte Blandusia' rises at the head of a narrow glen, which opens into the broader valley of the Digentia just beyond the Farm, and stretches up for two or three miles into the heart of the mountains, dividing Lucretilis from Ustica. This is evidently the *reducta vallis*, to which Tyndaris was invited; and is known by the peasants as the 'Valle Rustica,' than which no name could be more appropriate; though it probably was not conferred with reference to the scenery, but as a corruption of 'Ustica.' Whether *Ustica cubans* were a mountain or a valley, or both, as hath been opined, I leave to the critics to determine; but the mountain on the right of the glen, which contrasts its recumbent form with the steep-browed Lucretilis, is still called 'Ustica,' and sometimes 'Rustica,' by the peasantry. The penultimate, however, is now pronounced short. The streamlet is called 'Le Chiuse;' it is the same which flows beneath the villa, and threatens the '*pratum apricum.*' I ascended its course from the Farm, by the path which Horace must have taken to the fountain. It flows over a rocky bed, here overshadowed by dwarf-willows, there by widespreading fig-trees, and is flanked by vineyards for some distance. Then all cultivation ceases—the scenery becomes wilder—the path steeper—the valley contracts to a ravine—a bare grey and red rock rises on the right, schistose, rugged, and stern; another similar cliff rises opposite, crested with ilex, and overtopt by the dark head of Lucretilis. As I approached the fountain I came to an open grassy spot, where cattle and goats were feeding.

'Tu frigus amabile
Fessis vomere tauris
Præbes, et pecori vago.'

The spot is exquisitely Arcadian; no wonder it captivated the poet's fancy. It is now just as it must have met his eye. During the noon-tide heat, the vast Lucretilis throws his grateful shade across the glen,

> ' et igneam
> Defendit æstatem capellis.'

Goats still wander among the underwood, cropping *arbutos et thyma* which cover the ground in profusion, or frisking amongst the rocks as smooth-faced—*levia saxa*—as when they reëchoed the notes of the poet's pipe.

"Crossing the stream by the huge rocks which almost choke its bed, I climbed through brambles and sloes to the fountain. It is a most picturesque spot. Large masses of moss-clad rock lie piled up in the cleft between the hills, and among them the streamlet works its way, overshadowed by hanging woods of ilex, beech, horn-beam, maple, chestnut, nut, and walnut,—which throw so dense a shade, that scarcely a ray of the all-glaring sun can play on the turf below.

> ' Te flagrantis atrox hora Caniculæ
> Nescit tangere : tu frigus amabile
> Præbes.'

The water springs from three small holes at the top of a shelving rock of no great height, and glides down into a sandy basin, which it overflows, trickling in a slender thread over the rocks into a small pool, and thence sinking in a mimic cascade into the rugged channel which bears it down the glen. From the rocks which separate the upper from the lower basin of the fountain, springs a moss-grown walnut tree, which stretches its giant limbs over the whole. The water itself merits all that has been said or sung of it; it is verily *splendidior vitro*. Nothing—not even the Thracian Hebrus—can exceed it in purity, cool-ness, and sweetness.

> " Hæ latebræ dulces, et jam (si credis) amœnæ !'

Well might the poet choose this as a retreat from the fierce noon-tide heat. Here he could lie the live-long day on the soft turf and sing

> ' ruris amœni
> Rivos, et musco circumlita saxa, nemusque,'

while his goats strayed around, cropping the cyclamen which decks the brink of the fountain, or the wild strawberries and sweet herbs which scent the air around. Here, while all nature below was fainting with the heat, might he enjoy the grateful shade of Lucretilis. Or here might he well sing the praises of the fountain itself, as he listened to its 'babbling waters,' and feasted his eye on the rich union of wood and rock around it.

> 'Me dicente cavis impositam ilicem
> Saxis, unde loquaces
> Lymphæ desiliunt tuæ.'

"Just as it was then, so is it now,—even to the very ilices overhanging the hollow rocks whence it springs. And so exactly, in every particular, does this fountain answer to the celebrated Fons, that my faith in its identity is firm and steadfast."—*G. Dennis.*

"On this farm lovers of Horace have been fain to place the fountain of Bandusia, which the poet loved so well, and to which he prophesied, and truly, as the issue has proved, immortality from his song (*Ode* iii. 13). Charming as the poem is, there could be no stronger proof of the poet's hold upon the hearts of men of all ages than the enthusiasm with which the very site of the spring has been contested.

> 'Bandusia's fount in clearness crystalline
> O worthy of the wine, the flowers we vow!
> To-morrow shall be thine
> A kid, whose crescent brow
>
> 'Is sprouting, all for love and victory
> In vain; his warm red blood, so early stirred,
> Thy gelid stream shall dye,
> Child of the wanton herd.
>
> 'Thee the fierce Sirian star, to madness fired,
> Forbears to touch; sweet cool thy waters yield
> To ox with ploughing tired
> And flocks that range afield.
>
> 'Thou too one day shall win proud eminence,
> 'Mid honoured founts, while I the ilex sing
> Crowning the cavern, whence
> Thy babbling wavelets spring.' (*C*)."

Horace, by Theo. Martin.

The ascent of *Monte Gennaro* may be made from Licenza, but it is better to make it from Tivoli itself, whence a carriage may be taken to *Polo*, and horses ordered there. Hence it is a constant ascent over ridges of hill till we reach the long upland valley called *Val del Paradiso*, which is exceedingly beautiful, covered in spring with primroses, crocuses, heartsease, and many of the mountain flowers of Switzerland. Here herds of cattle feed under the shade of the ilexes. The last part of the ascent is very steep and entirely over rock. The view from the top, 3,965 feet above the sea, is magnificent, though many will doubt whether it is sufficiently finer than that from Monte Cavo, to repay the fatigue of an excursion which is certainly very long and tiring, though it is exaggerated by the hotel-keepers at Tivoli, and though the start at 3 A.M., which is urged by them, is altogether unnecessary: 6 or 7 A.M. being quite early enough.

It is best to descend by the almost perpendicular staircase called *La Scarpellata*, but the steps are very rugged and of course can only be traversed on foot. There is a pleasant ride through meadows from S. Francesco, ascending afterwards by the olive-woods, and coming up to Tivoli by the Madonna del Quintiliolo. We leave a little to the right the low isolated hills called *Montes Corniculani* (which may be made the object of a separate excursion from Tivoli). Their southern height is occupied by the village of *Monticelli*, the next by *Colle Cesi*, the northern by *S. Angelo in Cappoccio*. All the villages are ruinous, but contain many picturesque bits. S. Angelo is supposed to occupy the site of *Corniculum*, which was burnt by Tarquin. The widow of its slain chieftain, Ocrisia, was taken, after the siege, to Rome, where she was delivered of a boy, who was educated in the house of Tarquin, and became King Servius Tullius. Some ancient walls of Cyclopean masonry remain: the interstices between the large stones are filled in with smaller ones.

CHAPTER XIV.

VELLETRI.

(Velletri is a station on the Naples line of railway, one hour and 20 minutes from Rome. The Locanda del Gallo is a comfortable and reasonable hotel. The vetturino Roberto Tasselli, 116 Strada Vittorio Emmanuele, is an honest man, and lets out capital carriages for excursions. A carriage for the day to Cora costs 25 francs, to Ninfa 22 francs, but the price must be settled beforehand.)

VELLETRI is in many respects a much better centre for excursions than Albano, being situated on the railway itself, so that tourists are saved the long drive down to the station, which makes excursions from the latter town so fatiguing. Its streets are wide and clean, and the air healthy and invigorating. Like Albano, it has no costumes of its own, but on festas the people flock in from the neighbouring villages, and enliven it with their white *panni* and brilliant red and blue bodices. Of the old Volscian city of Velitræ, which once occupied this site and which was so long at war with Rome, there are many scattered traces, and vestiges may be discovered of the vallum and fosse with which the place was surrounded by Coriolanus. But the inhabitants of the Volscian city were removed to Rome, where they became the forefathers of the Trasteverini, and though in imperial times the place had again a certain importance, and though Augustus himself is declared by the natives to have been born there (in contradiction to the account of Suetonius, who expressly states that he was born at Rome, at the sign of the Ox-heads, in the Palatium), the principal existing remains are all mediæval.

From the station a gradual ascent leads into the town, fringed with trees, and with beautiful views of the Volscian range, over the hill-side slopes so rich in the vines which produce the famous wine of Velletri. The extraordinary folly which has affected almost every town in Italy since the change of government, has changed all the old historical appellations of the streets to the meaningless "Corso Cavour, Via Vittorio Emmanuele, Via Garibaldi," &c. One whole side of the principal square is occupied by the façade of the *Palazzo Lancellotti*, built by Martino Longhi. The exterior gives no idea of the extreme beauty of the interior, which is one of the most remarkable in Italy. On the first floor is an open gallery of immense length, the arcades divided by pillars richly decorated with caryatides. A marble staircase, with open loggias on every landing, ascends to the top of the palace, whence there is a glorious view, and beneath are beautiful gardens extending to the open country. Near the top of the staircase is a very fine statue of Minerva Pudicitia (with its own head, that at the Vatican being an addition) found at Velletri. The palace is now inhabited by Prince Gianetti, who kindly allows it to be shown to strangers, and it is well worth visiting.

Opposite the palace rises the beautiful tall detached campanile of *Santa Maria in Trivio*, raised to commemorate the deliverance of the city from the plague in 1348, whilst it was being besieged by Nicola Gaetani, Lord of Fondi. Other old palaces of impoverished nobles abound in the smaller streets, the most remarkable being the Palazzo Filippi,

S. Maria in Trivio, Velletri.

which is really magnificent, in spite of its desertion and decay.

The old palace of the popes, now called *Palazzo Communale*, built by Giacomo della Porta, occupies the highest part of the town, the citadel of old Velitræ, and beside it stands the palace of the Cardinal-Archbishop, with a bas-relief on its front commemorating the opening of the Via Appia Nuova by Pius IX., and an inscription rather inconsistent with present ideas —" Papalis et imperialis est mihi libertas." Close to these palaces are two little churches, *San Michaele* and *Il Santissimo Sangue*. Over the door of the latter is an ancient sun-dial— " Horologium Beronianum"—found in the neighbouring ruins. In the interior is an inscription recording a miraculous appearance of the Virgin, and an altar to an early Christian who has been canonized on the belief that she was a martyr—" Temporalem mortem S. Tertura Victorina contemnens coronam vitæ æternæ possidet in pace." By the side is the catacomb inscription:—

    URTURA VICTORINA
    VAE VIXIT ANNUS XLII
    III MATRI FECERUNT
    BENEMERENTI IN PACE.

The Legate's Fountain, Velletri.

In the lower part of the town is the *Cathedral*, dedicated

to S. Clemente, and partly ancient, though altered in 1660. It contains a chapel of the Borgias, who are still one of the great families of the place, with their monuments. On the left of the altar is a beautiful fresco of the Virgin and Child, with St. John, St. Sebastian, St. Jerome, and St. Roch, by an unknown artist of the Perugino school. In the sacristy is the *lavamano*, which Julius II. presented to the church while he was Cardinal-Archbishop of Velletri. Latino Orsini, to whom the hymn "Dies Iræ" is wrongly attributed, but who was one of the most distinguished prelates of the thirteenth century, was also bishop here. We were present on Easter Sunday, when the existing archbishop performed high-mass in the presence of thousands of countrywomen, kneeling in their white and brown *panni*, and the sight was very imposing and impressive.

Nothing can be more charming than the environs of Velletri in early spring. It is almost the only place near Rome where the trees are allowed to grow at their own will, and are not cut into squares, and the lanes around are delightfully shady and attractive. Gulfs of verdure with little streams running in their deep hollows may be discovered in all directions, and there are also pleasant walks to many convents and churches on neighbouring heights. Near the Roman gate is the ascent to the *Cappuccini*, whence the view is especially fine, the long lines of the Pontine marshes and the beautiful Circean promontory being seen behind the old houses and churches of the town. In this direction is the battle-field where Charles III. of Naples gained the victory over the Austrians which gave the kingdom of the two Sicilies to the Spanish Bourbons. On the Naples road is the Jesuit Convent containing a famous Madonna attributed to St. Luke, of which About tells :—

"Un hôte du Campo-Morto appelé Vendetta conçut le projet d'une spéculation hardie. Depuis longtemps, il rançonnait les gens de Velletri et des environs. Il demandait à celui-ci deux écus, à celui-là dix ou douze. Quiconque avait une récolte sur pied, des arbres chargés de fruits, un frère en voyage, payait sans marchander ce singulier impôt. Cependant Vendetta finit par prendre en dégoût un métier si lucratif. Il rêva de rentrer dans la vie normale avec un revenu modeste et un honnête emploi. Pour atteindre ce but, il ne trouva rien de plus ingénieux que de voler la madone de Velletri et de la déposer en lieu sûr.

"On approchait d'une fête carillonnée où la madone devait paraître aux yeux du peuple avec tous ses diamants. Le sacristain ouvrait la niche et constata avec des cris de douleur que la madone n'y était plus. Grande rumeur dans Velletri. On cherche de tous côtés et l'on ne trouve rien. Le peuple s'émeut ; une certaine effervescence se manifeste dans les villages voisins. Le clergé du pays accuse les jésuites de s'être volés eux-mêmes ; les jésuites récriminent contre les prêtres de Velletri. Le couvent est envahi, fouillé, bouleversé par un public idolâtre. Enfin le dimanche, à la grand'messe, Vendetta, armé d'un poignard, monte en chaire et se dénonce lui-même. Il prie le peuple d'agréer ses excuses et promet de rendre la madone dès qu'il aura réglé ses comptes avec l'autorité. L'autorité traite avec lui de puissance à puissance. Vendetta demande sa grâce et celle de son frère, une rente de tant d'écus et un emploi du gouvernement. On promet tout, mais Rome désavone ses agents et ne veut rien ratifier. Cependant la population des montagnes se met en marche, et un flot de paysans menace d'inonder Velletri. Le brigand cède au nombre, révèle la cachette où il a celé la madone, et se rend lui-même à discrétion. Il aura la tête coupée ; personne n'en doute à Velletri."—*Rome Contemporaine.*

The inhabitants of Velletri were formerly famous for their brigand tendencies : now they are most inoffensive. But a Roman proverb says

" Velletrani sette volte villani."

CHAPTER XV.

THE VOLSCIAN HILLS—CORI, NORBA, NINFA, AND SEGNI.

FOR the excursion to Norba it is quite necessary to make an early start, and can anything be more charming than six o'clock on a cloudless morning in April, if, with jingling bells, we drive out of the old town of Velletri and descend into the hollow lanes shaded by fresh green trees and gay with peasants going out in bands to the work of the day. The road winds through dips in the low hills. It is the country which was formerly known as the "Volscorum Ager." We only pass one village, *San Giulianello*. A little beyond this, *Rocca Massima* is seen on the top of a precipice, but travellers may reach it by a good mountain path, if they are anxious to explore the site of the ancient Arx Carventana. An excellent road ascends to Cori, which soon becomes visible, though its temples cannot be seen from here as Murray describes, for they are on the other side of the hill. Through the olives there is a beautiful view across the Pontine marshes to the sea, with the Circean promontory and the neighbouring islands. Of these, the largest is San Felice. Then comes Ponza, whither Tiberius banished his nephew Nero, the son of Germanicus, and where many Christians lived in exile, or suffered martyrdom, under

Tiberius and Caligula. Lastly we see Pandataria, to which Julia, daughter of Augustus, and then wife of Tiberius, was banished by her father. Hither, too, her beautiful daughter, Agrippina, wife of Germanicus, was banished by Tiberius, and here she was starved to death. Here also Octavia, the divorced wife of Nero, and daughter of Claudius and Messalina, was banished by the Empress Poppæa, who forced her to commit suicide by opening her veins.

Thinking of these associations, and stopping to gather honey-suckle—*fiori della Madonna* (because it generally flowers in May)—we reach the gates of *Cori*. We must leave our carriage here, for the streets, chiefly staircases, are too steep for anything but mules and foot passengers. It is best to make our way first to the quaint old inn in the Piazza Romana, to order dinner from the fat, good-tempered landlady with the silver *spadello* in her hair, and to get the honest old landlord, Filippo Capobianchi, to provide a guide, which is desirable, if time be of importance, and delivers one from the swarm of would-be cicerones who pounce upon the stranger like so many harpies. The inn at Cori is quite tolerable as a resting-place, but is strangely backward in civilized knowledge. A friend of ours who stayed there was astonished by seeing that the eggs when boiled were always bored through with a very small hole, and, asking the reason, was told that of course it must be so, or they would burst in the boiling!

Virgil and Diodorus speak of Cori as a colony of Alba Longa. Pliny asserts that it was founded by the Trojan Dardanus. It was certainly one of the thirty cities of the Latin League in B.C. 493, and Livy speaks of it as in the enjoyment of municipal rights during the second Punic war. During this war it is mentioned as one of the rebellious cities which refused to contribute the necessary supplies. It was taken and sacked many years after by one of the wandering bands of Spartacus. Propertius and Lucan describe it as totally ruined.

Yet there are few places in the neighbourhood of Rome which have so many or such fine remains of antiquity as Cori. In mounting to the upper town, three distinct tiers of its ancient walls may be traced. The first, in the lower town, built of polygonal blocks, has their interstices filled up

Temple of Castor and Pollux, Cori.

with smaller stones; the second, near Santa Oliva, has polygonal blocks alone, very carefully fitted; and the third, at the top of the hill, is still polygonal, but of ruder construction. Behind some wretched houses are two columns still standing, with beautiful Corinthian capitals, a fragment of the *Temple of Castor and Pollux*, as is proved by still legible inscriptions. Another capital of the same temple is before a house door a little further up the ascent. The adjoining house to this temple is called the Palace of Pilate. On the top of the hill stands the church of S. Pietro, where the font (in the first chapel on the right) is sustained by a sculptured marble altar, adorned with rams' heads. Behind the church is a small garden, where we find entire the beautiful Doric peristyle of the Temple of Minerva, generally known here as

Temple of Minerva, Cori.

the Temple of Hercules. Eight columns still remain, four in the front. Here the figure of Minerva, which now stands under the Senators' palace on the Roman Capitol, was found. The ruin is most picturesque, and is grandly situated on a terrace.

> "Whence Cora's sentinels o'erlook
> The never-ending fen."

Raphael made a sketch of it, which is still extant. As we sat to draw here, the children, who were vainly locked out by the Sacristan, and climbed after us over the wall, got pieces of stone for blocks, and sticks for pencils, and imitated every line we made.

Halfway up the hill is the beautiful old convent of Santa Oliva, whose shrine is in the crypt at Anagni. She was a holy maiden of Cori, to whom the Virgin appeared in 1521. Her cloister, with a double row of arches, is most picturesque, and it contains an old well. The body of the church has a ceiling whose intention is the same as that of the Sistine, representing scenes of Old and New Testament story. In the apse is the Coronation of the Virgin, evidently by a pupil of Pinturicchio; the donor kneels beneath. The aisle of the church, a labyrinth of columns of different sizes and designs, is shown as the Temple of Jupiter. The temples of Cori are all attributed to Sylla. Outside the gate of the town, on the Norba side, is the beautiful bridge called *Ponte alla Catena*, built of huge masses of tufa, spanning the deep ravine of the Pichionni, and overhung by quaint old houses.

Norba and *Norma* are five long miles from Cori, and can be reached only on foot or on muleback without making an immense detour. A very steep and intensely stony way leads up the hill-side from near the Ponte alla Catena. The olive-gardens beside it are fringed with wild blue iris—*gigli* the Italians call them, and the *gigli*, which are the arms of Florence, are represented as iris. The path emerges on the steep of the mountain, and clambers along, with precipices above and below, amid the wildest scenery. All around are grey rocks, with short grass between, on which the flocks of goats pasture, whose shepherds, clad in goatskins, are the only human beings we meet here. Hawks swoop overhead. It is a vast view over what looks like a boundless plain, for all the undulations and sinuosities of the country are lost to us at this great height. The village which glitters midway between us and the sea is Cisterna, "the Three Taverns" of St. Paul. At length Sermoneta comes in sight on the top of a precipice, and then Norma. Then the ancient *Norba*, now often called *Civita la Penna d'Oro*, one of the earliest of the Roman colonies, rises on the right. It has been an utter ruin ever since the time of Sylla, when it was betrayed into the hands of his general, Lepidus, and the garrison put themselves and the inhabitants to the sword. It must have been a tremendous fortress, for the walls are seven thousand feet in circuit, and the blocks of which they are built, and on which time has failed to make any impression, are often ten feet in length. The gates may be traced, and an inner series of walls surrounding the citadel. A square enclosure sunk in the earth is surrounded by Cyclopean walls: its object is unknown. Our guide said that when the Deluge occurred it would have failed to make any impression upon Norba—a very ancient city at that time—so strong was it; but here the rain which fell was made of lead, and the inhabitants, who were giants, were all destroyed, and every house, and all the temples of the ancient religion of that time, and only the walls remained, for they were so strong that not even a leaden deluge could affect them. Hither Ricchi mentions that as late as the beginning of the last century people were wont to use magical arts in the search for hidden treasure.

Norma and Norba belonged to the Gaetani from 1282 to 1618, when they were sold to Cardinal Scipio Borghese.

"From the citadel, the panorama of the Maritima is especially magnificent. One can distinctly trace the whole boundary line of the sea, from Antium (Porto d'Anzio) to the Cape of Circe near Terracina, and still farther off one can distinguish Ostia, Pratica, and Ardea, and many towers rising like solitary obelisks on the sea-shore. These watch towers were built in the ninth century, when the Saracens began to invade the coasts of Italy; and even in the present time the whole of Italy and all the Italian islands are encircled by these picturesque towers. . . . A tower gleams on the sea-shore with the dark woods reaching down close to it : it is the celebrated castle of Astura. A mile farther on is another tower, Foceverde, so called from the river, flowing from the marshy wooded wilderness into the sea. Farther on is another tower by a great lake, the surface of which shines like molten gold, while round it extends a thick green wood. There a ghostly stillness surrounds the traveller, he stands by the lake as if in a strange world ; and he looks at the osprey circling above ; or at the fisherman, pale with fever, floating on his frail raft ; or at the half-naked leech-seeker, who passes his life there. These are the Tower and Lake of Fogliano, in ancient times Clostra Romana, where Lucullus had a villa. The Nymphæus, that charming stream which we see rushing through the green ring of Ninfa, flows into the lake of Fogliano ; we can trace its course thither, through the whole of the Pontine marsh-land. Farther on, by its side, the Lago de' Monaci is visible, then the Lago di Crapolace ; finally the great lake of Paola, with its tower ; and not far from this rises the Cape of Circe, almost like an island.

"Whoever has not traversed the Pontine marshes by the Via Appia as far as Terracina, has the most erroneous idea of their nature, if he only thinks of horrible morasses. There are indeed plenty of marshes and lakes, but they lie hidden in forests and bushes, where the hedge-hog, the stag, the wild boar, the buffalo, and the half wild bull are roaming. In May and June the Pontine land is a sea of flowers, which cover the ground as far as the eye can reach. In summer it is a Tartarus, where pale fever stalks, and torments the poor shepherds and farm-labourers, who have to earn their bread here.

"The nearer to the sea, the more forest, and from Norba we see it distinctly stretching to the Cape of Circe. From the mouth of the Tiber the forests of Ostia, of Ardea, of Nettuno, Cisterna, and Terracina succeed one another. In the middle of these woods or on their borders lie single farms, principally devoted to breeding cattle, but also to agriculture ; such are Conca, Campo Morto, Campo Leone, Tor' del Felce, and others. Where the forest leaves off in the interior stretch endless meadows, then a firm arable land, and we see distinctly the Appian Way, renewed by Pius VI., traversing the Maritima. Near it is Cisterna, the largest place in the marshes, close to which the Three Taverns stood formerly, and farther on is For' Appio, the ancient Forum Appium.

"No century has been able to drain the Pontine marshes. Julius Cæsar formed a plan for it, but he died before putting it into execution. The Roman Emperors, so extravagant in buildings of every kind, did nothing for it ; and it is therefore strange enough, that under a barbarian king, inheritor or conqueror of Rome, the great Theodoric, the ruined Appian Way was first restored, and a part of the marshes as far as Terracina drained. The original record of this noble deed of a Goth, may be read at the present day inscribed on two tablets in Terracina. In papal times Sixtus V., a man of practical Roman spirit, was the first to undertake again the draining of the marshes, and more than two centuries later he was followed by Pius VI. This pope restored the Appian Way, dug the great canal alongside, had other canals made, changed part of the marsh into arable land, and thus gained a lasting credit in this part of the Maritima."—*Gregorovius*.

A man in scarlet cap and with long curly hair guided us through the high beans which occupied the platform of the ancient city, to the " Grotte di Norba." It is a ruin of later Roman brickwork, covering the entrance to long caves and cellars, but is always shown to strangers as the place where the spirit of Junius Brutus is held imprisoned, waiting for the final judgment, and whence his howls are heard at night mingling with the thunder-storms.

Leaving the citadel, and descending slightly on the other side, we soon reach the edge of the precipice towards the marshes, and here, through a jagged rift in the mountain-side, we look upon Norma, perched like an eagle's nest upon the top of tremendous precipices of bare rock.

" Immediately beneath us is a ring as of green ivy walls encircling many wonderful mounds, which all seem formed of flowers and ivy.

Grey towers rise out of this, ruins all overhung with green, and in the midst of the strange circle we may see a silver spring gushing forth and glowing through the Pontine marshes, ending in a sparkling lake far away by the sea-shore. We ask in astonishment what this curious garlanded circle is with its many green hillocks, and are told it is Ninfa Ninfa, the Pompeii of the middle ages."—*Gregorovius*.

View of Norma.

Instead of returning the same way, it is best to descend from hence to the valley, clambering down through the broken rock and sliding shale, clinging to the myrtle and Judas bushes, into the depths where, nestling under the hill, is *Ninfa*, almost as entirely a ruin as Norba itself. It is an unspeakably quiet scene of sylvan beauty, and there is something unearthly about it which possesses and absorbs every sense. If fairies exist anywhere, surely Ninfa is their capital; Ninfa, where Flora holds her court, where the only inhabitants are the roses and lilies, and all the thousand flowers which grow so abundantly in the deserted streets, where honeysuckle and jessamine fling their garlands through the windows of every house, and where the very altars of the churches are thrones for the flame-coloured valerian. Outside the walls you would scarcely believe it was a town, so encrusted in verdure is every building, that the houses look like green mounds rising out of the plain. It is as if Nature had built the city for a perpetual Feast of Tabernacles. One tall tower stands near the entrance and watches its reflection

Ninfa.

in the still waters of a pool white with lilies and fringed with forget-me-not. By the road-side a crystal spring rises in great abundance in a little basin of ancient brickwork, and falls into the pool, where it turns a mill, and a little farther on becomes a lake, on which Pliny mentions the floating islands in his time, which were called Saltuares, because they were said to move to the time of dancing feet. An inscription on the mill tells that it was built by one of the Gaetani, lord of the place, in 1765. The town must have been inhabited then, yet none can tell now the story of its desertion. It has belonged to the Gaetani since the thirteenth century, and Pope Alexander III. was consecrated here, September 20, 1159. From the tower, say the natives of Norma, "la bella Ninfa," who was disobedient to her parents, flung herself into the pool to evade becoming the *sposina* of the unsympathetic *partito* they had chosen for her, and ever since the name of the little city has kept her memory alive. Let it be so, though etymologists suggest the little river Nymphæus as a godfather. The water-nymphs will avenge all insults by the fever-bearing vapours of their lake. Ninfa can never be rebuilt. Even the shepherds cannot dare to pass the night there. Death, garlanded with flowers, is death still. Gregory I., who built a church here in 1216, to "St. Mary of the Myrtle-branch," dedicated it in vain. No sound will ever be heard but the hum of the myriad insects which float amongst the flower-possessed streets and houses, the croaking of the green frogs in the surrounding waters, and the everlasting sighing and rustling of the wind in the tall bulrushes.

"Here is Ninfa, the fairy-like ruin of a town, with its walls, towers, churches, convents, and dwellings half sunk in the marsh, and buried under thickest ivy. Truly this place looks even more charming than Pompeii, for there the houses stare like crumbling mummies, dragged from the volcanic ashes. But over Ninfa waves a balmy sea of flowers;

every building, every wall, every church, every house is veiled with ivy, and on all the ruins wave the purple banners of the triumphant god of spring.

"It causes an indescribable impression to enter this ivy town, to wander down the grassy, flowery streets, between the walls where the wind plays in the leaves, and no voice is heard, but the cry of the raven in the tower, the splash of the foaming stream Nymphæus, the rustling of the tall reeds by the pond, and the melodious singing and sighing of the blades of grass all around.

"All the streets are filled with flowers, which seem to march in procession to the ruined churches. They climb on every tower, they lie laughing and smiling in all the desolate windows, they barricade every door, for within the houses reside elves, fairies, water-nymphs, and a thousand charming spirits of the fable world. Yellow marigolds, mallows, sweet narcissus; grey-bearded thistles who once dwelt here as monks; white lilies, who were nuns in their lifetime; wild roses, laurestinus, masticks, tall ferns, wreaths of clematis and bramble; the red fox-gloves, which look like enchanted Saracens; the fantastic caper-plant growing in the clefts of the buildings, the sweet wall-flower, the myrtle, and the fragrant mint; brilliant yellow broom, and dark ivy which creeps over all the ruins, and falls over the walls like green cascades,— yes, one may fling oneself into this sea of flowers, quite intoxicated by the perfume, and the most charming fairy power enchains the soul.

"The walls of the town are still standing and encircle it like a great ring, but they are everywhere covered thickly with ivy, and only here and there peeps out a crumbling pinnacle on a square ruined tower. The gates of the town are no less barred and barricaded by the wild vine, the ivy, and the bramble, as if the flowers in Ninfa feared some enemy who wanted to break in upon them, as formerly the Saracen, or the soldiers of Barbarossa, or of the Duke of Alba, and the Colonna. They have entrenched themselves behind these ivy walls; perhaps it may be the swarms of meteors, or will-o'-the-wisps from the Pontine marshes, who by night besiege or storm this enchanted town to carry off the flower spirits into the marshes.

"Many squares and many streets are still standing, with their ruined houses covered with an ivy web, many palaces of a half-gothic architecture, once the dwellings of rich nobles. The churches, the ruins of four or five of which remain, look very strange. I never saw such fantastic ruins; but how can one describe them in words? How shall I depict such a brown shattered bell tower, with round windows, or windows divided by small pillars, with its frieze of the middle ages formed of sharp-pointed tiles, and with its romantic decorations of ivy and flowers waving in the wind? or how shall I picture the ruins of the arched niches, or the nave of the church, all overhung with tapestries of flowers?

"These churches are old, they belong to the eleventh or twelfth century if they are not of a still earlier date, for they are built in the simple basilica style. In their deserted space the flowers worship now, and the censers are swung by the bacchanalian roses. From the walls, or perhaps from an ivy-hung tribune, some old fresco paintings still look down. They represent early Christians with palms in their hands, and instruments of martyrdom by their side. With faded nimbi on their pale foreheads, in golden dalmatica, with stole upon their shoulders, they look down morosely from behind their veils of flowers, and seem shocked by the heathen rites which the children of Flora are daring to celebrate in these deserted churches.

"The beetle hums continually his romance of summer, and the cricket chirps incessantly her Anacreontic love-songs. The flowers and beetles yield up these temples no more. A complaint was once brought to S. Bernard that countless swarms of flies had taken possession of a church which was just about to be consecrated, and would not leave it : 'I excommunicate them,' said he ; and behold, when the messengers returned to the church all the flies lay dead. But a saintly exorcist would hardly succeed in excommunicating the flowers from the churches of Ninfa, and though the painted martyrs look angry, the ivy is already creeping up and will soon have entirely veiled and walled them in. Of many there is now nothing more visible than the hem of a robe, and the name in old Roman characters :—S. Xystus or S. Cesarius and S. Laurentius. I went into the last of these churches—what a sight ! The original mosaic of the pavement with its arabesques and circles or squares seemed now to be imitated by living flowers, and from the shrine where the bones of the saint once lay the Indian vine waves joyously with its bluish red berries.

"Here also the counterpart of Pompeii is not wanting. As there the classic age expresses itself decidedly in the bright frescoes, so in Ninfa the Christian epoch of humanity speaks from the paintings on the walls of the ruins. There they are the attractive forms of life and pleasure : Cupids fishing in the pool, dancing satyrs, crickets driving a little chariot, hovering Bacchantes clashing cymbals, or holding in their hands a mysterious casket, or bearing juicy figs upon a dish, but in the Pompeii of the middle ages the frescoes only represent death and woe. Instead of those cheerful pictures, we find here the melancholy figures of the catacombs, the mythic gods of suffering and martyrdom, in the flames, on the cross, or kneeling with folded hands before the executioner who stands with uplifted sword.

"Is it not time that all these martyrs, saints, and decaying crucifixes were buried in flowers? Here Nature strews them plentifully on the graves of the unfortunate penitents and monks, and of all those who in the time of dark superstition scourged and tortured themselves—would that catholic humanity might imitate her, and give to the dead peace and a grave of flowers!

"At the entrance to Ninfa still stands the castle, once the seat of the barons in whose dungeons the victims of feudalism languished. High rises the square tower, built as strongly of bricks as the Torre delle Milizie in Rome, and it seems to belong to the same period. It stands close to a pool, which lies here like a Stygian marsh at the entrance to the city of the dead. Tall reeds surround it. It is a mythic spot, as if from the shadow-world of Eneas or Ulysses. The gloomy tower and other ruins fling their trembling reflection across the still water of the marsh. The reeds rustle sadly. Sometimes the sobbing voice of a water-hen is heard, like the souls of the departed, who dwell in this Hades and yearn after the upper existence. I sit on ruins and look into this green spirit world, then up to the blue entrancing mountains, on which stand the cyclopean stones of Norba and its citadel, then over the Pontine marshes to the sea in the sunshine of evening, whence rises the glittering Circean mount. Can the enchantress Circe have left her castle there? Does she now dwell in Ninfa? Has she become the ivy-queen? There is so much ivy here, it seemed to me as if this Ninfa must be the ivy store-house of Italy, and as if the ivy spirits of history supplied all the ruins of this noble country with creepers from this place.

"One must sit here when the evening floods every ruin of these ivy halls first with purple, and then with gold, and steeps mountains, and sea, and the Cape of Circe in unspeakable richness of colour—but I will not speak of it, or describe how this fairy land appears, so soon as the moon shines on it.

"Out of the pool rushes the spring Nymphæus. It appears to take its rise here, and suddenly brings a startling contrast of young, noisy life into this green grave-world. For with the stormy force of a mountain torrent it dashes past the ruins, as if urged on by demons, as if winged, as if trying to escape from the deathly grasp of the ivy, and it looks like a living creature, as, sparkling and foaming, it flees across the Pontine marsh towards the sea.

"Near the pool it turns a mill, which has been erected in a building of the middle ages, for part of this house keeps still its pillared gothic-roman windows. They say that there stood in olden times, by the spring and the lake, a temple of the Nymphs, from which the town took its name, and on the site of that Nymphæum the church of St. Michael was built. In the year 1216 Ugolino Conti founded here the church of S. Maria del Mirteto—of the myrtle-grove.

"But the history of Ninfa is all very obscure. In the 12th century the Frangipani possessed this town. At the end of the 13th century the race of Gaetani got possession of Ninfa, and the descendants of that famous house retain it to this day. The archives of the family in Rome preserve many records which show how Pietro Gaetani, nephew of Boniface VIII., Lateran Count Palatine and Count of Caserta, gradually bought up the houses and possessions of Ninfa. I found there no deeds of the 15th century. But an old record of 22 Feb., 1349, is inscribed on the now ruined baronial castle. It runs thus: Actum Nimphe in scalis palatii Rocce Nimphe presente Nicolao Cillone Vicario Sculcule."—*Gregorovius.*

Evening closed in upon us at Ninfa; the low houses turned purple against the sunset, and the lake became like molten gold. We hurried away from the fever. It was too late to ascend the mountain way again with its unguarded precipices, but another path led us along the foot of the hills through the low-lying moorlands—parched and ugly at midday, but beautiful in the soft twilight, when each arum and thistle, thickly diamonded with dew, sparkled and glittered in the last gleams, and the figures of our party on their mules stood out dark against the soft after-glow. And then, as the bells of Cori were ringing the last strokes of the Ave Maria, which serves as the summons for the peasants of the Campagna to save themselves from the malaria in their high mountain homes, we wound up to the town through the ancient olive-groves, the most solemn thing in nature, and looked down through the gnarled stems over the vast marshes to the great Circean promontory engraven in black upon a flaming sky.

From Cori a mountain road, which is described as most

.beautiful, leads through the Volscian forests to *Segni*. We took the railway thither from Ferentino. The station is at the bottom of the mountain called Monte Lepini, while the town is at the top, and we had the discomfort of finding that no omnibus met the train from the south, and having to wait until the great heat of the April day was over before we could walk up. However, we employed the time in sketching two fine old castles near the railway, one of them, Colleferro, now turned into farm-buildings, being especially picturesque, its front formed by deeply recessed arches. The ascent to Segni is most wild and rugged, and the road wound along the mountain edge without any parapet beyond a fringe of Judas bushes just bursting into bloom to be ready for the Good Friday close at hand, and with tremendous precipices below, rather alarming in a carriage. Segni was the ancient Signia, colonized by Tarquinius Superbus as a restraint upon the inhabitants of the Volscian and Hernican hills, and it is said that the name is derived from the number of standards which he saw raised by the inhabitants in his behalf against the people of Gabii. The town is mentioned in the " Captives " of Plautus, where the parasite and epicure Ergasilus swears in turn by Cora, Præneste, Signia, Phrysinone, and Alatrium, and explains, when asked by his host Hegio why he swears by foreign cities, that they are just as disagreeable as the dinner he is about to receive from him. Strabo and Pliny mention the peculiar wine of Signia, as well as several of the poets :

> " Quos Cora, quos spumans immiti Signia musto,
> Et quos pestifera Pomptini uligine campi."
> *Sil. Ital.* viii. 380.

"Potabis liquidum Signina morantia ventrem;
Ne nimium sistant, sit tua parca sitis."
Martial. xiii. *Ep.* 106..

In the twelfth and thirteenth centuries, when the popes sought safety in the strongest towns of the Campagna, Segni was frequently their residence. Eugenius III. fled hither from the Roman Senate, and built a papal palace, in 1145; and here Alexander III., Lucius III., and Innocent III. passed a considerable portion of their reigns in security. Segni was long a fief of the great family of Conti, to which so many of the popes belonged, and it disputes with Anagni the honour of having been the birthplace of Innocent III. In 1353 the head of the house of Conti was Podesta, and afterwards Vicar in the name of the Pope. After the Conti had died out, and Segni had passed into the hands of Mario Sforza, Sixtus V. created it a Duchy. On the 13th of August, 1557, the place was taken and almost totally destroyed by the Duke of Alba, and it is owing to this that so few gothic buildings remain. The town was rebuilt, and was given as a duchy by Urban VIII. to his nephew, Cardinal Antonio Barberini. A long lawsuit which followed between the Barberini and the Sforza, the former lords of Segni, was only decided at the end of the last century in honour of the Sforza-Cesarini, who are still Dukes of Segni.

The town is surrounded on all sides by steep rocks, except where a *passeggiata* bordered by trees, with splendid views of valley and mountains, leads to the one gate, the Porta Maggiore. This gate rests against the Cyclopean walls, and over it are the remains of the baronial castle of the Conti, in which, as in many other buildings here, the curious style of construction may be observed, which is frequently spoken of in old documents about other places as "Signino opere," and which consists of alternate layers of bricks and the dark lime-stone of the country.

All those who visit Segni should turn at once to the right after entering the gate (there is a poor inn where a tolerable meal may be obtained), and make the circuit of the Pelasgic walls which give the place its chief interest. They are formed by masses of rock jammed into one another, and though of no great height, almost surround the existing town, and are among the most extensive in Italy. In some places they are most picturesque, especially where a tall cross crowns the huge pile of stones, and stands out against the vast expanse of distance, for you look across the great

From the Walls of Segni.

depths to billow upon billow of purple Hernican hills, and

beyond these upon all the ranges of the Abruzzi, still, in April, covered with snow. The church of S. Pietro, built quite at the end of the fortifications, is another striking point.

"When I reached this spot where the cyclopean citadel of the Volscians stood in hoary antiquity on the lofty heights, the magnificence of the situation took me by surprise ; it reminded me of the Acropolis of some Sicilian mountain town. Here, on a height overlooking all Latium, stood the citadel and temple of ancient Signia, of which but few vestiges remain, among them a large circular cistern near the Seminary. The townspeople have here one of their favourite promenades; they walk about there on the cyclopean walls of the highest plateaux of the mountain, as if round a great stone table, among the grey blocks of stone overgrown with moss and wild flowers. One can imagine nothing more original than this promenade in the cloud-region, amid this grand rock scenery. Among the promenaders I saw, as it was a Sunday, many a gaily decked young lady in silk attire parading up and down, while, immediately below, the mountain fell sheer away in a precipice, and Latium lay extended below. The eye reaches over a wide-spread picture of provinces with their innumerable mountains and cities, each of which is full of its own historical or mythical memories. For the panorama extends from Rome, visible in the plain, to Arpino, Cicero's paternal city, which stands out among the far blue mountains of the Neapolitan kingdom.

"The air up here is fresh, almost sharp. The brown grasses on the masses of rock, the wild roses, and the golden broom wave to and fro in it. The very spirit of antiquity and of the primæval wilderness, of a great, mighty, pre-historic age, seems to brood on these storm-worn cyclopean stones.

"I scrambled further over the rocks, to reach the famous cyclopean walls. As in all the Latin cities, their long lines girdle the actual Arx or citadel, and sink away sheer down the precipice. The arrangement of their unhewn stones is as perfectly preserved as if the builder had been at work but yesterday : here and there they are pierced by a small door of Etruscan appearance. At the end of one great line of wall there still stands the great cyclopean gate, in use at the present day. It is built of massive, almost square blocks, in such a manner that the two side walls lean towards each other till the angle is cut off by the stone which forms the lintel.

"The hugeness of these grey walls, weather-stained by thousands of years, the wild growth of plants clinging to them, the mighty strength of the mountain on which the giant fabric rests, and the grandeur of nature which surrounds it, all combine to bring the mind into a state of feeling impossible to describe.

"When I had passed through that gate, the rocky path led me deep down the other side of the wall of mountain, so that the view of Latium was lost. Below I found another and far larger circular cistern hewn in the rock, of at least 30 feet in diameter. In its broad rocky margin many basins are scooped out, in which the women of Segni still do their washing. In all the Volscian towns I have found such ancient and perfectly preserved cisterns : they seem to be peculiar to that neighbourhood, as I do not remember ever to have met with them elsewhere in Latium of this size and shape."—*Gregorovius.*

The streets of Segni have little interest. In its piazza is the modernized *Cathedral*, having few memorials of a bishopric which dates from 499. It contains however two remarkable statues—one is that of St. Vitalian, a native of Segni, Pope from 657 to 672, the feeble though canonized pontiff who received the Emperor Constans II. at Rome, and allowed him to carry off to Constantinople so many of its treasures, including the bronze roof of the Pantheon. Nevertheless he deserves honour for having been in some respects, with Wilfrid, the apostle of England, and, having been the Pope who sent the Greek Archbishop Theodore to Canterbury. The statue was placed here in 1721, and taken from the image on his coins. Its inscription ends :

"Signia gave me to Rome : Rome gave me the tiara.
Signia divides with Rome the honours of my rule."

"The other statue, also of indifferent execution, stands opposite that of St. Vitalian. Bruno, a native of Asti, in Piedmont, came to Rome, recommended to Gregory VII., and was afterwards made Bishop of Segni by Urban II. In defiance of the Canon, he abandoned his episcopal seat and went to Monte Cassino, where the Abbot Oderisius received him among the Benedictines. Although Pascal II. ordered the truant to return to his diocese, he remained at Monte Cassino, was there chosen Abbot, and in the leisure of the cloister composed his exegetical writings.

"Not long after, Bruno played a part at Rome. It is well known that in the sequel of the strife about investiture, Pope Pascal was taken prisoner by the Emperor Henry V., and compelled to issue a Bull by which he yielded to the Emperor the contested right of spiritual investiture. After his release, when Henry had returned to Germany, Cardinals and Bishops beset Pascal with entreaties to revoke the Bull thus wrung from him, and to break his oath; among these fanatics the most zealous was Bruno. His vehemence angered Pascal, who thereupon forbade him to be at the same time Bishop and Abbot. So Bruno laid down his office at Monte Cassino, and returned to Segni, where he died in 1123. He was canonized in 1183.

"It was Lord Ellis, also both Abbot of Monte Cassino and Bishop of Segni, who raised this monument to his predecessor. But the Church of Segni has another and more remarkable connection with distant England; for it was in a synod of bishops of the Campagna held here in 1173, that Thomas à Becket was canonized shortly after his murder. This is recorded by an inscription in the Cathedral.

"Lord Ellis became Bishop of Segni in 1708. He restored the Cathedral, and bequeathed to the town a seminary, its best memorial of him. Pupils come to it from all parts of Latium; they wear a priestly garb, although not necessarily intended for Holy Orders. The seminary stands near the Church of St. Pietro."— *Gregorovius*.

Nothing can be more kind than the reception which the inhabitants of Segni give to strangers. The women here wear a different costume to those in the towns on the other side of the valley. They have no *panni*, but a large silver bodkin fastens up their hair, and their bodices, usually green, are laced behind instead of in front. Almost all the natives are proprietors in the country on a very small scale, and though little can be grown in these lofty uplands, the vineyards, oliveyards, and fruit-gardens are very productive. The most excellent cherries and peaches abound; and the woods supply chestnuts for a coarse bread which is considered very nourishing, and abundant acorns for the maintenance of the black pigs which are fed here in vast numbers.

It is most amusing to see the return of the country-people at sunset when they return home from their fields, thousands

The Inhabitants of Segni returning from the Country.

at a time, streaming along the terrace in front of the gateway, and up the steep streets into the upper town, each accompanied by his domestic animals—his donkeys, his goats, or his pet pigs, which come frisking behind their masters in the most diverting manner, for all share their homes with them. Then the whole street is blocked up for a time, and the cries, the shouts, the braying, the barking, and, above all, the squeaking and grunting, baffle all description.

CHAPTER XVI.

THE HERNICAN HILLS—FERENTINO, ALATRI, AND ANAGNI.

At Ferentino.

THIS is one of the most interesting excursions near Rome, and is perhaps the one which is least known, though it is now rendered very easy by the railway. To accomplish it, one must leave Rome by the first train at eight A.M., and it must be remembered, that *that* train alone is met by the omnibus from Segni, Anagni, Ferentino, and other places on the route, but distant several miles from the railway; and that if any other train is chosen, the traveller will find himself deposited at a small country station in a desolate district, without any further means of progress. For the same reason it will be best to visit the nearest places first, taking up the same train at the different stations. Any one who is delicate about food, had better take it with them from Rome, or at any rate some tea and coffee. Meat can scarcely ever be obtained in the mountain towns, but eggs, goats' milk, and excellent coarse bread are always to be found there, and often macaroni also, with the thin sour wine of the hill districts. The inns are mere taverns, often approached by filthy alleys, but the people are always civil, the linen clean, and the beds sufficiently comfortable to be appreciated by a tired traveller, whose appetite, strengthened by the fresh mountain air, will also be quite ready for the humble fare of the place. The charges are those of an Italy unspoilt by English and Americans ; one franc for bed, two francs for dinner, and forty centimes for breakfast, are not unusual prices. It is quite unnecessary to bargain, and will only create surprise and discomfort.

Those who have not been accustomed to it in Rome, will learn on this excursion how much beauty and pleasure are lost by want of early rising. The most delicate hues and shadows do not last for many hours after sunrise. When we have emerged from the unfinished station, and traversed the vineyards and kitchen-gardens within the walls of Rome, we are astonished by the colouring of the pale pink precipices in the familiar range of the Sabina, as they melt into a silver haze. Here and there a projecting cliff can be distinguished, in the rest all form is lost in colour; Monticelli and S. Angelo glitter on their hill-tops, and the long flat lines of the Campagna are tinged with peacock hues, as the blue cloud-shadows flit across them. In the foreground the rank vegetation of thistles, marigolds, and lupins, grows together so vigorously, that you seem to see them sucking their strong life out of the rich brown earth. On the other side, we have first the striding aqueducts, tinged on their inner edge by the dazzling sunlight, and then the long line of ruined tombs, which traces out the Appian Way against the low-lying horizon. Soon the train rushes across the sepulchral road of so many memories, and over the stones which we know were once trodden by the sandalled feet of St. Paul,—and so into the upland, to olive-gardens, whose silvery stems glisten against the brilliant green of the young corn, to dark cypress groves and pine-trees on the edge of terraced villas, and to fields divided by hedges of the graceful Spina Christi, the hallowed plant, said to have been brought to Italy by the returning crusaders, and to have come from the seed of the tree on Calvary, whence the sacred crown was woven. Thus we wind round the base of the green slopes encircling Monte Cavo, from which Castel Gandolfo looks down upon the Alban lake, and reach the station of Albano. Beyond this, upon the right, we overlook a plain historical with the sites of Pratica, Ardea, Antium, and Astura, to a wide expanse of blue sea. On the left Civita Lavinia rises with its tower on a fortified height; then Velletri with its orange roofs and wooded hills riven into gulfs of verdure; and then we enter a wilder and less wooded country, the valley of the Sacco—a plain alternately narrow and wide; a very definite plain indeed, closed in by the Hernican hills on one side, and the Volscian mountains on the other, which rise abruptly out of it with rocky buttresses.

An omnibus met us at the *Fe entino* station, and took us the three miles up into the town, through a country where the most remarkable feature was the faggots, stacked high up in the maple-trees, pollarded for the purpose.

We found tolerable rooms at the little inn, and almost immediately set off in the omnibus again for *Alatri*. It is a long drive (much longer than Murray describes) of about two hours; you skirt the base of the Hernican mountains, and cross many running streams:

"Roscida rivis
Hernica Saxa colunt."
Æn. vii. 683.

You are beginning to wonder where Alatri can be, when you see its huge Cyclopean walls rising against the sky at the end of a valley upon the left, and forming a terrace fit for Titans to walk upon, an architectural Stonehenge. The modern road winds into the town by a gradual ascent. The ancient approach is the earliest instance of a *cordonnata*, a hill-side broken by steps, such as the approach to the Roman Capitol. The streets are full of mediæval houses, with gothic windows and loggias; and the two ancient churches have each a fine rose-window in the west front. But towering high above the buildings of all later ages are the Cyclopean walls of the Pelasgic city, forming a quadrangle, and quite perfect, as if they were finished yesterday: for though the stones are fitted together without cement, each is like a mass of rock, and the arched form of their fitting adds to their firmness. One of the ancient gates remains under a single horizontal stone measuring eighteen feet by nine. The figure of the Pelasgic god Priapus is repeatedly sculptured on the walls, and it has long been a semi-religious custom for the inhabitants to go out *en masse* to mutilate it on Easter Monday. The place is mentioned by Plautus, under the Greek form Ἀλάτριον: Strabo calls it Ἀλέτριον.

"Alatri, like Ferentino, was surrounded with walls, but the circle round the town has been almost entirely destroyed, and only the walls of the citadel remain, an astonishing monument of that period of civilization, and without parallel amongst the towns of Latium, so that to see so wonderful, so unparalleled a work, which may be compared with the buildings of Egypt, is well worth a fatiguing day's journey.

"The old citadel of Alatri (it is now called 'Civita'—the town, by itself) occupies the highest point in the place, and is now the site of the cathedral, for here, as at Ferentino, the bishopric has nestled within the old fortress. And this hill, on the broad flat surface of which is the cathedral, is surrounded, supported, and surmounted by Cyclopean walls reaching to a height of from eighty to a hundred feet. When I saw and I walked round these constructions, of black Titanic stonework, to which the eye looks up with astonishment, so well preserved that they seem as if their age might be reckoned not by thousands of years but by years, I was impelled to much greater admiration of human power than the sight of the Coliseum of Rome had inspired. For in times of advanced civilization, with many complete mechanical appliances, amphitheatres or public baths like those of Caracalla or Constantine might be piled up, without imputing anything extraordinary to the strength of man; and even the walls of Dionysius of Syracuse, the grandest of such creations which I had yet seen, do not make an equal impression. But here we see before us walls, each stone of which is not a huge square but a block of irregular shape, many-sided, hewn out of the rock; and if we ask in wonder by what mechanical means such huge masses of rock could be lifted up and piled one upon another, still less can we understand how it was possible to arrange the many-cornered blocks so artistically that they fit into one another exactly without leaving spaces to be filled up, and form a complete gigantic mosaic.

"Tradition ascribes this species of ancient Latin buildings to the time of Saturn, and so places them altogether before the time of historical civilization; but scientific research, which occupies itself so much with Indo-Germanic and Pelasgic races in Italy, is forced to confess that it knows nothing of the nations which piled up these works. Their appearance shows that the race of men which built such walls must have possessed already a considerable material civilization and well-ordered political arrangements. As these Cyclopean towns are found near one another, and scattered over the whole of Latium, it follows that in this country a great number of independent republics or states were established in very ancient times, whose connection with one another we do not know. But such immense fortifications imply constant war between the different towns, and particularly a predatory, unsafe, and isolated state of life. To bring the strength of the men into a suitable proportion to the colossal dimensions of the works, one must imagine those who erected them, or who came as enemies to storm them, to have been regular giants. But these erections only point to that colossal period with which the civilization of men in all nations and in all parts of the world begins, till it gradually rises from the materially sublime to the representation of things pleasing and beautiful, which more perfect means render possible. Altogether these Cyclopean works should not be placed in too dark a time ; perhaps some of them may have been built in Latium after Rome was founded, and the step from this manycornered style of building to the hardly less colossal square stone walls of the Etruscans and Romans is by no means a long one.

"Out of the walls of this Capitol of the ancient Alatri led a principal gate which exists still, an enormous erection made of horizontal stones ; besides this there is also a smaller entrance, and three square niches in the south wall lead to the conclusion that images of gods may have been set up there, while at the same time Cyclopean remains in the middle of the castle may with some probability be held to be the public altar on which festive sacrifices were offered.

"Till the year 1843 these walls were half buried under ruins and creepers, and no road led round them. A visit of Gregory XVI. inspired the Alatrians with the happy thought of cleaning and clearing out such unparalleled monuments of the remotest antiquity ; so 2000 men worked for ten days at removing the rubbish, and thus the Acropolis was not only laid bare again but surrounded with a road called Via Gregoriana, by which one can walk round it comfortably. Then too the great gate was dug out, and the ascent to the plateau re-opened. This broad flat space is only surrounded by a stone bulwark, which rises above the Cyclopean wall, and as it contains no building but the cathedral, it admits a most charming view of the mountain scenery. And indeed the beautiful surroundings make such an enchanting picture, that I will not attempt to describe it in words, or even to indicate the lines of the mountains which rise from Elysian fields to the sunny blue above. In the perfect stillness and indeed deserted condition of this strange scene of remote civilization, the impression of the sublime is doubly effective."—*Gregorovius.*

Within the precincts of the Pelasgic fortress stands the *Cathedral.* It only dates from the last century, though the see was created in A.D. 551 ; but it is a conspicuous feature in all distant views of the town. A finer church is that of *S. Maria Maggiore,* which has three gothic portals in its west front, and a fine rose-window above them. The mouldings are richly ornamented with acanthus. It had formerly two towers, but only one remains. The interior is completely modernized. From the heights overhanging the Cyclopean walls are wild views over the Volscian and

Hernican hills, the most prominent feature being a bare mountain, crowned by a little town and a grove of cypresses. This is *Fumone*, the scene of the imprisonment and death of the abdicated hermit-Pope, Celestine V., immured here by the jealousy of his successor, Boniface VIII., though the next Pope, Clement V., enrolled him amongst the saints. In old days Fumone was carefully watched, for its lord had feudal rights over all the surrounding country, and, when he wished to summon his vassals, either in defence or attack, he lighted a bonfire on his hill-top, whence the proverb,— " Quando Fumone fuma, tutta la campagna trema." The

Cyclopean Gate of Alatri.

people of Alatri are magnificently handsome, and as the women come down the steep stairs under the great gateway, with their flowing veils, their rich costume, and their gleaming brass *conche* poised upon their stately heads, they are wonderfully in keeping with the scene.

The drive back from Alatri to Ferentino in the gloaming of one of the most beautiful days in the beginning of April, gave us a perfect succession of charming pictures, not only of landscape—though that was beautiful exceedingly in the still late light—but of herdsmen in their closely-fitting blue dress, with their guiding-poles over their shoulders, following great grey oxen down the hollow ways between the red earth and bright young grass, and singing as they went; and of women

Inn at Ferentino.

in white dresses, with snow-white *panni* folded over their dark hair, large gold earrings, and embroidered aprons, sometimes coming up from wayside fountains with the great brazen vessels of water, which one sees here everywhere, poised upon their heads, like beautiful Greek Caryatides. And our evening was a perfectly Italian one—seated in the brick-floored, wall-painted room, lighted by Italian lamps with three burners and hanging chains, and waited on by a gaily-jewelled hostess, who had nothing to offer but eggs and salad.

Another beautiful morning found us quite rested, and up at six to enjoy the early light glinting through the old olive-trees under our window, and the distant views of rosy peaks fading fainter into a misty plain. Then we set off to explore the town, the ancient Ferentinum, up the steep dark street, all balconies, and loggias, and Gothic windows, with plenty of dirt beneath, and only a strip of opal sky lighting it up at the end. On the steepest part of the hill is the *Church of St Valentine*, with a very curious porch, whose canopy is formed by a projecting apse. A little further is *S. Francesco*, with strange bas-reliefs in its little fore-court. Hence the Via dell' Antico Acropole, a street full of long steep staircases, beloved by artists, leads up to a terrace under Cyclopean walls of huge stones, something like those of Alatri. The dark passage caverned under these walls emerges close to the *Duomo* (SS. Giovanni e Paolo), which, externally, has much of its Lombard architecture remaining; and, within, a splendid opus-alexandrinum pavement, mended with fragments of sculptured marble-work, and a glorious twisted mosaic pillar nearly the whole height of the church, secured against the wall by iron clamps. Behind the church is the bishop's palace, with a stately old staircase guarded by marble lions.

A crowded street, where old women, like the Fates of Michael Angelo, sit spinning in their doorways, surrounded by their domestic circles of goats, cats, dogs, and pigs, all joining vociferously in the conversation, leads to the lower

Bishop's Staircase, Ferentino.

town. The stone used as the font in the little church of St Giovanni Evangelista has an inscription from the inhabitants of Ferentinum to Cornelia Salonina, wife of the "unconquered Gallienus." From the piazza, where a number of Roman altars are collected, we have a magnificent view over mountain and plain. Hence, also, one may learn, by looking down, to find one's way through the intricate maze of filthy alleys, many of which have such stately names as Via dell' Atreo, Vicolo dei Bagni de Flavio, Vicolo del Calidario, &c., to the finest of the churches, *Sta. Maria Maggiore*, which, in its beautiful west front, has a door with detached red marble columns banded together, and above it the

VOL. I. 17

emblems of the Evangelists on either side of the Lamb of God, and a grand rose window.

S. Maria Maggiore, Ferentino.

Old Italian histories assert that S. Maria Salome, the reputed mother of S. John the Evangelist, was buried at Ferentino, "as is attested by the archives in the cathedral of Veroli."

Near the gate close to this church an inscription hewn in the solid rock records the erection of a statue by the grateful people of Ferentinum to Quinctilius Priscus, who, amongst other largesses, gave them *crustula* and *mulsum* (cakes and mead) upon his birth-day, with *sportulæ* (presents of money) for the decurions, and *nucum sparsiones* (scrambles of nuts) for the boys.

"'The pride of Ferentino, amongst its antiquities, is the so-called 'Testament.' With difficulty I climbed over rocks and through the brambles in a vineyard to reach this curiosity, and at last I saw before me a great table hewn in the living rock. A long inscription in well-cut characters tells here that Aulus Quinctilius, Quatuorvir and Ædile, was the benefactor of his native town, bequeathing to it all his property by will, for which the town gratefully honoured him by placing his statue publicly on the Forum."—*Gregorovius*.

Another public carriage met us at the station for *Anagni*,

the ancient Anagnia, the capital of the Hernicans, and one of the five Saturnian cities whose names begin with the first letters of the alphabet—Anagni, Alatri, Arpino, Arca, and Atino. The town clings to terraces on the bare side of the Hernican hills, with the most splendid views in every direction. Its streets perfectly abound in quaint architectural fragments, griffins, lions, open loggias, outside staircases, trefoiled windows, and great arched doorways, and still remind one of the expression "municipium ornatissimum," which Cicero, in his defence of Milo, applies to this town. Virgil also speaks of its riches :—

"Quos, dives Anagnia, pascis."

The centre of life here, as in all the mountain towns, is the piazza, where groups of brilliantly-dressed peasants, the women all wearing *panni* again, stand gossipping round the fountain, poising their brazen *conche* meanwhile upon its marble ledges. The men lie basking in the sunshine along the stone ledges of the terrace, for here only three sides of the piazza are surrounded with houses, the fourth is open towards the valley and the mountains.

"From this piazza the view is so beautiful, that it enchants even those who have seen all Italy from the Alps to the African and Ionian sea. Immediately opposite rise the Volscian hills, whose sunny heights are so distinctly seen that the windows in the houses can be distinguished. Everywhere Volscian towns catch the eye, as they follow one another along the hills. Monte Fortino, the celebrated Segni, Gavignano, Rocca Gorga, Scurgola ; then Morolo, Supino, Patrica, behind which the tall pyramid of Monte Cacume rises blue and beautiful. Further still are peak after peak ; then more towns ; here Ferentino on a hill; there Frosinone, whose citadel even is visible, and Arnara, Posi, Ceccano, and many other places which the eye can discover. Towards Rome extends a large plain bounded by the mountains of Palestrina, which is itself visible in the far distance. The Latin hills also appear, and thus the view embraces a large part of Latium."—*Gregorovius.*

Beyond the piazza, on the left, open the huge round arches of the portico of the old *Papal palace*. Little that is curious

Papal Palace, Anagni.

remains in the interior; yet in these rooms William of Nogaret insulted the mighty Boniface VIII., and imprisoned him in his own palace, when "the *fleur-de-lis* was seen in Anagni." Here, also, Innocent III., Gregory IX., and Alexander IV., held their courts in the thirteenth century, all born here, and all sprung from native families, and once canons of the cathedral. Behind the palace a fragment of a beautiful Gothic loggia of the time of Boniface remains; part of the interior is now used as a theatre. There is not a book-shop in Anagni, and we could find no one, not even the sacristan of the cathedral, who knew anything whatever of its history. The utmost they could tell, was that "Bonifazio" had lived there, that his statue

stood on their walls, and that Dante had written of him—
what, or who he was, they were quite ignorant of.

Entrance to the Cathedral, Anagni.

It is a very short distance up the hill to the *Cathedral* (Sta. Maria), which is the most interesting mediæval building in this part of Italy, except the convent of Subiaco. The see dates from A.D. 487. On the wall, above what was once the great south entrance, Boniface VIII. sits aloft, in robes and tiara, in his throne of state. Over his head, blazoned in gold and mosaic, are the illustrious alliances of the Gaetani before his time. The steps beneath this statue, which must have had a magnificent effect in the open space, as seen from the valley beneath, were destroyed thirty years ago by a certain Marchese (even his name seems to be forgotten), and the present entrance is by the north, where a quaint winding staircase leads into a dark gallery, lined with curious old frescoes and inscriptions, and so into the cathedral.

"The cathedral of Anagni, though several times renovated by the bishops of the town and by the popes, still retains its original Gothic-Roman character. The façade is of rude architecture; it terminates in an obtuse-angled gable, the triangle of which is cut off by a simple cornice. In it is an arched, unornamented window, beneath which is a large square one, evidently of a later date. The door (there is only one) has a cornice in very bad taste, formed of different blocks of stone patched together, and ornamented with heads of oxen and lions, the rude work of the middle ages. Two pillars are built into the wall, with the capitals joined together, without any visible object, and very unsymmetrically too, as they are only on one side of the door. Over the door is a round arch adorned with simple arabesques. The masonry is throughout of the black limestone from the neighbouring mountains. One can see that the façade still retains its original form, and has only been restored at a later period in a hurry, when absolutely necessary."—*Gregorovius.*

The interior is far more picturesque than beautiful. In the lofty choir is a grand pascal candlestick, supported by a crouching figure. Portraits of all the popes connected with Anagni hang over the throne and stalls. The whole pavement of the church is of the most splendid opus alexandrinum, though much decayed, and in the choir it reaches a degree of minuteness and perfection like delicate jewellers' work. Here, on the Maundy Thursday of 1160, Alexander III. stood to curse the great Emperor Barbarossa. Here Innocent III. read aloud the bull which excommunicated

Frederick II., and on this same spot Alexander IV. banished the young Manfred. Here also the cardinals elected Innocent IV., after they had received the furious letter of the Emperor Frederick II., calling them "sons of Belial." In this church also (September 7, 1303) Boniface VIII. knelt at the altar in his pontifical robes, when the French, prompted by his hereditary enemies, the Colonnas, had forced the gates of the town, and burst into the streets, crying, "Vive le roi de France, et meure Boniface."

"The Pope had retired, as usual, from the summer heat to his native city, Anagni. Here he seemed, as it were, to pause, to be gathering up his strength to launch the last crushing thunders upon the head of the contumacious king of France. The Bull of excommunication was ordered to be suspended in the porch of the cathedral of Anagni. The 8th of September was to be the fatal day.

"On a sudden, on the 7th of September, the peaceful streets of Anagni were disturbed. The Pope and the Cardinals, who were all assembled around him, were startled with the trampling of armed horse, and the terrible cry, which ran like wild-fire through the city, 'Death to Pope Boniface! Long live the King of France!' Sciarra Colonna, at the head of three hundred horsemen, the Barons of Ceccano and Supino, and some others, the sons of Master Massio of Anagni, were marching in furious haste, with the banner of the King of France displayed. The ungrateful citizens of Anagni, forgetful of their pride in their holy compatriot, of the honour and advantage to their town from the splendour and wealth of the Papal residence, received them with rebellious and acclaiming shouts.

"The bell of the city, indeed, had tolled at the first alarm; the burghers had assembled; they had chosen their commander; but that commander, whom they ignorantly or treacherously chose, was Arnulf, a deadly enemy of the Pope. The banner of the Church was unfolded against the Pope by the captain of the people of Anagni. The first attack was on the palace of the Pope, on that of the Marquis Gaetani, his nephew, and those of three Cardinals, the special partisans of Boniface. The houses of the Pope and of his nephew made some resistance. The doors of those of the Cardinals were beaten down, the treasures ransacked and carried off; the Cardinals themselves fled from the backs of the houses through the common sewer. The Pope and his nephew implored a truce ; it was granted for eight hours. This time the Pope employed in endeavouring to stir up the people to his defence: the people answered coldly that they were under the command of their captain. The Pope demanded the terms of the conspirators. 'If the Pope would save his life, let him instantly restore the Colonna Cardinals to their dignity, and reinstate the whole house in their honours and possessions; after this restoration the Pope must abdicate, and leave his body at the disposal of Sciarra.' The Pope groaned in the depth of his heart. 'The word is spoken.' Again the assailants thundered at the gates of the palace ; still there was obstinate resistance. The principal church of Anagni, that of Santa Maria, protected the Pope's palace. Sciarra Colonna's lawless band set fire to the gates ; the church was crowded with clergy and laity, and traders who had brought their precious wares into the sacred building. They were plundered with such rapacity that not a man escaped with a farthing.

"The Marquis Gaetani found himself compelled to surrender, on the condition that his own life, that of his family, and of his servants, should be spared. At these sad tidings the Pope wept bitterly. The Pope was alone ; from the first the Cardinals, some from treachery, some from cowardice, had fled on all sides, even his most familiar friends : they had crept into the most ignoble hiding-places. The aged Pontiff alone lost not his self-command. He had declared himself ready to perish in his glorious cause ; he determined to fall with dignity. 'If I am betrayed like Christ, I am ready to die like Christ.' He put on the stole of S. Peter, the imperial crown was on his head, the keys of S. Peter in one hand and the cross in the other : he took his seat on the Papal throne, and, like the Roman senators of old, awaited the approach of the Gaul.

"But the pride and cruelty of Boniface had raised and infixed deep in the hearts of men passions which acknowledged no awe of age, of intrepidity, or religious majesty. In William of Nogaret the blood of his Tolosan ancestors, in Colonna the wrongs, the degradation, the beggary, the exile of all his house, had extinguished every feeling but revenge. They insulted him with contumacious reproaches ; they menaced his life. The Pope answered not a word. They insisted that he should at once abdicate the Papacy. 'Behold my neck, behold my head,' was the only reply.

"The Pope was placed under close custody, not one of his own attendants permitted to approach him. Worse indignities awaited him. He was set on a vicious horse, with his face to the tail, and so led through the town to his place of imprisonment. The palaces of the Pope and of his nephew were plundered ; so vast was the wealth, that the annual revenues of all the kings in the world would not have been equal to the treasures found and carried off by Sciarra's freebooting soldiers. His very private chamber was ransacked; nothing left but bare walls.

"At length the people of Anagni could no longer bear the insult and the sufferings heaped upon their illustrious fellow-citizen. They rose in irresistible insurrection, drove out the soldiers by whom they had been over-awed, now gorged with plunder, and doubtless not unwilling to withdraw. The Pope was rescued, and led out into the street, where the old man addressed a few words to the people : 'Good men and women, ye see how mine enemies have come upon me, and plundered my goods, and those of the Church, and of the poor. Not a morsel of bread have I eaten, not a drop have I drunk, since my capture. I am almost dead with hunger. If any good woman will give me a piece of bread and a cup of wine,—if she has no wine, a little water,—I will absolve her ; and any one who will give me their alms, from all their sins.' The compassionate rabble burst into a cry, 'Long life to the Pope !' They carried him back to his naked palace. They crowded, the women especially, with provisions, bread, meat, water, and wine. They could not find a single vessel : they poured a supply of water into a chest. The Pope proclaimed a general absolution to all except the plunderers of his palace. He even declared that he wished to be at peace with the Colonnas and all his enemies. This perhaps was to disguise his intention of retiring, as soon as he could, to Rome.

"The Romans had heard with indignation the sacrilegious attack on the person of the Supreme Pontiff. Four hundred horse, under Matteo and Gaetano Orsini, were sent to conduct him to the city. He entered it almost in triumph ; the populace welcomed him with every demonstration of joy. But the awe of his greatness was gone ; the spell of his dominion over the minds of men was broken.

"The religious mind of Christendom was at once perplexed and horror-stricken by the sacrilegious violence on the person of the Supreme Pontiff : it shocked some even of the sternest Ghibellines. Dante, who brands the pride, the avarice, the treachery of Boniface in his most terrible words, and has consigned him to the direst doom, nevertheless expresses the almost universal feeling. Christendom 'shuddered to behold the Fleur-de-lis enter into Anagni, and Christ again captive in his Vicar, the mockery, the gall and vinegar, the crucifixion between robbers, the insolent and sacrilegious cruelty of the second Pilate.'"
—*Milman's Hist. of Latin Christianity.*

"Veggio in Alagna entrar lo fiordaliso,
　　E nel vicario suo Cristo esser catto ;

> Veggiolo un' altra volta esser deriso,
> Veggio rinnovellar l'aceto e 'l fele,
> E tra vivi ladroni esser anciso.
> Veggio 'l nuovo Pilato si crudele,
> Che ciò nol sazia, ma, senza decreto,
> Porta nel tempio le cupide vele."—*Purgatorio*, xx. 89.

Two chapels on the left of the cathedral nave are filled with Gaetani memorials. In one is a Greek inscription. In the other is a painting of the Madonna, of 1322, and the grand mosaic tomb wrought by the Cosmati ("magister Cosmas, civis Romanus, cum filiis suis Luca et Jacopo"), known as "Il sepolcro della famiglia di Bonifazio." It bears in Latin the inscription:

"Whoever thou art who directest thy steps to this venerable church, know at once the founders of all its glories. Peter the Bishop founded it with great effort, whom noble Salerno reared and gave to us. May the only Son of the Supreme Father have mercy on him."

In the sacristy are preserved some curious copes, and the croziers of Innocent III. and Boniface VIII. The crypt is given up to the especial saints of Anagni, who are numerous, and whose story, in a series of very early frescoes, occupies the walls. The south altar is devoted to Santa Oliva, whose bones and head are shown in a glass case beneath her statue. Opposite her is St. Magnus, bishop and martyr, who is represented above seated between two virgin saints. Beneath another altar are the martyrs Secunda, Aurelia, and Neonissa. In the tribune, which has a magnificent pavement, is the papal throne, and over it, in ancient fresco, the whole story of the Apocalypse—the seven candlesticks, the seven churches, the twenty-four elders in adoration of the spotless Lamb, &c., and, in the centre, above the altar, the Redeemer seated on a rainbow, with the two-edged sword proceeding out of his mouth.

The tall Romanesque tower of the Cathedral is not joined to the rest of the building, but stands alone upon a little green platform at the west end of the church. Hence there is a grand view over the valley, but to Roman Catholics a more interesting feature will be the knot of brown buildings on the barren side of the mountain, about six miles above Anagni; for this is *Acuto*, where the recently founded but ever-increasing order of the Precious Blood had its origin, and where its foundress, Maria de Matthias, lived till her death in August, 1866. The story of her vocation is quite as romantic and curious as that of any old saintly legend, and that of her founding here a large sisterhood and school which she supported by faith and prayer, without any definite sources of assistance, in the same way in which the immense institutions of the Protestant Muller are carried on at Clifton. Of her extraordinary influence on the surrounding districts, no one who has visited them can have a doubt, or of the power of her sermons, which were simple discourses of loving practical Christianity, such as Miss Marsh might have delivered. When she was likely to preach thousands flocked to hear her, and when she appeared, a silence fell upon the crowd, with the whisper, " Hush, the great mother is going to speak to us."

CHAPTER XVII.

PALESTRINA.

(Palestrina is about 27 miles from Rome by way of Zagarolo. Public carriages leave the Piazza S. Marco daily at 6 A.M. for Palestrina and proceed to Olevano—fare, five francs. A shorter way of reaching these places is to take the railway as far as the Valmontone Station, where a post-carriage, with seats for two, meets the first train. It is about seven miles from the station to Palestrina. But the best plan of all is to drive from Velletri. There is no decent inn at Palestrina, but comfortable quarters may be obtained at the house of an artist's widow, sister of a lawyer, Anna Pastina, at the same charges as those usual in country inns. Her house—1, Via delle Concie—is the last on the left at the top of the staircase on the right of the piazza.)

AN early drive from Velletri to Palestrina, the ancient Præneste, is delightful. Then the cloudless sky is generally opal behind the soft pink mountains. Reaching the foot of the Volscian hills, we come upon the most picturesque town of *Monte Fortino*, a fortress of the Conti, clambering up the side of a hill so steep that each row of houses begins over the roof of its neighbour, and each has a clear view of the sky.

About a mile distant, at the spot now called La Civita, is the site of the Volscian city *Artena:* portions of the Cyclopean walls of the citadel remain.

It is about three miles from Monte Fortino (passing the station) to *Valmontone*, the ancient Toleria, which stands on a tufa rock in the midst of the plain between the two ranges of mountains, and is girt by old republican walls, with mediæval towers. From the families of Conti, Sforza, and Barberini, it has passed to the Pamfili, by whom the huge palace which crowns the town was built in 1662. The eldest son of Prince Doria Pamfili bears the title of Prince of Valmontone. In the cortile of the palace are some inscriptions from the Labican catacombs. Adjoining it is a rather handsome cathedral of the 17th century, designed by Matteo de

Valmontone.

Rossi. There are several *bits* at Valmontone to delight an artist, especially at the entrance of the town, where a magnificent fragment of the ancient wall forms the foreground to some very picturesque houses. Near this also is the interesting old church of Sant' Antonio, now called the Madonna delle Grazie.

Palestrina is quite a different type of place from all the others we have seen, and its people, unlike the courteous peasants we have hitherto met with, are savage and lawless, violent and avaricious. Can the bitter warfare of reprisal, of which both ancient Præneste and mediæval Palestrina have been the scene, be setting its mark still upon the inhabitants? for perhaps no place has been more often besieged, and more often utterly ruined and destroyed.

Præneste is one of the towns of fabulous origin. Virgil ascribes it to Cæculus the son of Vulcan :

> "Nec Prænestinæ fundator defuit urbis,
> Vulcano genitum pecora inter agrestia regem
> Inventumque focis omnis quem credidit ætas,
> Cæculus."
>
> *Æn.* vii. 678.

Strabo gives it a Greek origin, and says that it was first called Πολυστέφανος. Pliny also says that it was called Stephane, a name which is supposed to have been derived from the appearance of the castle on the top of the hill being like a mural crown. Servius derives the name from the πρινοι, ilexes, which grew here, Cato and Festus from the situation —"quia montibus præstet."

Even in the time of the Siculi, Virgil describes Præneste as having been governed by a king called Herilus, who fell in defending his country against the Latins. Livy says that eight towns were dependent upon it. It was reduced to the condition of a Roman colony upon the failure of the struggle in favour of the Tarquins. After the defeat of Caius Marius, who killed himself within its walls, Præneste fell into the hands of Sylla, who totally annihilated the population and the city alike :—

> ".   .   .   Vidit Fortuna colonos
> Prænestina suos cunctos simul ausa recisos,
> Unius populum pereuntem tempore mortis."
>
> *Lucan.* ii. 193.

But Sylla rebuilt the town with the utmost magnificence, and erected the Temple of Fortune, which was so splendid that the Athenian philosopher Carneades said he had "never seen a Fortune so fortunate as that of Præneste." Its glories were celebrated by several of the Latin poets.

> "Sextus Junonis mensis fuit. Aspice Tibur,
> Et Prænestinæ mœnia sacra Deæ."
> *Ovid. Fast.* vi. 61.

> "Ædificator erat Cetronius, et modo curvo
> Littora Caietæ, summa nunc Tiburis arce,
> Nunc Prænestinis in montibus, alta parabat
> Culmina villarum, Græcis longeque petitis
> Marmoribus, vincens Fortunæ atque Herculis ædem."
> *Juv. Sat.* xiv. 86.

> ". . . sacrisque dicatum
> Fortunæ Præneste jugis."
> *Sil. Ital.* viii. 366.

> ". . . sacro juvenes Præneste creati
> Occubuere simul : votisque ex omnibus unum
> Id Fortuna dedit, junctam inter prælia mortem."
> *Id.* ix. 404.

"Cicero gives a curious account of the institution of the divination called the Sortes Fortunæ Primigeniæ Prænestinæ : 'Numerius Suffucius having, in consequence of frequent dreams, excavated in a rock, found a piece of oak, on which the necessary ceremonies seem to have been inscribed in ancient characters. The place was inclosed, honey flowed from an olive tree on the spot, and the Temple of Fortune was erected on or near the site." (De Divin. ii. 41.) "In the time of Cicero, the credit of the Sortes Prænestinæ had much diminished."—*Gell's Topography of Rome.*

Its coolness, which was an agreeable change after the heat of Rome, made Præneste a favourite summer resort to the emperors Augustus, Tiberius, Nero, Domitian, and Hadrian. Suetonius describes Augustus as employing two days on the journey hither from Rome. Horace alludes to the freshness of the climate.

> ". . seu mihi frigidum
> Præneste, seu Tibur supinum,
> Seu liquidæ placuere Baiæ."
> *Horace*, iii. *Od.* 4.

Sometimes the poet himself resided here:

> "Trojani belli scriptorem, maxime Lolli,
> Dum tu declamas Romæ, Præneste relegi."
> i. *Epist.* 2.

> "Quis timet aut timuit gelida Præneste ruinam?"
> *Juv. Sat.* iii. 190.

In 970, the town, already called Palestrina, was given by Pope John XIII. to his sister Stephania, and through the marriage of her grand-daughter Emilia ("Imilia nobilissima comitissa"), came into the Colonna family, whose history is henceforth that of the place. When, in 1217, the Cardinals Giacomo and Pietro Colonna had opposed the election of a member of the rival family of the Gaetani of Anagni to the papacy, they fled hither with their kinsfolk. The newly-elected pope, Boniface VIII., immediately issued bulls confiscating all the estates of the Colonnas, and promised plenary indulgences to all who would take up arms against them.

"Stronghold after stronghold was stormed; castle after castle fell. Palestrina alone held out with intrepid obstinacy. Almost the whole Colonna house sought their last refuge in the walls of this redoubted fortress, which defied the siege, and wearied out the assailing forces. Guido di Montefeltro, a famous Ghibelline chieftain, had led a life of bloody and remorseless warfare, in which he was even more distinguished by craft than by valour. He had treated with contemptuous defiance all the papal censures which rebuked and would avenge his discomfiture of many papal generals, and the depression of the Guelfs. In an excess of devotion, now grown old, he had taken the habit and the vows of S. Francis, divorced his wife, given up his wealth, obtained remission of his sins, first from Cœlestine, afterwards from Boniface, and was living in quiet in a convent at Ancona. He was summoned from his cell on his allegiance to the Pope, and, with plenary absolution for his broken vows, commanded to inspect the walls and give his counsel for the best means of reducing the stubborn citadel. The old soldier surveyed the impregnable defences, and then, requiring still further absolution for any crime of which he might be guilty, uttered his memorable oracle, " Promise largely, keep little of your promises."*—*Milman's Latin Christianity.*

Thus the Colonnas were induced to open their gates, and proceeded in mourning robes to meet the Pope at Rieti. He received them with outward forgiveness, and gave them absolution; but while they were detained as his guests, Ranieri, Bishop of Pisa, was sent to destroy Palestrina ut-

Cathedral, Palestrina.

terly, and ordered to spare nothing except "the cathedral of S.

* Among the evil-counsellors in Malebolge, swathed and tormented in the flame of his own consciousness, Dante saw the shade of Guido di Montefeltro, who had found that the Devil was a logician and unable to reconcile the wish to repent with the wish to sin. So the cordelier's frock had to give place to the robe of flame, in which the unhappy warrior must rue eternally the crafty counsel,

" Lunga promessa con l'attender corto."
Inf. xxvii.

Agapitus." Everything else was "totali exterminio et ruinæ exposita," a plough was driven over the ruins, and the ground was sown with salt; even the famous marble staircase of a hundred steps, up which people could ride on horseback into the palace, perished. The Colonna family fled in all directions, but Sciarra Colonna returned just at the time when Boniface was quarrelling with Philippe le Bel, and joining the French, captured the Pope at Anagni. Under Benedict IX., the ban against the Colonnas was removed, and under Clement V. Stefano Colonna was allowed to rebuild Palestrina. In 1350 and 1354 the town was successfully defended against Rienzi, but in 1436, when the Colonnas had rebelled against Eugenius IV., it was again besieged and taken by his legate Cardinal Vitelleschi, who completely razed it to the ground, not even the cathedral being spared this time. In 1447, Nicholas V. gave permission that Palestrina should once more be rebuilt, but it never again became a place of any importance, and the only noteworthy event which has since occurred there, has been the birth, in 1524, of the musician Pierluigi da Palestrina, author of the mass of Pope Marcellus. The last Colonna of Palestrina was Francesco, who died in 1636, and in 1630 the town was sold to Carlo Barberini, brother of Urban VIII., and it still belongs to that family.

Remains of the old Præneste meet us on every side, and it is typical of the place and its overflow of antiquities, that the curbstone at the cross-roads as we approach it is a headless ancient statue. In the walls of almost every house fragments of pillars and capitals may be discovered. And what is chiefly remarkable is that almost all the remains belong to one building, the gigantic *Temple of Fortune*, built by Sylla, which rose upon terraces, tier above tier, occupying the whole space now filled by the town, and perhaps the largest building in Italy.

Behind Palestrina the mountain rises abruptly, bare and arid, and the town itself stands very high. Virgil alludes to the cool climate of Præneste :—

" Quique altum Præneste viri, quique arva Gabinæ
Junonis, gelidumque Anienem, et roscida rivis
Hernica saxa colunt :— "

There is not much to be seen in the lower town. In the piazza are some pillars of the Temple of Fortune built into a wall, and the small ugly *Cathedral*, which has a low but graceful gothic campanile. In the highest part of the town is the *Palazzo Barberini*, of which the wing is used as a barrack, but which is for the most part as deserted and forlorn a specimen of an old Italian palace, once exceedingly mag-

The Barberini Well, Palestrina.

nificent, as can well be found. Its front was built in a vast semi-circle, so as to follow the plan of the temple of

Sylla, and is approached by curved staircases enclosing an old well. The halls on the ground-floor are painted by the Zuccheri, but Apollo with his dove-chariot, and Juno with her peacocks, are fading with the damp which streams from the walls. We asked the old housekeeper if she did not suffer from it. "Ah, yes," she said, "all my hair has come off, and all my teeth have fallen out; for even when out of doors it is a *caldo feroce*, here within it is *fresco assai*." She said she was a *forestiera*, for she came from Frescati, and though she had been here forty years, she could not accustom herself to the wickedness of the people,—"Il mondo è bello, ma se fosse buono sarebbe meglio." On the upper floor is the famous mosaic, found amid the ruins of the Temple of Fortune, representing the joy of the people and the beasts of Egypt in the annual overflow of the Nile. It is like a dictionary of the manners and customs and people of the Egypt of its time. Priests and priestesses, warriors, fishermen, shepherds, and huntsmen are equally represented, with all the peculiar animals of the country, and its plants, besides its temples and houses. The mosaic was discovered in 1638 and it is quite perfect: the arms and the bees of the Barberini have been added in the corners. There is a grand view from the balcony of this room over the Volscian and Alban ranges, while the Hernican and Sabine hills are seen in profile.

"What is most remarkable in the palace of Palestrina is its incomparable situation on the height, where an ever-fresh and health-giving breeze blows, and whence the indwellers enjoy a view, whose beauty is indescribable. Here a great part of Latium lies spread out beneath the eyes on one side, and of Tuscany or the patrimony of S. Peter's on the other, a great and classic district, whence rise the Latin and Volscian mountains, between which a wide plain opens, reaching to the distant glancing sea. There is the world-town Rome steeped in the mist; there stands the island-like Soracte; hard by rise the mighty chains of the Apennines; on the left, at their feet, is the deep beautiful valley of the Sacco, over which shine the gleaming hill-towns of Monte-Fortino and Segni; further are the heights of the Serra, and the airy chiefs of all these hills, whose varied forms lose themselves in the sunny atmosphere beyond Anagni and Ferentino. One looks upon these plains and hills, bedecked with towns and villages, of which most are rich in associations, and the early history of Rome, the story of the empire, or of the middle ages, comes back to one's recollection, and when one feels that Umbria, the Sabina, Latium, the Equian territory, the land of the Hernicans, Etruria, the Volscian country, the Alban hills, and the sea are united in one panorama, one appreciates the grandeur of this view. When a Colonna of the middle ages looked down from the windows of the old palace or castle, he might venture, as he gazed upon his possessions, to feel that he was the richest and mightiest chieftain in Latium."—*Gregorovius*.

The plain beneath the windows is so rich that it looks like one vast garden of fruit-trees, amongst which, about a mile from the town, near S. Maria della Villa (the name commemorating it), the remains of the immense villa of Hadrian may be discovered. They are little worth visiting, yet here the Braschi Antinous and other important statues have been found, and smaller antiquities are dug up daily. Madama Pastina, who lets the lodgings to strangers, has a collection of them, chiefly terra-cottas and small bronzes, which she sells at low prices. The little statuettes of Fortune suckling a child are very interesting.

The hill-side above Palestrina is so bare and the sun beats so pitilessly upon its white rocks, that it is best to put off the ascent till near sunset. It may be made on donkeys, but they are atrociously bad. We were obliged to dismiss ours; and when we reproached its owner for having brought it, he coolly said—"Yes, he knew that it was bad, and would certainly fall down, but he brought it because if a saddle was once put on it must be as much paid for as if it had been used. So few strangers came, that they must be taken ad-

Street Scene, Palestrina.

vantage of." We did not wonder that so few came amongst this savage population. Every woman and child you meet, however well dressed they may be, rush at you with defiant shouts, insisting, not petitioning, "*Signor, dammi un baiocc.*" From every window hands are outstretched. Stern-looking Sibyls scowl their demands at you, distaff in hand, upon their doorsteps. Dozens of ragged children yell and tumble over one another, and follow you for hours, dancing like frantic little demons, wherever you go. Some friends of ours ascended the mountain, followed by hampers well equipped for a delicious pic-nic. They reached the top, and were surrounded by the inhabitants of S. Pietro. The hampers were unpacked and the luncheon spread out, and —before any resistance could be offered or even suggested, the thronging swarms had descended upon the feast like locusts, and, in one moment, men and women tore up the chickens and swallowed the limbs at a mouthful, crunching bones and all like wild beasts, so that not the slightest vestige remained, and the rightful owners were left, dumbfoundered and famished, to stare at their empty table-cloth.

We had happily no such attractions to offer, but were well persecuted notwithstanding, and heartily cursed by troops of hungry ragged urchins because we had brought nothing for them, as well as by a shaggy-looking ruffian, who was imprisoned under the Barberini Palace, for having lately murdered his wife and son, and who stretched out his bony hand with nails like claws, and shook it at us through the iron bars as we passed. Yet an officer, who was quartered at the palace, told us that the people here are perfectly angelic compared to those of the neighbouring Cavi. *There*, on the slightest contradiction, the natives never hesitated to pull out a stiletto or a revolver, and he never knew a time when six or seven of his men were not suffering from their violence while they were quartered there.

The view from the top is certainly magnificent. No wonder that Hannibal climbed up to survey it in order to assist his military operations. It is the most historical panorama imaginable. Rome is seen amidst the mists of the plain. Nearer us are Gabii, Collatia, and Zagarolo. On the Alban hills are Tusculum, Frescati, Monte Porzio, Monte Compatri, Labicum (now Colonna), Corbio (now Rocca Priora),

Velitræ (now Velletri). Then on the distant sea-coast we can make out Astura, Nettuno, Antium (Porto d'Anzio), Ardea, Pratica, Ostia, Porto, and Fiumicino. On the Volscian hills are Monte Fortino, Colle Ferro and Signia (Segni); on the Hernicans, Anagni, Ferentino, Paliano, Genazzano, and Cavi, and the fore-ground is formed by the Cyclopean walls of Præneste! Looking down upon all these scenes, girt by the huge polygonal stones of the walls of the ancient citadel, is the modern village of *San Pietro*, a place so dilapidated and crumbling, so bare and colourless, that it looks as if it had been transported from Africa to this windy height. Here the Roman Catholic Church believes that St. Peter dwelt for some time, and here, in the church, he is commemorated in a statue by Bernini, as well as in a good picture representing his martyrdom by Pietro di Cortona. The holy water basons are supported by ancient *cippi*.

Colonna Castle, Palestrina.

Still higher, on the last peak, stand the huge ruins of the fortress, rebuilt by the famous Stephen Colonna, which bears over its gate, beneath the Colonna arms, the inscription, "Magnificus DNS Stefan de Columna-redificavit civitatem penestre cv monte et arce. Anno 1332."

In summer the stagnation of Palestrina is enlivened by the presence of the Barberini family, who live, not at the palace with the mosaic, but at another lower down in the town, quite in a feudal manner, and, as Prince and Princess of Palestrina, hold receptions in their garden, to which all the small gentry of the place are invited.

The *Ponte S. Antonio* may be visited from Palestrina. It is a magnificent Roman arch 120 feet in height, not far from Poli, by which the Aqua Claudia and the Anio Novus were carried across a deep ravine in the Campagna.

CHAPTER XVIII.

GENAZZANO, PALIANO, AND OLEVANO.

(At Olevano there is an excellent country inn, kept by Nino and Pepina Baldi, much frequented by artists, who reside here for months in summer. The charges for *pension*, including everything, are five francs a day, or four francs if for a long time. A carriage may be obtained from Olevano to meet the train at the Valmontone Station by writing beforehand to Casa Baldi. The public carriage, which leaves the Piazza S. Marco at six A.M. for Palestrina, proceeds to Olevano—fare, from four to five francs. At Subiaco there is a comfortable small hotel with capital food—Locanda della Pernice—pension, six francs a day.)

IT is a pleasant drive of three miles from Palestrina to *Cavi*, which is built on the edge of a steep bank over a torrent, approached by a handsome bridge, and entered by a gateway, over which is an inscription, dedicating the place to the especial protection of the Madonna. To her the inhabitants trust to supply them with all the necessaries of life, and exist themselves in a *far niente* not very *dolce*, but unending. The very dogs seemed too apathetic to move when our carriage approached where they lay in the sun. Some ragged children were rolling in the gutter, while their mother was engaged in lavishing the tenderest embraces and kisses upon a pet pig—the son of her heart. In the market-place rises a column decorated with the arms of the Colonna, of whom Cavi is a fief. The dialect of the people here is very peculiar. Six miles beyond Cavi, after passing a chapel beautifully situated near an old pine and some cypresses, *Genazzano* rises in a valley on the left about half a mile distant from the road. It contains the shrine of the Madonna di Buon Consiglio, who *flew* hither through the air from Albania.

"From this time the Madonna of Genazzano, called 'Our Lady of Good Offices,' began to work miracles, and a church was built in her honour, with a monastery adjoining it. The Order of the Augustines possessed themselves of this wonder-working and holy source of gain, which is not less profitable, if not more so, than the Madonna of the Augustine monastery at Rome. For this Divinity of Genazzano enjoys throughout the whole of Latium a reputation, which exactly corresponds with that of a heathen oracle. Twice a year, in spring and in summer, her festival is celebrated, and thus a double harvest of offerings is reaped, besides innumerable presents of money and jewels brought by the worshippers. And as even the poorest countryman lays his mite upon the altar of the picture, it may be said that this one Madonna taxes the whole Latian Campagna as well as the State itself. I was told that the offerings are collected by certain confraternities which exist in the Campagna; each member puts into the common fund as much as five baiocchi a month, and thus a travelling confraternity brings sometimes as much as a hundred scudi. The yearly receipts of this place of pilgrimage are estimated at 37,500 francs."—*Gregorovius.*

The festa of the Madonna of Genazzano, on the 25th of

Genazzano.

April, is one of the most celebrated and the most frequented in this part of Italy. A figure-artist should never fail to see it, and the most sanguine expectations as to colour and costume cannot possibly be disappointed.

"Even on the eve of the festival the pilgrims begin to arrive, and the place and the whole landscape becomes animated in a wonderful manner, while the air resounds perpetually with the chanting of Litanies. Through all the streets pass gay but orderly crowds. They come from the Abruzzi, from the sandal land, from Sora, from the Liris, and from all parts of the Latian Campagna.

"The festival of Jupiter Latiaris seems to be renewed before our eyes, so numerous are the thousands that approach, so varied their dress and their dialects. They come down from the hills with their solemn chant of the 'Ora,' there down the broad road, here along the river, by field paths, ever and again fresh bands of pilgrims in bright red, green, and blue costumes, with their tall pilgrim staves (*bordoni*) in their hands, and the sight combined with the grandeur of the scenery is one which would be alike wonderful to the artist, the poet, and the historian.

". . . They wander along the Sacco, and down from the hills (*come i grù, che van cantando lor lai*), like the cranes who sing as they go. The middle ages passed before me; and I thought of those bands of pilgrims who thronged to Rome at the Jubilee year, and more than once the sight made me repeat that beautiful verse in the pilgrim sonnet of the Vita Nuova,

> Deh! peregrini, che pensosi andate
> Forse di cosa che non v'è presente,
> Venite voi di si lontana gente,
> Com' alla vista voi ne dimostrate?

"They go by tens, twentys, fiftys, hundreds, and even more. All ages are represented amongst them; the old man leans on the same pilgrim staff which has supported him already fifty times along the same road, and this may perhaps be the last time: the matron passes with her grandchildren; the beautiful and blooming maiden; the sturdy youth, the boy; even infants are here carried on the heads of their mothers, for in one of these processions I saw a young woman carrying on her head a basket in which lay a laughing child, its eyes wide open as if it was enjoying the beautiful sunshine. Most of the women carry on their heads a basket of provisions, or a bundle of clothes, which still more increases the beauty of the spectacle. If any one could lift up the veil from these souls they would see concealed crime side by side with innocence, and vice, remorse, pain, and virtue passing in a motley crowd.

"It is like a great and beautiful but serious masked procession which passes over one of the most beautiful scenes of nature, always with fresh dresses and colours, and with different faces. One sees the people of

Contadino, Valley of the Sacco.

Frosinone, of Anagni, the inhabitants of Veroli, of Arpino, of Anticoli, of Ceprano, and the Neapolitans from Sora.

"See the groups from Sora! dark olive complexions and beautiful oval faces. The women look fantastic, like the Arab women; they are adorned with strings of coral or golden chains round their necks, and heavy gold earrings; their heads are covered with white or brown kerchiefs, with long fringes, which hang down upon the neck like a madonna's veil: they wear white chemisettes quite loose though folded in

Contadina, Valley of the Sacco.

innumerable plaits, and over these a low, dark red bodice. The skirt is short, of a bright red or blue colour, with a yellow border. And what large dark eyes, under black, strongly marked eyebrows!

"The pilgrims of Ceccano! The women wearing red bodices with long aprons of the same colour, white kerchiefs on their heads with long ends hanging down behind, and sandals. The men in pointed hats, with red jackets, and a girdle round the waist, twisted of bright ribbon.

"Pilgrims from Pontecorvo! The women in dark red dresses beautifully ornamented; with a red head-dress; beautiful and majestic.

"Pilgrims from Filettino : black velvet bodices, a most simple dress, quiet and graceful.

"Ciociari! The men and women of the sandal land! Perhaps from some place near Ferentino, or farther away, from the Neapolitan boundaries of the Liris and the Melfa. It is a land of beautiful and wild mountains, which extends from Ferentino far into the Neapolitan territory. There the people wear the Ciocia, a very simple covering for the foot, from which the country is called Ciociaria. I found this covering for the foot in use near Anagni. One more primitive certainly cannot be found, perhaps one might also say there is none more comfortable. It certainly made me envy the Ciociari. The shoe is simply formed of a square piece of ass or horse skin. Holes are made in this skin, through which a string is passed, and this parchment is so tied round the foot that it forms itself to the shape of the foot. The leg is swathed up to the knee with coarse grey linen, bound round many times with string or thread. Thus the Ciociaro moves freely and comfortably across the fields, and over the rocks, whenever he goes to dig the ground ('zappar la terra'), or drives his sheep and goats, as a shepherd with bag-pipes, dressed in a short grey cloak, or clothed in skins. These sandals are classical, and Diogenes would have worn them if he had not gone barefoot; and Chrysippus or Epictetus might have praised them in a treatise on the few needs of wise men. If these shoes are well arranged, and the linen leggings new, they look well, but very bad and beggarly when they are old and ragged; and as this is generally the case, it has given the sandal folk a character of ragged poverty, and their name is despised and even used as a word of reproach. One day, when a man of San Vito was showing me the beautiful panorama of the Campagna, he said to me, 'See, sir, there lies the Ciociaria!' and he smiled with a look of lofty contempt.

"The Ciociari wear bright red vests, and pointed black felt hats, which seldom lack a gay feather, a bow, or a flower. I found among them, especially in the Campagna of Rome, a remarkable number of men with fair hair and blue eyes; they wear their hair cut short behind, like the Prussian Landwehr, but let it hang down in long locks from the temples. Hang a ragged grey waterproof cloak or a black or white sheepskin on the Ciociaro, and we have our sandal man complete; but we will not give him a gun in his hand, or he will fall upon us as a robber in the pass of Ceprano, crying out, 'faccia in terra,' and will empty

our pockets with astonishing agility. The women also wear the sandals, a short gay skirt, a bright striped apron, a white or a red woollen kerchief on the head, and lastly the *busto*, the principal article of female dress throughout the whole of Latium. This is the bodice of stiffly-quilted linen, hard as a saddle, broad and high, with epaulets resting on the shoulders. It forms a support to the breast, it seems like a bulwark to shield virtue; like a firm breast-plate it surrounds the bosom; yet it is loose, and stands out, so that it serves at the same time as a pocket."
—*Gregorovius.*

The town of Genazzano was long a fortress of the Colonnas, and was the place where Stefano Colonna was murdered in 1438. The only pope given by the great Colonna family to Rome was born at Genazzano. This was Oddone Colonna, elected at Constance in 1417 as Martin V. while two other popes were already in existence. As sovereign he continued to be devoted to his native place, where he built churches and enlarged the palace of his family, which is now neglected and fast falling into decay. In its decline it is very picturesque, and is supplied with water by a half-ruined aqueduct, along which there is a walk leading to the deserted convent of San Pio. The whole population is occupied in the cultivation of the hill-side vineyards.

Continuing our way along the valley, we see that a hill-top in front of us is occupied by a mountain-town, surrounded with strong, sixteenth-century fortifications. This is *Paliano*, another important stronghold of the Colonnas. Prospero Colonna defended it against Sixtus IV. In 1556 Paul IV. took it away from the Colonnas, and gave it to his own nephew Giovanni Caraffa, for whom it was raised into a principality.

"Declaring that the Colonnas, 'those incorrigible rebels against God and the Church,' however frequently deprived of their castles, had always managed to regain them, Paul IV. resolved that this should be amended; he would give those fortresses to vassals who would know how to hold them. Thereupon he divided the possessions of the house of Colonna among his nephews, making the elder Duke of Paliano, and the younger Marquis of Montebello. The cardinals remained silent when he announced these purposes in the assembly; they bent down their heads and fixed their eyes to the earth."—*Ranke's History of the Popes.*

Only fifteen years after, however, upon the victory of Marc-Antonio Colonna over the Turks at Lepanto, Paliano was restored to its original owners, and has since given the title of Duca di Paliano to the head of their house.

A long ascent now brings us to *Olevano*, of the beauty of which one has no idea till one really arrives, but it is perhaps the most picturesque place of this wonderful district. Passing from the rough stone houses with their crumbling staircases of rock, and from the stony ways full of pigs and children, a gate admits us to a high olive garden, full of beans and corn, where a winding path leads to a kind of large farm-house at the top of the hill, with an outside loggia and staircase. And this is the famous inn of Olevano, the Albergo degli Artisti. It is a perfect artist's paradise. Its rooms are homely, but are cleanliness itself. They all debouch from a common sitting-room, surrounded by queer old portraits and with a grand old chair, which may have been that of Cardinal Scipio Borghese, whose picture hangs over the fire-place. The pleasant honest mistress, Pepina Baldi, with her husband Nino, are really charming specimens of respectable well-to-do Italians of the lower orders, full of simple kindnesses and courtesies, and frankness and openness itself. Their handsome boys and girls have served as voluntary models to half the artists in

Rome when they have been staying here; and many sketches of the family by famous hands, which would fetch enormous prices in Paris or London, hang upon the walls, where they have been left as thank-offerings with the mother. For the entertainment of guests too we have a collection of albums, which any sovereign might envy, and than which few possess any more valuable, for every artist who has staid here has left his portrait, by his own hand or that of a friend, and the collection is really wonderful, of the natives of every country in Europe, from the delicate hand of our English Leighton to that of the least known student of the Via Margutta. But still the greatest charm of Casa Baldi is its view. One looks along the whole of the Hernican range, tossed above into every variety of peak, and clothed on its lower slopes with corn and fruit-trees, olives and cypresses, from which Anagni and Ferentino and Frosinone look across the valley to the more distant Volscians, also sprinkled with rock-throned villages. In the middle distance Paliano watches the valley from a steep elevated ridge. Deep below rises the town of Olevano,

Olevano.

with yellow-roofed houses, weather-stained, machicolated, arch-adorned, rising from rocks overhung with ivy and flowers, and leading up to the jagged walls and tower of a ruined castle. Behind the town are the wild mountains of the Sabina, with Civitella, Capranica, San Vito, and Rocca di Cavi perched upon different heights, and on the furthest of all the curious sanctuary and the Polish convent of Mentorella, and round the corner of this range we catch a glimpse of the Alban hills projecting over the purple Campagna.

> "There are many places on the sunny heights, or in the dark recesses of the mountains; castles, monasteries, and towns, rising in the clear air—all seems to rest in a romantic quietude. The outlines of the mountains are cut with enchanting clearness and sharpness upon the pure blue of the sky; one longs to cross over, to wander amongst the shining crags and soft plains in the freshness of that high and heavenly region. Above the hollows of the Serra, rises, here and there, a snow-capped mountain, violet-tinted, out of the wilds of the Abruzzi, suggesting still another distance; in the background mountain-peaks rise further and further out of the silvery mists, shadowy, many-formed, obelisk-like, dome-like, beckoning the spirit onwards into the unknown regions of the sandal-land, or to the shore of the lovely Liris."—*Gregorovius*.

The name of Olevano carries us back pleasantly into the mediæval times, when it was compelled to pay a tax called *Olibanum*, for purchasing incense for the churches of the province. Then the noble family of Frangipani, who derived their glorious name of "Bread-breakers" from their vast charities during a famine, resided in its fortress. From them it passed by exchange to the Benedictine monks of Subiaco, by whom it was sold in the 13th century to the Colonnas, who built the present castle and guarded it through weal and woe for four hundred years, when it was purchased by the Borgheses, who hold it still.

The most remarkable excursion which can be made from Olevano is that to *Guadagnolo*, a rock 4000 feet high, with a village curiously wedged in between high rocks, which surround and conceal it on every side, as with a natural wall. A mile and a half below the town, are the hermitage and church of *La Mentorella*, on the edge of the precipice, jutting out over the valley of the Girano. Here, before he went to Subiaco, S. Benedict lived in the sixth century, in a cave at the foot of the rock. A tradition of far earlier date (during the reign of the Emperor Trajan) represents the crag of La Mentorella as that where the vision of a white deer, with a crucifix between his horns, led to the conversion of S. Eustace.

> "S. Eustace was a Roman soldier, and captain of the guard to the Emperor Trajan. His name before his conversion was Placidus, and he had a beautiful wife and two sons, and lived with great magnificence, practising all the heathen virtues, particularly those of loyalty to his sovereign and charity to the poor. He was also a great lover of the chase, spending much of his time in that noble diversion.
>
> "One day while hunting in the forest, he saw before him a white stag, of marvellous beauty, and he pursued it eagerly, and the stag fled before him, and ascended a high rock. Then Placidus, looking up, beheld, between the horns of the stag, a cross of radiant light, and on it the image of the crucified Redeemer; and being astonished and dazzled by this vision, he fell on his knees, and a voice which seemed to come from the crucifix cried to him, and said, 'Placidus! why dost thou pursue me? I am Christ, whom thou hast hitherto served without knowing me. Dost thou now believe?' and Placidus fell with his face to the earth, and said, 'Lord, I believe!' and the voice answered, saying, 'Thou shalt suffer many tribulations for my sake, and shalt be tried by many temptations; but be strong and of good courage, and I will not forsake thee.' To which Placidus replied, 'Lord, I am content. Do thou give me patience to suffer!' And when he looked up again the wondrous vision had departed. Then he arose and returned to his house, and the next day he and his wife and his two sons were baptized, and he took the name of Eustace."—*Jameson's Legendary Art.*

A flight of stairs, which troops of pilgrims devoutly ascend upon their knees on the festa of the twenty-ninth of September, leads to the campanile, which is surmounted by a pair of antlers, like those of the portico of the church of S. Eustachio at Rome, commemorating his conversion. The festa of La Mentorella is one of the most romantic in Italy. The peasants come by the steep mountain-paths chaunting litanies, and each carrying a stone which they add to a great commemorative pile. They spend the night in groups, sleeping round fires lighted on these wild crags, and those who have been present describe the scene as quite unrivalled in its weird picturesqueness—the brilliant costumes illuminated by the fire-light and backed by the savage precipices which overhang the Girano and Siciliano, and the rude chaunts echoing amid the rocks under the starlit sky. The name of Mentorella comes from Wultvilla or Wulturela, the ancient name of the mountain. The gothic chapel which now exists, is of the tenth century, but a church certainly existed here as early as A.D. 594, when it was bestowed upon the abbot of Subiaco by Gregory I. In A.D. 958, the mountain of Wulturela with its church, dedicated to Sta. Maria, belonged to S. Gregorio in Rome, but the building appears to have been deserted in the fourteenth century, though it was restored by the Emperor Leopold in 1660.

CHAPTER XIX.

SUBIACO.

(Subiaco is 26 miles from Tivoli. A diligence runs daily. There is a very tolerable inn, *La Pernice*,—pension, 5 francs a day—but passing travellers must arrange their prices beforehand.)

THE road from Olevano to Subiaco passes through a dismal bare rocky district, but is a fine specimen of engineering, being one of the many excellent mountain-roads, constructed under Pius IX. A few miles before reaching Subiaco, we skirt a lake, which is probably one of the Simbriviæ Aquæ.

" Quique Anienis habent ripas, gelidoque rigantur
Simbrivio, rastrisque domant Æquicula rura."
Sil. Ital. viii. 370.

The three pools called Simbrivii Lacus were made by Nero by the damming up of the Anio. Here he fished for trout with a golden net, and here he built the mountain-villa to which he gave the name of *Sublacum*—under the lake —which still exists in Subiaco.

" Avoir une villa dans les montagnes du pays des Æques, c'était pour Néron ce que serait pour un moderne la fantaisie d'un châlet en Suisse."
—*Ampère, Emp. Rom.* ii. 62.

While Nero was residing here the conspiracies were forming which led to his overthrow, and here he was warned of his fate by a portent most terrible in those times of omens, when his drinking-cup was shivered in his hand by lightning whilst he was seated at a banquet near the lake, a presage which seized upon his mind with appalling effect. That very day he had bathed in the aqueduct of the Aqua Marcia, that all his people might enjoy the privilege of drinking water that had been thus defiled.* The choice of his villa amid the Æquian mountains shows that, in spite of all his monstrosities, Nero must have been as great a connoisseur of the beauties of nature as of art, and for centuries the glorious gorge through which the Anio foams beneath its ruins, between tremendous crags clothed with evergreens and flowers, has been a sanctuary to half the poets and painters in the world.

Hither, four centuries after the time of Nero, when the recollection of his orgies had given place to silence and solitude, a young patrician, sprung from the noble family of the Anicii, which gave Gregory the Great to the Church, and many other saints to the sacred calendar, fled from the seductions of the capital, to seek repose for his soul, with God alone as his companion. The name of the fugitive was Benedictus, or "the blessed one." He was only fourteen when he renounced his fortune, his family, and the world. It was to Mentorella that he first fled, and thither he was followed by his faithful nurse Cyrilla, who could not bear to think that the child of her affections was alone and uncared for, who begged for him, and prepared the small modicum of food which he could be prevailed upon to take. Some neighbour had lent her a stone sieve to make bread,

---

* Claudius first made an aqueduct to bring to Rome the water of two fountains called Curtius and Cæruleus, in the hills above Sublacum.

after the manner of the mountain district, she let it fall out of her hands, and it was broken to pieces. Moved by her distress, Benedict prayed over the fragments, and they are said to have been instantly joined together. This was his first miracle. Terrified at the excitement it caused, and at seeing the sieve hung up in the village church as a relic, Benedict evaded the solicitude of his nurse, and escaped unseen by any one to the gorge of Subiaco, where he found (c. 480) a cave in the rocks above the falls of the Anio, into which not even a ray of the sun could penetrate. Here he lived, his hiding-place unknown to any one, except to Romanus, a monk who dwelt amid a colony of anchorites founded by S. Clement on the ruins of Nero's villa. By him he was provided with a garment made of the skin of a beast, and each day Romanus let down to him from the top of the rock the half of his daily loaf, giving him notice of its approach by the ringing of a bell suspended to the same rope with the food. It is said that when the devil wished to make himself particularly disagreeable to Benedict he would cut the cord which supplied him. His hiding-place was discovered by a miracle. A village priest seated at a banquet of Easter luxuries had a revelation that while he was thus feasting a servant of God was pining with hunger, and his steps were miraculously directed to the hermitage. Benedict refused to eat the delicate food, until convinced that it was indeed the festival of Easter. The priest told what he had seen to the shepherds, who, while following their goats along one of the tiny pathlets which may still be seen on the face of these mountains, had seen a strange creature with unkempt hair, and nails like claws, and taking it for a wild beast, had fled from it in terror. They were now re-assured by his gentle words, and from that day, while they watched their flocks, he began to instil into their rude and ignorant minds the light of the Christian faith. Gradually their report became spread abroad, pilgrims flocked from all quarters to the valley, and through the disciples who gathered round Benedict, this desolate ravine became the cradle of monastic life in the West.

> "The life of Benedict, from infancy to death, is the most perfect illustration of the motives which then worked upon the mind of man. In him meet and combine together all those influences which almost divided mankind into recluses or cœnobites, and those who pursued an active life; as well as all the effects, in his case the best effects, produced by this phasis of human thought and feeling. Benedict, it was said, was born at that time, like a sun to dispel the Cimmerian darkness which brooded over Christendom, and to revive the expiring spirit of monasticism. His age acknowledged Benedict as the perfect type of the highest religion, and Benedict impersonated his age.
>
> "How perfectly the whole atmosphere was then impregnated with an inexhaustible yearning for the supernatural, appears from the ardour with which the monastic passions were indulged at the earliest age. Children were nursed and trained to expect at every instant more than human interferences; their young energies had ever before them examples of asceticism, to which it was the glory, the true felicity of life, to aspire. The thoughtful child had all his mind thus pre-occupied; he was early, it might almost seem intuitively, trained to this course of life; wherever there was gentleness, modesty, the timidity of young passion, repugnance to vice, an imaginative temperament, a consciousness of unfitness to wrestle with the rough realities of life, the way lay invitingly open—the difficult, it is true, and painful, but direct and unerring way to heaven. It lay through perils, but was made attractive by perpetual wonders; it was awful, but in its awfulness lay its power over the young mind. It learned to trample down that last bond which united the child to common humanity, filial reverence; the fond and mysterious attachment of the child and the mother, the inborn reverence of the son to the father."—*Milman's Latin Christianity.*

Twelve monasteries speedily arose amid these peaks and gorges, each only containing twelve monks, for it was an idea of Benedict that a larger number led to idleness and neglect. The names of several of these institutions recall their romantic situations, and they were the scenes of the miracles attributed to the founder and his disciples. *S. Clemente della Vigna* was the place whither Maurus and Placidus were brought to Benedict by their parents. It was situated near one of the lakes, and it was there that the sickle of a Gothic monk, which he dropped into the water while cutting weeds upon the bank, swam in answer to the prayers of Maurus, who summoned it by holding the wooden handle over the waves. This monastery was entirely destroyed by the earthquake of 1216. *S. S. Cosmo and Damian* was the next to be built, the monastery which was afterwards dedicated to Scholastica. *S. Biagio* (S. Blaise) was the home of the monk Romanus, the friend of Benedict. Its church was consecrated in 1100 by Manfred, Bishop of Tivoli. *S. Giovanni dell' Acqua* was so called because there, as well as in two other houses, water is said to have burst forth from the arid rock to supply the thirsting monks, in answer to the prayers of Benedict.* *Santa Maria de Marebotta* was afterwards called *S. Lorenzo* in honour of the holy monk S. Lorenzo Loricato who lived there as a hermit, in the most severe austerity, from 1209 to 1243. At *Sant' Angelo*, Benedict saw the devil, in the form of a black boy, leading away a monk, who had neglected to attend properly the services of the Church. In *S. Victor at the foot of the Mountain* lived the monk who brought the Easter food to Benedict when he was starving in the cave. *S. Andrew*, or *Eternal Life*, was ruined in a Lombard invasion. *S. Michael the Archangel* was built by Benedict beneath the Sacro Speco,

* This subject is represented in the frescoes of Spinello at San Miniato.

but has long since disappeared. *Sant' Angelo di Trevi* stood near Sta. Scholastica and was incorporated with it. *S. Girolamo* was rebuilt as late as 1387 in accordance with a bull of Urban VI. *S. Donato* has entirely disappeared. Gradually all these societies became incorporated in the great monastery dedicated to Scholastica, the holy sister of Benedict, which may be regarded as the mother house of the whole Order, and which was governed by a regular abbot chosen by the General Chapter.

The visits of the numerous Popes who have come hither form landmarks in the story of the place. In 853 Leo IV., summoned by the Abbot Peter, came to consecrate the altars of the Sacro Speco. In 981 Benedict VII. came to consecrate Sta. Scholastica. In 1052 Leo IX. was summoned to turn out a monk who had unlawfully seized the abbacy—and issued a bull appointing Sta. Scholastica " Caput omnium monasteriorum per Italiam constitutorum." In the thirteenth century the privileges of the monastery were greatly augmented by Alexander IV., who had lived there as a simple monk, and who declared in his diploma that other Benedictine communities had only to look to Sta. Scholastica to receive a perfect model which they should copy. The same affection for the place was evinced by Urban V., who had also been a Benedictine, and who colonized the monastery with German monks, to amend the morals of the brethren, which had then grievous need of it. The last of a long series of papal visits was that of Pius IX. in the first year of his pontificate.

The road which leads from the town to the monasteries (S. Benedetto is about two and a half miles distant) is beautiful,—bordered by ilexes and olives, beneath which there is ever a carpet of tulips, hyacinths, and anemones, in spring. Gorgeous are the views looking back amid the mountain rifts, between which Subiaco rises house above house with the great archiepiscopal castle at the top of its rock. The modern *Collegiata*, a huge mass of building, seems to block the valley, standing almost over the stream of the Anio, and consisting of a church and palace built by Pius VI., when Cardinal Bishop of Subiaco,—being necessary, because the abbots of Santa Scholastica had been bishops also, until the see was united with a cardinalate. The nearer hills are all aglow with the richest vegetation, olives, chestnuts, and corn, and here and there the tall spire of a cypress. The air is scented by the sweet box, which grows upon the cliffs close to the road, and a freshness always rises from the river which dashes wildly through the abyss of green beneath, rejoicing to be freed from its imprisonment in the walls of cliff beneath S. Scholastica. Here a ruined gothic chapel stands amid thickets of flowers, there a gaily painted shrine, very dear to artists, surmounts the tufa rocks.

When we reach the bridge called "Ponte S. Mauro," by which the road from Olevano crosses the Anio at a great height, a carriage can go no further, and the footpath which ascends to the great monasteries turns off up the gorge to the left. Little chapels at intervals mark the rocky way, which is overhung by wild laburnum and coronilla, and fringed with saxifrage and cyclamen. The first of these chapels commemorates an interesting mediæval story in which Benedict bore a share. Amongst those who came hither from Rome to share his teaching, were two Roman senators of high rank, Anicius and Tertullus, who brought with them their sons Maurus and Placidus, entreating

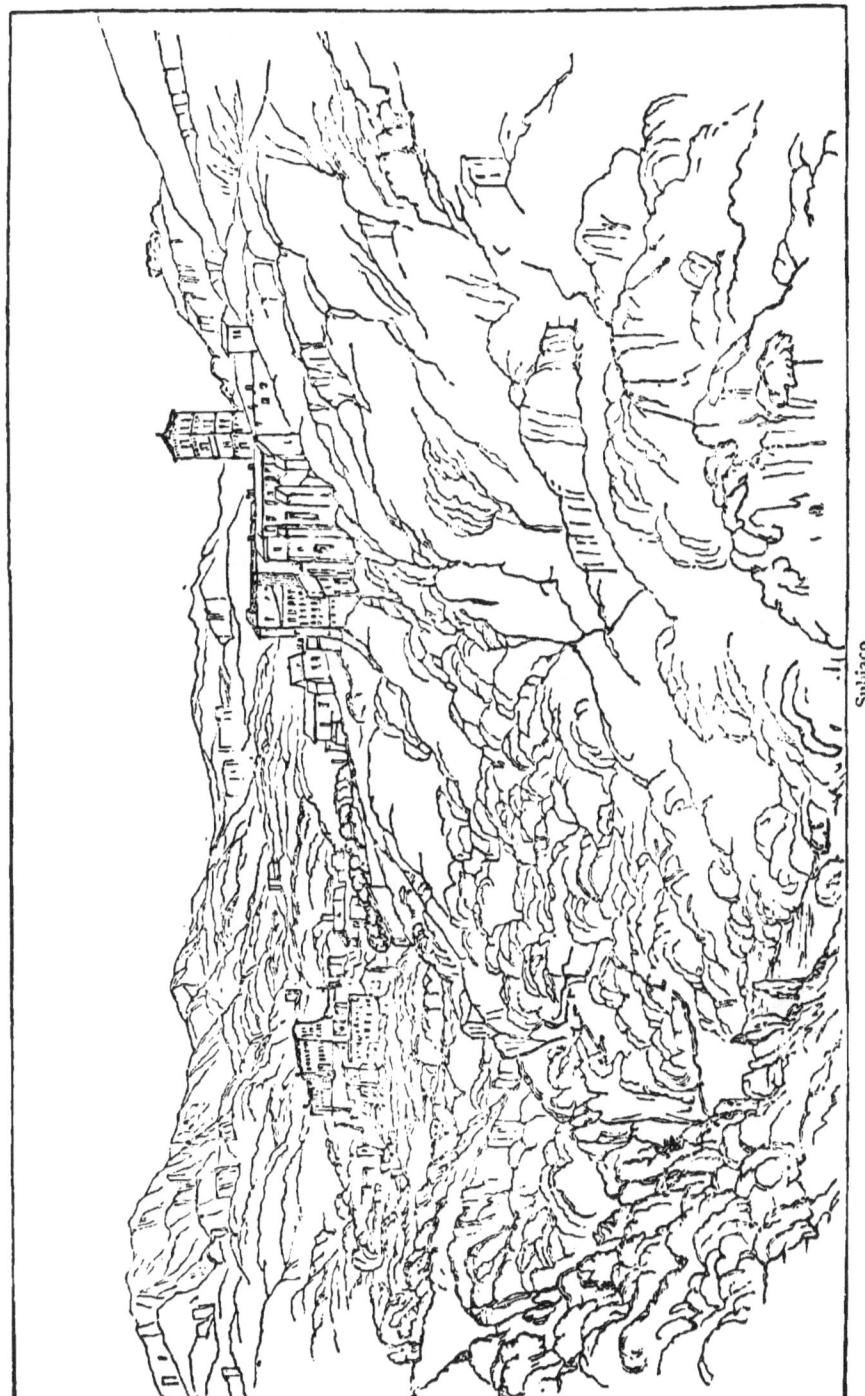

Subiaco.

him to bring them up in the way of Life. Maurus was then twelve years old and Placidus only five. One day (in 528) the child Placidus fell into the Anio below this cliff. Benedict, seeing him fall, called to Maurus to assist him, and he, walking upon the water, caught the drowning boy by the hair, and dragged him out. His safety was followed by a contest of humility between the pupil and master. Maurus attributed it to the holiness of Benedict, Benedict to the self-devotion of Maurus; Placidus decided the question by saying that he had seen the sheepskin-coat of Benedict hovering over him in the water.

Long before we reach it, the grandly toned bell of *Santa Scholastica*, echoing amid the rocks, gives notice of the approach to a great sanctuary. Nothing can exceed the solemn grandeur of its situation, perched upon huge crags, and with the roaring river below. The monastery was founded in the fifth century by the Abbot Honoratus, the sainted successor of Benedict, and though repeatedly attacked and burnt by the Lombards, the Saracens, and by its own neighbours, it always rose again from its ashes more splendid than ever. In 981 it was rebuilt from the ground under Benedict VII., and dedicated to S. Benedict and his holy sister Scholastica. From this time rich donations were constantly made, and lands were added to its territory, till, in 1100, its abbots became princes, possessed of many castles and fortresses, and with a right of supreme jurisdiction over their vassals. They did not hesitate to appear personally in the battle-fields of that troubled time, in which the Bishops of Tivoli, Anagni, and Palestrina were also frequently seen. Many curious records remain of their savage administration of justice. In the time of the Ghibelline

Abbot Adhemar (1353) seven monks were hung up by their feet, and fires lighted under their heads. In 1454 their severities led to a rebellion in which the convent was stormed and many of the monks massacred. Calistus III. made the Abbot a Cardinal Commendatory, and the first who bore this title was the Spanish Torquemada, under whose rule, in 1464, the famous Sweynheim and Pannartz established here the first printing-press in Italy, and published from hence "Lactantius de divinis institutionibus;" "Cicero de Oratore," and, in 1467, "Augustinus de Civitate Dei." In the same year, however, a quarrel with the monks drove them to Rome, where they established themselves in the Massimo Palace. It is interesting to remember that the first printing-press in England was also established in a Benedictine Abbey—that of Westminster.

Torquemada was succeeded as abbot by Rodrigo Borgia, afterwards Pope Alexander VI., and in his time Lucrezia Borgia often resided in the castle-palace, and Cæsar came hither to hunt. Under the Abbot Pompeo Colonna, Julius II. united the abbacy with that of Farfa; in 1514, Leo X. joined it to that of Monte Cassino. After this it remained for 116 years in the hands of the Colonnas, and a memorial of the way in which they held their own against the Popes may be seen in the papal banner which fell into their hands in battle, and which still hangs in the convent church.

From the middle of the last century the great power of the abbots of S. Scholastica began to decline, but until the late suppression the monastery remained one of the richest and most influential in Italy, and it continued to own no less than sixteen towns and villages, viz. Subiaco, Trevi, Jenna, Cervara, Camerata, Marano, Agosta, Rocca di Canterano,

Canterano, Rocca di Mezzo, Cerreto, Rocca di Santo Stefano, Civitella, Rojate, Asile, and Ponza.

The front of S. Scholastica is modern, but its tower dates from 1053, when it was built by the Abbot Humbert. The most interesting parts of the building are its three cloisters. The first, which only dates from the seventeenth century, has its arcades decorated with frescoes of papal and royal benefactors, amongst which is a full-length portrait of "James III., king of England." Here is a curious sarcophagus with Bacchic ornaments. The second cloister, which dates from 1052, contains many beautiful fragments of Gothic decoration, but its chief feature is a richly decorated arch adorned with small figures and spiral columns. A bas-relief of 981 represents two animals, apparently a wolf and a dog, drinking; on the body of one of the beasts is an inscription relating to the dedication of the church, Dec. 4th, 981, by Benedict VII. To the right of the church, we enter the third and smallest cloister—"Il chiostro dell' Abbate Lando"—built early in the thirteenth century. It is surrounded by a beautiful arcade of double pillars like those at the Lateran, and has an inscription in mosaic, the work of the famous Cosmo Cosmati and his two sons, Luca and Jacopo, to whom are due the beautiful decorations in the cloister of the Benedictine convent of S. Paolo at Rome :—

> "Cosmus et Filii Lucas et Jacobus alter
> Romani Cives in Marmoris arte periti
> Hoc opus explerunt Abbatis tempore Landi."

In the porch of the church is an interesting old Giottesque picture and the capital of a Corinthian column attesting the presence of a temple on this site. The interior, though modern, is not unimposing. S. Onorato sleeps beneath the high altar. Under his statue is an inscription which recalls the legend that the translation of his beloved master Benedict into the better world was miraculously revealed to him:

> "Scandentem hic alter Benedictum vidit in astra ;
> Primus et has ædes illo abeunte regit."

As the path from Sta. Scholastica to the Sacro Speco is steep and fatiguing, a small chapel has been erected at a short distance beyond the larger monastery, where aged and infirm persons are allowed to accomplish their pilgrimage. It bears the inscription—

> "Si montis superasse jugum negat ægra senectus,
> Nec detur ad sacros procubuisse specus,
> Siste, tibi cœli hæc ædes æraria pandet,
> Hæc tibi cœlestes prodiga fundet opes."

The scenery now becomes more romantic and savage at every step as we ascend the winding path, till, about half a mile further on, a small gate admits one to the famous immemorial *Ilex Grove*, which is said to date from the fifth century, and which has never been profaned by axe or hatchet. The grand old trees bowed with age, with twisted and contorted stems, form a dense mass of shadow, grateful after the arid rocks, and they hang in masses of grey-green verdure over the depth. Here and there the mossy trunks are covered with fern, upon which a ray of sunlight falls with dazzling brilliancy. At the end of the grove the path narrows, and a steep winding stair, just wide enough to admit one person at a time, leads to the platform before the convent, which up to that moment is entirely concealed. It is always said that monks have known how to choose the sites of their dwellings better than any one else, but surely no situation was ever equal to this, to which they were led by its historical associations. There is an old Latin distich which says:

> "Bernardus valles, colles Benedictus amabat,
> Oppida Franciscus, magnas Ignatius urbes."

The name of the monastery, *Sacro Speco*, commemorates the holy cave of S. Benedict. Over his caverned oratory a chapel was erected by Onorato, his immediate successor. Soon after another chapel was built in the cave which was his dwelling, and the two were united by the sixth abbot, Pietro. In the eleventh century a more imposing church was constructed by the Abbot Humbert, which was to enclose both the caves—*utramque cryptam*. His successor, the Abbot John V., finished the church much as we now see it, for the present buildings, raised on arches against the rocks, all date from the eleventh and the early part of the twelfth centuries; the lower church is of 1053.

At the entrance, the thrilling interest of the place is at once recalled to us by the inscription—" Here is the patriarchal cradle of the monks of the West of the Order of S. Benedict." The entrance corridor, built on arches over the abyss, has frescoes of four sainted popes—Gregory, Agatho, Leo, and another. It ends in an antechamber with a painted statue of S. Benedict, some beautiful old Umbrian frescoes of the Virgin and Child between the four Evangelists, and the lines

> "Do you ask of Benedict, 'If you seek for light, why do you choose a cave,
> For a cavern can give no light to him who prays for it?'
> Know that if one ray penetrates into utter darkness,
> It gives more light in the gloom than the stars in the night."

We now reach the entrance of the all-glorious upper-church, built by the Abbot John V. in 1116, and adorned with frescoes under John VI. in 1220.

> "One seems to be deeply embued with the mysterious associations of famous days of old, as one enters the first church from the gallery, and finds oneself suddenly in a little cathedral of graceful Gothic architecture, its walls and pillars gleaming with the varied colour of already fading frescoes. Unseen monks sing vespers in the choir, their powerful bass voices echoing solemnly through the twilight gloom of the church, and the pauses of the litanies are filled up by the louder croaking of ravens. For three young ravens are brought up here in the convent in memory of S. Benedict; it seems that the number of this living symbol of the order must always be maintained."—*Gregorovius*.

On one side of the church the story of the Birth of Christ is told, introduced by the figures of the prophets who announced His coming, and the story of His life is continued round the church to the eastern wall, which is occupied by the history of the Crucifixion. Here, angels are represented as catching the streams of blood which flow from the Divine wounds; the soul of Dismas,* the penitent thief, is received by an angel, while that of the bad thief Gesmas is carried off by a black demon.

Beneath the fresco of the Crucifixion, is S. Benedict throned with his principal disciples around him, over a triple arch, with hanging lamps, behind which the bare rock of the cavern is seen. A representation of Benedict writing his Rule in the cave, has the inscription:

> "Hic mons est pinguis, qui multis claruit signis,
> A Domino missus sanctus fuit Benedictus,
> Mansit in hac cripta, fuit hic nova Regula scripta,
> Quisquis amas Christum talem sortire Magistrum."

---

* One of the litanies preserved in Santa Scholastica has the strange invocation—"Sancte Dismas, latro de Cruce. . . ."

From the principal church we enter upon a perfect labyrinth of chapels hewn out of the rock, which frequently forms one of their walls, while the other is completely covered by ancient frescoes. The four chapels hewn in the rock to the right and left of the high altar, are devoted to the story of S. Benedict, together with that of Scholastica, Placidus, Maurus, and other of his followers. The holy water basin was once the sarcophagus of a Roman child, and is decorated with reliefs of birds. The frescoes continue in succession to the second or middle church. A Madonna throned between two angels has the inscription—"Magister Conciolus pinxit hoc opus." *Concioli* is a rare Umbrian master noticed by Vasari, who, however, seems scarcely to have been aware of the power of his works. The most striking frescoes are those of the death and burial of the Virgin: in the latter the Jews who attempted to intercept the funeral procession are represented as stricken with blindness. A picture of the martyrdom of S. Sebastian bears the date 1486.

"Le goût moderne, qui s'attache surtout à l'effet extérieur et à la perfection matérielle, peut aujourd'hui regarder d'un œil dédaigneux ces types étranges mais singulièrement expressifs qui, pendant plusieurs siècles, furent invariablement reproduits par la piété autant que par le génie tout symbolique des premiers peintres chrétiens. Or, bien différent était sur ces questions le jugement des hommes du moyen âge. Animés du sentiment profondément religieux qui avait inspiré les œuvres des artistes, leurs contemporains, ils regardaient ces pieuses représentations avec les yeux de la foi, et n'y cherchaient qu'un nouvel aliment à la ferveur dont leur âme était remplie." — *Alphonse Dantier, Les Monastères Bénédictins.*

In the sacristy are some small pictures by Bellini and the Caracci. Through the chapel on the left of the high altar a series of grotto-chapels are reached. In one of them is a picture by *Giotto* of "gli angeli che fanno festa" over the virtues of S. Benedict in his cave, while devils are tormenting S. Romano and cutting his cord.

It is by a staircase in front of the high altar that we descend to the under church. At the foot of the first flight of steps stands the frescoed figure of Innocent III., who first raised Subiaco into an abbacy, above the charter of 1213, setting forth all the privileges he accorded to the abbey. In the same fresco is represented the Abbot John of Tagliacozzo, under whom (1217—1227) the chronicles of the abbey narrate that many of the paintings were executed.

The passage on the right of this landing has, among many others, a fresco of S. Claridonia, who lived here in a hermitage above the monastery. On her dress is a curious inscription evidently scratched by a chaplain of Æneas Silvius when he was celebrating mass here. Here also is a fresco of Christ seated in judgment—the lily in his hand blossoms on the side of the good. This passage leads to the hermitage occupied by S. Gregory the Great when he visited Subiaco. On the outer wall is a fresco of Gregory writing his commentary on Job. The inner chamber, which is decorated with frescoes of seraphim, contains a portrait of S. Francis, supposed to have been painted during his visit to the Sacro Speco, by the artist then at work upon the chapel. It is in exact accordance with the verbal description which remains of him :—"facie hilaris, vultus benignus, facie utcumque oblonga et protensa, frons plana et parva, nasus æqualis et rectus."

"It is a life-size figure of a youthful monk in a high conical cowl,— the frock and cord of a mendicant friar, inscribed with the words FR. FRACISCU. Partially restored and retouched, the head may still attract attention by its character. Though lean from abstinence, the features are regular, the brow open, the eyes large, and the nose straight. The tonsure is visible across the forehead and along the temples to the ears, which are not remarkable for smallness. A straggling beard and a downy upper lip complete a far more pleasing portrait of Brother Francis, than those which in hundreds, at a later time, were placed in every monastery and convent of the Order. A miniature kneeling figure of a donor at the monk's feet seems to have been added at a later time. It is remarkable that S. Francis is depicted without the Stigmata; and if it be, as is pretended, a genuine portrait, it must have been executed, if not in 1216, at least before 1228, when the monk was canonized, and perhaps by one who had seen and conversed with him. If considered as a work of art, it differs in no wise from other early pictures in the Sacro Speco. Parts of the picture, where the colour had entirely fallen off, have been renewed. The background is all repainted."—*Crowe and Cavalcaselle.*

Another portrait, believed to be from his own hand, represents Brother Oddo, a monk of Subiaco, receiving the blessing of an angel he has invoked. S. Gregory is represented consecrating the altar of the church with the words—" Vere locus iste sanctus est in quo orant." An inscription which commemorates the dedication of the chapel, also mentions the two months' retreat which Gregory IX. made in the monastery:

> Pontificis summi fuit anno picta secundo
> Hæc domus: hic primo quo summo fulsit honore,
> Manserat et vitam cœlestem duxerat idem,
> Perque duos menses sacros maceraverat artus.
> Julius est unus, Augustus fervidus alter.

On the second landing, the figure of Benedict faces us (on a window), with his finger on his lips, imposing silence. On the left is the *coro*, now used by the monks. On the right the cave where Benedict is said to have passed three years in darkness. A statue by *Raggi* (sculptor of the fountain in the Piazza Navona), of the school of Bernini, commemorates his presence here: a basket is a memorial of that lowered with his food by S. Romanus. An ancient bell is shown as that which rang to announce the approach of his daily sustenance.

> "The grotto of Benedict vividly reminded me of the famous grotto of S. Rosalia on the Monte Pellegrino near Palermo. Behind the richly-decorated altar one sees the marble figure of the young Benedict kneeling in prayer before the cross: it is a tolerable work of the Bernini school, and it gains through the half darkness of the cavern. Truly everything here has a dramatic character. The smallness and grace of this little church gleaming with colour, its chapels and grottoes like a spiritual vision, such as I have never found elsewhere in the whole field of religious conception. It is an illustrated picture-book of poetical legends, which are bloodless and painless, though fantastic, like the lives of pious anchorites in the wilderness, and amid the birds of the field. Here Religion treads on the borders of fairy-land, and brings an indescribable atmosphere away from thence."—*Gregorovius.*

As we descend the Santa Scala, trodden by the feet of Benedict, and ascended by the monks upon their knees, the solemn beauty of the place increases at every step. On the right, is a powerful fresco of Death mowing down the young, and sparing the old; on the left, the Preacher shows the young and thoughtless the three states to which the body is reduced after death. Much of the rock is still left bare and hangs overhead in jagged masses, preserving the cavern-like character of the scene, while every available space is rich with colour and gold, radiant, yet perfectly subdued and harmonious. On all sides the saints of the Order, and those especially connected with it, Benedict, Gregory the Great, the Archdeacon Peter, Romanus, Maurus, Placidus, Honoratus, Scholastica, and Anatolia, look down upon us repeatedly from the great thirteenth-century frescoes.

"C'est d'abord l'image du Christ qui ouvre le cycle de ces peintures, en indiquant, dans la livre de sa vie, ce passage dont le texte a été si fidèlement suivi par l'auteur de la regle Bénédictine—*ego sum via, veritas, et vita*. Par un harmonieux rapprochement qui fait honneur à la pensée de l'artiste, de même que le Sauveur y est entouré de ses principaux apôtres, de même Saint Benoît y rassemble auprès de sa personne ses disciples bien-aimés, auxquels il recommande de bénir incessamment le Seigneur, et d'avoir toujours ses louanges sur leurs lèvres :

  Benedicam Dominum in omni tempore :
  Semper laus in ore meo.

En effet, à l'entour figurent Saint Romain, Saint Placide, Saint Maur, et Saint Honorat, occupés à méditer les sages préceptes de leur maître. Puis, on voit Saint Gregoire ayant à ses côtés le diacre Pierre, son confident habituel, et tous deux placés en face du pape Saint Sylvestre et du diacre Saint Laurent. Plus loin sous la dernière travée, apparaissent les images à demi symboliques des quatre évangélistes dont le corps, qui a la forme humaine, est surmonté de la tête de chacun des animaux qui leur sert ordinairement d'emblème distinctif."—*Alphonse Dantier, Les Monastères Bénédictins.*

" Let any young painter or sculptor, thoroughly accomplished in the mechanism of his art, in which these his predecessors were so deficient, but drawing his inspiration from Christianity and the Romano-Teutonic nationality of Europe—let any such young artist, I say, visit Italy so prepared—tossing to the winds the jargon of the schools, content to feel and yield to the impulses of a high, and pure, and holy nature, and disposed, with God's blessing, like Fra Angelico or Perugino, to dedicate his talents, as the bondsman of love, to his Redeemer's glory and the good of mankind—let him so come, and commune with these neglected relics of an earlier, a simpler, and a more believing age—talk to the spirit that dwells within them in its own universal language ; ask it questions, and listen reverently for a reply—and he will gain more than a mere response—that spirit will pass into his own bosom—his eyes will be touched as with the magician's salve, and he will find himself in a world of undreamt-of beauty, hitherto unseen only because inadequately bodied forth ; a world of high spirits, beings of the mind ; ideas as yet only half-born (as it were), but which will throng around him on every side

  'Demanding life, impatient for the skies,'

for that life of immortality which his practised hand can so well bestow.—*Lord Lindsay's Christian Art.*

In the chapel on the left of the Scala Santa, that of S. Lorenzo Loricato, who is buried here, is a picture of the Madonna and Child, shown as one which existed in the time of S. Benedict, and was venerated by him in his childhood. It is signed "Stammatico Greco Pictor P.," a powerful painter of whom we have no account whatever.

Lastly, we reach the Holy of Holies, the second cave, in which S. Gregory narrates that Benedict after his return from Vicovaro (to which he had gone for a short time as abbot) "dwelt alone with himself," being "always busied in the presence of his Creator, in bewailing the spiritual miseries of his soul and past sins, in watching over the emotions of his heart, and in the constant contemplation of Divine things." Here the Devil hovered over him as a little black bird, suggesting sinful thoughts and desires, which he subdued by flinging himself amid the thorns and nettles. Here he received a poisoned loaf from the wicked priest Florentius, and, throwing it on the ground, forced a tame raven on his command to bear it beyond mortal reach. And here he laid down the rule of his order, making its basis the twelve degrees of humility : viz.—

1. Deep compunction of heart, and holy fear of God and His judgments, with a constant attention to walk in the Divine presence, sunk under the weight of this confusion and fear.
2. The perfect renunciation of our own will.
3. Ready obedience.
4. Patience under all sufferings and injuries.
5. The manifestation of all thoughts to a spiritual director.
6. To be content, even rejoice, under all humiliations, to be pleased with mean employments and mean clothes ; in short, to love simplicity and poverty.
7. To esteem ourselves more unworthy and base than all—even the greatest sinners.

8. To avoid all wish for singularity in words and actions.
9. To love and practise silence.
10. To avoid uncurbed mirth and laughter.
11. To seek for modesty of speech and words.
12. To be humble in all external actions.

"Three virtues constituted the sum of the Benedictine discipline. Silence with solitude and seclusion, humility, obedience, which, in the strong language of its laws, extended to impossibilities. All is thus concentrated on self. It was the man isolated from his kind who was to rise to a lonely perfection. All the social, all patriotic, virtues were excluded: the mere mechanic observance of the rules of the brotherhood, or even the corporate spirit, are hardly worthy of notice, though they are the only substitutes for the rejected and proscribed pursuits of active life.

"The three occupations of life were the worship of God, reading, and manual labour. The adventitious advantages, and great they were, of these industrious agricultural settlements, were not contemplated by the founder; the object of the monks was not to make the wilderness blossom with fertility, to extend the arts and husbandry of civilized life into barbarous regions, it was solely to employ in engrossing occupation that portion of time which could not be devoted to worship and study."
—*Milman's Latin Christianity.*

Here an appropriate inscription commemorates the wonderful series of saints, who, issuing from Subiaco, became the founders of the Benedictine Order all over the world.

From the arches below the convent one may emerge upon a small terraced *Garden*, once a ridge covered with a thicket of thorns, upon which S. Benedict used to roll his naked body to extinguish the passions of the flesh. Here, seven centuries afterwards, S. Francis, coming to visit the shrine, knelt and prayed before the thorns which had such glorious memories, and planted two rose-trees beside them. The roses of S. Francis flourish still, and are carefully tended by the monks, but the Benedictine thorns have disappeared.

"Ce jardin, deux fois sanctifié, occupe encore une sorte de plateau triangulaire qui se projette sur le flanc du rocher, un peu en avant et au-dessous de la grotte qui servait de gîte à Benoît. Le regard, confiné de tous côtés par les rochers, n'y peut errer en liberté que sur l'azur du ciel. C'est le dernier des lieux sacrés que l'on visite et que l'on vénère, dans ce célèbre et unique monastère du *Sagro Speco*, qui forme comme une série de sanctuaires superposés les uns aux autres et adossés à la montagne que Benoît a immortalisée. Tel fut le dur et sauvage berceau de l'Ordre monastique en occident. C'est de ce tombeau, où s'était enseveli tout vivant cet enfant délicat des derniers patriciens de Rome, qu'est née la forme définitive de la vie monastique, c'est-à-dire la perfection de la vie chrétienne. De cette caverne et de ce buisson d'épines sont issues ces légions de moines et de saints dont le dévouement a valu à l'Eglise ses conquêtes les plus vastes et ses gloires les plus pures. De cette source a jailli l'intarissable courant du zèle et de la faveur religieuse. Là sont venus, là viendront encore tous ceux à qui l'esprit du grand Benoît inspirera la force d'ouvrir de nouvelles voies ou de restaurer l'antique discipline dans la vie claustrale. Tous y reconnaissent la site sacré que le prophète Isaïe semble avoir montré d'avance aux cénobites par ces paroles d'une application si merveilleusement exacte : *Attendite ad petram de qua excisi estis, et ad cavernam laci de qua præcisi estis.* Il faut plaindre le chrétien qui n'a pas vu cette grotte, ce désert, ce nid d'aigle et de colombe, ou qui, l'ayant vu, ne s'est pas prosterné avec un tendre respect devant le sanctuaire d'où sortirent, avec le règle et l'institut de saint Benoît, la fleur de la civilisation chrétienne, la victoire permanente de l'âme sur la matière, l'affranchissement intellectuel de l'Europe, et tout ce que l'esprit de sacrifice, réglé par la foi, ajoute de grandeur et de charme à la science, au travail, à la vertu "—*Montalembert, Les Moines d'Occident.*

"Caché d'abord au fond d'un antre, oublié des hommes, et connu de Dieu seul, passant les nuits, ou à chanter de saints cantiques, ou à méditer les années éternelles, Benoît ne trouve plus de volupté qu'à crucifier sa chair, et la réduire en servitude ; devenu père d'un peuple de solitaires, il renouvelle en Occident ces prodiges d'austérité, que les déserts de Scéthé et de la Thébaïde avoient admirés ; et sa règle si estimée depuis, ne fut, dit Saint Grégoire, que l'histoire exacte des mœurs du saint Législateur. C'est ainsi que Benoît confond la mollesse du monde. En effet, quand on nous propose ces grands modèles, nous nous récrions sur la puissance de la grâce dans ces hommes extraordinaires : mais nous n'allons pas plus loin ; et parceque nous ne croyons pas que ces modèles de pénitence soient proposés pour être imités, nous

ne les croyons pas même faits pour nous instruire. Mais quel a pu être le dessein de Dieu en suscitant dans tous les siècles, de ces pénitents fameux qui ont édifié l'Eglise? n'est-ce pas de nous faire comprendre de quoi notre faiblesse, soutenue de la grâce, est encore capable? De plus, je vous demande pourquoi ces grands exemples de pénitence nous paroissent-ils si éloignés de nos devoirs et de notre état? Est-ce parce-qu'ils ont vécu dans des siècles fort éloignés des nôtres? mais les devoirs ne changent pas avec les âges. Est-ce parce que les Saints ont été des hommes extraordinaires? mais les Saints ne sont devenus parmi nous des hommes extraordinaires, que parceque la corruption est devenue universelle. Est-ce parceque les mortifications et les saintes austérités ne forment que le caractère particulier de quelques Saints? mais lisez les histoires ; tous ont fait pénitence ; tous ont crucifié leur chair avec leurs desirs ; et partout où vous trouverez des Saints, vous les trouverez pénitents. Nous avons donc beau nous rassurer sur l'exemple commun ; si les Saints l'avoient suivi, ils ne méritoient pas aujourd'hui nos hommages. L'Evangile est fait pour nous comme pour eux ; et comme il n'a rien qui nous ressemble, il n'a rien non plus qui doive nous rassurer."
Massillon, Sermons.

Under the part of the cave which opens upon this garden all the monks are buried, and when corruption has passed away their bones are taken up and placed in an open chapel in the rock, where they are visible to all. To obtain a general view of the convent of the Sacro Speco, it is necessary to follow the lower path which diverges just beyond Santa Scholastica. A succession of zig-zags along the edge of the cliffs, amid savage scenery, leads into the gorge, which is closed in the far distance by the rock-built town of Jenne, the birth-place of Alexander IV. and of the Abbot Lando. We cross the river by a bridge, whence a pathlet, winding often by staircases up and down the rocks, allows one to see the whole building rising above the beautiful falls of the Anio. We emerge close to the ruins of a *Nymphæum* belonging to Nero's Villa, and nothing can be more imposing than the view from hence up the gorge, with the great rock-cresting monastery on the other side, and all the wealth of rich verdure on the nearer steeps, which take the name of *Monte Carpineto* from the hornbeams with which they are covered. The little chapel above the Sacro Speco is that of San Biagio (S. Blaise), who is invoked whenever any catastrophe occurs in the valley. Here, once every year, mass is chaunted by the monks of Santa Scholastica.

Sacro Speco, Subiaco.

The castle, called *La Rocca*, built by the warlike Abbot John V., was long a summer residence of the popes. One of its towers, still called "Borgiana," recalls the residence here of Cardinal Rodrigo Borgia, afterwards Alexander VI. Magnificent views may be obtained from the windows of the rooms, which contain a few good pictures.

The town formerly professed the utmost devotion to the papacy, and the waggon-load of its wild-flowers was one of the most suggestive and attractive of the presents to Pius IX. on his anniversary, sent by "*La sua divotissima Subiaco*," yet now the names of the streets are all changed, and we have the eternal "Via Cavour, Via Venti Settembre, &c." Costumes still linger here, but are less striking than further in the mountains. The men all wear bunches of flowers in their hats on festas, the women wear *spadoni*, ending in a hand, an acorn, or a bunch of flowers in silver. Beyond the Albergo della Pernice (see above), and the gate built in honour of Pius VI., is a curious old bridge with a gate-tower over the Anio. One of the best views of the town is just across this bridge.

The path which is approached by the bridge leads to the beautifully situated *Convent of the Cappuccini*. In its portico is a very quaint fresco of S. Francis, the beloved of animals, "vir vere catholicus totusque apostolicus," shaking hands with a wolf, much to the horror of his attendant monks.* Endless other paths lead up the hills in different directions, through woods by rushing brooks, and along mountain ledges, and indeed the whole of the *Valle Santa*, as the district of Subiaco is popularly called, is well worth exploring.

The road to Tivoli is one of the many benefits which Subiaco owes to its having been so long the residence of Pius VI. It follows, first the *Via Sublacensis*, constructed

---

* This was at Gubbio. A wolf who had long ravaged the surrounding country was rebuked by S. Francis, who promised it a peaceful existence and daily food, if it would amend its ways. The wolf agreed to the compact, and placed his right paw in the hand of S. Francis in token of confidence and good faith. "Brother Wolf," as S. Francis called him, "lived afterwards tamely for two years at Gubbio, in good fellowship with all, and finally died, much regretted, of old age."—From the "*Fioretti di S. Francesco.*"

by Nero, and then the *Via Valeria*, which was the work of the censor Valerius Maximus, in the year of Rome 447. In spring, when it is chiefly visited by foreigners, the country here strikes one as bare, and the chief interest is derived entirely from the villages which crest the hills on either side.

Subiaco.

But in summer, when the chestnut woods are in full leaf, and the luxuriant vines leap from tree to tree along the valleys, the scenery is unspeakably lovely.

"Les montagnes rapprochées forment une suite de vallées étroites et singulièrement accidentées, où, à chaque détour du chemin, le charme saisissant de l'imprévu vous découvre une source toujours nouvelle d'émotions. Sous la voûte épaisse de ces bois, au milieu des gorges profondes de ces montagnes, on croit errer dans les forêts primitives que les anciennes traditions nous représentent pleines de ténèbres, de mystère et d'horreur, et qui couvraient le pays, quand les colons sicules et pélasges vinrent s'y établir long-temps avant la période romaine.

"La silence de ces retraites inhabitées n'est troublé que par le murmure de ruisseaux nombreux qui, roulant sur des pentes rapides, y forment des cascades et se précipitent ensuite dans l'Anio, dont les chutes retentissantes dominent çà et là tous les autres bruits. C'est toujours le même cours d'eau impétueux, aux ondes froides et transparentes—'Frigidas atque perspicuas emanat aquas'—comme le peint Saint Grégoire le grand, en décrivant la contrée montagneuse où le jeune Benoît trouva une solitude si bien appropriée à ses desirs. Aujourd'hui encore la nature vivante n'y décèle sa présence qu'à de rares intervalles. Parfois seulement un troupeau de chèvres à demi sauvages apparaît suspendu sur la crête d'un mamelon recouvert de broussailles. Au vêtement grossier, à la figure étrange du pâtre qui les conduit, il semble qu'on retrouve quelque berger arcadien, descendant des compagnons du bon roi Évandre. Assis sur la pointe du roc d'où il paraît écouter la bruyante harmonie produite par les chutes de l'Anio, ce berger rappelle assez fidèlement celui que Virgile dépeint, dans une attitude semblable ;

'. . . . . stupet inscius alto
Accipiens sonitum saxi de vertice pastor.'
Æn. ii. 307.

pretant l'oreille aux bruits sinistres qui s'élèvent d'une campagne dévastée par l'inondation d'un torrent."—*Alphonse Dantier.*

A continuous avenue of mountain villages lines the way. First we have, on the right *Cerbara*, and on the left *Rocca di Canterano*, its long lines of old houses cresting the declivity. Then, on the right we have *Agosta*, and on the left *Marano*. A road on the right now turns off to the Lago Fucino, and, only two miles distant, we see *Arsoli*, the ancient Arsula, containing the handsome, still inhabited castle of Prince Massimo. Here the apartment once occupied by S. Filippo Neri, founder of the Oratorians, is preserved with religious care. Though he frequently staid with the Massimo family, he lived here almost as a hermit, eating only bread, with a few olives, herbs, or an apple, drinking only water, and lying on the bare floor. There is a small *Picture Gallery* at Arsoli, but it is almost always locked up.

Passing under *Roviano*, which has a castle of the Sciarras, we reach a more fertile country, where the men train the vines, with bunches of great blue iris fastened in their hats, and on the right we see *Cantelupo*, where the Marchese del Gallo, who married a daughter of Prince Lucien Buonaparte, has a château, in which he spends the summer. Here a number of shrines, surrounding a little green with some old ilex-trees, announce the approach to *San Cosimato*, the village of hermitages, mentioned in a bull of Gregory VII. as " Monasterium Sancti Cosimatis situm in valle Tiburtina." No one would imagine, from merely passing along the road, that this is one of the most curious places in the country, well deserving of attention and study. But in the earliest ages of Latin Christianity the caverns in the cliffs which here abruptly overhang the river, had been taken possession of by a troop of hermits, who turned this country, for they had many caverns at Vicovaro also, into a perfect Thebaid. Passing through the convent, and its pretty garden full of pillared pergolas (ladies are not admitted), a winding path, the merest ledge, often a narrow stair against the face of the precipice, often caverned over or tunnelled through the rock, leads to this extraordinary settlement, and opens upon one tiny hermitage after another, provided with its little window and its rock-hewn couch and seat. A campanile remains on a projecting crag, which summoned the recluses to prayer. The last cave, larger than any of the others, was their chapel, formed of living rock. Mass is still occasionally said here, and the scene is most striking, as, to admit the light, large doors just opposite the altar, and only a few feet distant, are thrown open, and one looks down the perpendicular cliff overhung with ilexes centuries old, into the

Anio immediately beneath, and the roar of its waters mingles with the chaunting of the Psalms. In the fifth century a

At S. Cosimato.

collection of monks had united on the heights above the river, and, before he had founded his own convent, attracted by the fame of his sanctity, they chose S. Benedict as their superior. He declined at first, warning them that they would not like the severity of his rule, but they insisted and he joined them here. In a short time his austerity roused their hatred, and they attempted to poison him in the Sacrament cup, but when, before drinking, he made the sign of the cross over it, it fell to pieces in his hands. "God forgive you, my brethren," he said, "you see that I spoke the truth when I told you that your rule and mine would not agree," and he returned to Subiaco. The scene of this story is a caverned chapel in the cliff on the other side of the convent, adorned with rude frescoes. Here women are permitted to enter.

Two miles beyond San Cosimato is Vicovaro. The rest of the road to Tivoli is described in chapter xiii.

END OF VOL. I.

INDEX.

A.

Acque Salvie, ii. 290
Acuto, i. 267
Ad Medias, Roman station of, ii. 249
Æsula, i. 190
Agosta, i. 320
Agylla, ii. 304
Alatri, i. 251 ; ii. 10
Alba Fucinensis, ii. 183
Alba Longa, site of, i. 73
Alban Lake, i. 67
Alban Mount, distant view of, i. 51 ; summit of, i. 85
Albano, i. 59—80
Albula, river, i. 185
Aldobrandini, family of—their villa at Frascati, i. 104
Alexander III., Pope—his consecration at Ninfa, i. 236
Allia, the river, i. 175, 181
Altieri, family of — their villa at Oriolo, i. 152
Aluminiera, ii. 311
Amasena, the river, ii. 10, 249, 259
Amatrice, ii. 161
Amelia, ii. 139
Amiternum, ii. 161
Amphitheatre of Albano, i. 66
                Albai Fucensis, ii. 184
                Sutr, ii. 68
                Tusculum, i. 107
Ampiglione, i. 207
Anagni, i. 259—267
Angelico, Fra, his frescoes at Orvieto, ii. 128
Angitia, ii. 189
Anguillara, i. 152
Anio, river, i. 185 ; falls of, at Tivoli, i. 194, 196 ; at Subiaco, i. 316

Anio Novus, Aqueduct of, at Tivoli, i. 204
Ansedonia, ii. 345
Antinum, ii. 191
Antium, ii. 268
Antrodoco, ii. 163
Antemnæ, i. 167
Anxur, ii. 251
Appii Forum, ii. 248
Appiola, i. 55
Aquæ Albulæ, i. 186
Aqua Bollicante, i. 154
Aquæ Cutiliæ, ii. 162
Aqua Ferentina, ii. 290
Aqueduct of the Anio Novus, i. 281
           Aqua Claudia, i. 52, 97, 281
           Aqua Marcia, i. 295
           Aqua Vergine, i. 162
           Della Torre at Spoleto, ii. 146
           Paoline, i. 97
Aquataccia, the, ii. 290
Aquila, ii. 163—169
Aquino, ii. 234—241
Arca, i. 259
Arce, ii. 202
Arco di Pino, i. 140
Ardea, ii. 276
Ariccia, i. 62
Arnara, i. 259
Arnolfo, tomb of Cardinal de Braye by, ii. 133
Arpino, ii. 198
Arpino, Il Cavaliere d' — picture at Trisulti by, ii. 18 ; birthplace of, ii. 200
Arrone, rivulet, i. 144
Arsoli, i. 320
Artena, ii. 268
Aspra, ii. 25

INDEX.

Astura, ii. 27
Atina, ii. 203
Augustus, bridge of — at Narni, ii. 136
Avezzano, ii. 183

B.

Baccano, i. 141
Bagnaja, ii. 89
Bagni di Paterno, ii. 162
Bagnorea, ii. 116
Balbi of Alatri, works of, ii. 18
Balzorano, ii. 192
Barberini, Cardinal, i. 127; the family Dukes of Segni, i. 242; their palace at Palestrina, i. 275; their residence at, i. 281
Bardella, i. 209
Basilica of S. Alessandro, i. 178
Bassano, Francesco and Leandro,— frescoes by, ii. 229
Bernini, Chigi Palace at Ariccia by, i. 63
Bertaldo, tower of, ii. 314
Bieda, ii. 97—100
Bisentina, island of, ii. 10
Blera, ii. 97
Bomanzo, ii. 107
Boniface VIII., the story of, i. 263— 265; his persecution of the Colonna family, i. 272; his treatment of Cœlestine V., ii. 7
Borghese, property of,—at Frascati, i. 116; at Cervaretto, i. 162; at Palombara, i. 179; at Porto d'Anzio, ii. 267; at Pratica, i. 282; at Rocca Priora, i. 168
Borghetto, on the Alban hills, i. 99
    in the Sabina, ii. 33
Borgia, Cæsar,—his siege of Isola Farnese, i. 132
Borgo Velino, ii. 163
Bovillæ, i. 55
Bracciano, i. 146
Bramante, La Quercia built by, ii. 88
Braschi, family of,—Villa Adriana the property of, road constructed by, i. 190; villa at Tivoli of, i. 204
Brigands in the Campagna, i. 35; their attack on the family of Lucien Buonaparte, i. 105; their encouragement by the Sardinian Government, ii. 36
Bruno, Bishop, his statue at Segni, his history, i. 245, 246

Bulicame, the,—baths of, ii. 93
Buonaparte, family of,—their property at Frascati, i. 105; at Musignano, ii. 334; their connexion with Canino, ii. 334; their burial-place at Corneto, ii. 317
Buonaventura, S.,—birth-place of, ii. 116
Buon Ricovero, farm of, 131

C.

Cære, ii. 304
Camaldoli, convent of the, on the Alban hills, i. 113
Camindoli, ii. 181
Campagna, the, — its geographical limits, i. 11, 12; characteristics of the, i. 19, 32; effect of the, i. 98; lost cities of the, i. 144; in the direction of Ostia, ii. 292; views over, i. 131
Campagnano, i. 141
Campiglia, hill of, ii. 353
Campo Bufalaro, ii. 287
    di Annibale, i. 84
    Morto, i. 40; ii. 245
Canino, ii. 334
Cantalupo, i. 320
Canterano, i. 320
Capistrello, ii. 191
Capranica, ii. 104
Caprarola, ii. 65—73
Carciano, a suburb of Tivoli, i. 206
Carsoli, ii. 186
Cartiera, the,—of Isola, ii. 198
Casale dei Pazzi, i. 178
Casamari, ii. 8—10
Casa Nuova, i. 179
Castel d'Asso, ii. 89—94
    Fusano, i. 47—49
    Gandolfo, i. 72
    Giubeleo, i. 173
    Madama, i. 207
    dell' Osa, i. 160, 164
    Porciano, ii. 287
    di Sangro, ii. 178
Castiglione, tower of, i. 157
Castle of—
    Anguillara, i. 152
    Antrodoco, ii. 163
    Aquila, ii. 169
    Ardea, ii. 277
    Arsoli, i. 320
    Avezzano, ii. 183
    Borgetto, near Frascati, i. 99

Castle of—*continued.*
  Borghetto, in the Sabina, ii. 33
  Bracciano, i. 147
  Cantelupo, i. 32
  Castel di Sangro, ii. 178
  Castel Fusano, i. 47
  Celano, ii. 181
  Ceprano, ii. 205
  'Civita Castellana, ii. 35
  Galera, i. 146
  Isola, ii. 202
  Montalto, ii. 329
  Nemi, i. 88
  Nepi, ii. 58
  Olevano, i. 291
  Ortucchio, ii. 190
  Orvieto, ii. 134
  Ostia, i. 42
  Palestrina, i. 280
  Passerano, i. 206
  Petrella, ii. 162
  Popoli, ii. 169
  Populonia, ii. 351
  Pratica, ii. 283
  Rocca Janula, ii. 208
  Ronciglione, ii. 64
  Roviano, i. 320
  Savelli, at Albano, i. 79
  Segni, i. 242
  Sermoneta, ii. 246
  S. Severa, ii. 312
  Spoleto, ii. 146
  Subiaco, i. 320
  Tivoli, i. 194
  Viterbo, ii. 79
Castro, ii. 338
Castro Vetere, i. 194
Castrum Novum, Roman station of, ii. 313
Cathedral of—
  Alatri, i. 253
  Albano, i. 78
  Anagni, i. 261—267
  Bieda, ii. 97
  Civita Castellana, ii. 36
  Corneto, ii. 315
  Ferentino, i. 256
  Frascati, i. 99, 100
  Massa, ii. 35
  Narni, ii. 139
  Orvieto, ii. 120
  Ostia, i. 43
  Palestrina, i. 275
  Pontecorvo, ii. 242
  Porto, ii. 298
  Ronciglione, ii. 64

Cathedral of—*continued.*
  Segni, i. 245
  Spoleto, ii. 147
  Sutri, ii. 64
  Terni, ii. 140
  Terracina, ii. 252
  Tivoli, i. 202
  Todi, ii. 143
  Toscanella, ii. 336
  Valmontone, i. 269
  Velletri, i. 223
Cavaliere, ii. 186
Cavamonte, i. 160
Cavi, i. 283
Ceccano, ii. 205
Celano, ii. 181.
  Lago di, ii. 186
Centumcellæ, ii. 313
Ceprano, ii. 205
Cerbara, near Subiaco, i. 320
Ceri Nuovo, ii. 311
Cervara, caves and tower of, i. 162; festa of, i. 163
Cervaretto, i. 154, 162
Cervetri, ii. 302—311
Cesarini, family of the,—their property at Genzano, i. 90; at Ardea, ii. 277.
Chiarriccia, ii. 313
Chigi, family of,—their palace at Castel Fusano, i. 47; at Arriccia, i. 63.
Ciampino, i. 98
Ciminian Hills, ii. 59—74
Cioccari, the, i. 287
Circean Mount, ii. 253
Circeii, town of, ii. 255
Cisterna, ii. 244
Citadel of Tusculum, i. 109
  Veii, i. 136
Civita Castellana, ii. 33—39
  d'Antino, ii. 191
  Ducale, ii. 162
  Lavinia, i. 93
  la Penna d'Oro, i. 231
  di Roveto, ii. 191
  Vecchia, ii. 313
Civitella, i. 291
Claudian Aqueduct, near Tivoli, i. 206, 207
Collatia, i. 164
Collemaggio, La, ii. 166
Collepardo, village of, ii. 13; Grotto of, ii. 19
Collicelli, ii. 161
Colonelle, Lago della, i. 186

INDEX. 327

Colonia, ii. 350
Colonna, i. 119
Colonna, family of,—at Marino, i. 130; at Galera, i. 145; at Colonna, i. 118; at Olevano, i. 291; their Pope, i. 288; at Cavi, i. 282; at Paliano, i. 288; at Palestrina, i. 272—280
Colonna, Vittoria, her residence at Viterbo, ii. 85.
Columbarium of Veii, i. 134
Concioli, frescoes at Subiaco by, i. 308
Convent of—
    Acuto, i. 267
    Buon Pastore, near Cavamonte, i. 160
    Camaldoli, i. 113
    Cappuccini, at Albano, i. 65
    Cappuccini, at Frascati, i. 105
    Cappuccini, at Subiaco, i. 318
    Cappuccini, at Velletri, i. 224
    Casamari, i. 8
    Fossanuova, ii. 255
    Gesuiti, at Velletri, i. 225
    Grotta Ferrata, i. 126
    Il Retiro, on Monte Argentaro, ii. 347
    La Madonna del Sorbo, i. 143
    La Quercia, ii. 88
    Monte Cassino, ii. 208
    Passionists, on Monte Cavo, i. 85
    S. Casciano at Narni, ii. 137
    S. Elia, ii. 56
    S. Pietro Celestino, ii. 176
    Sacro Speco, i. 306
    S. Scholastica, i. 303
    S. Silvestro, near Monte Compatri, i. 121
        on Mount Soracte, ii. 48
    Trisulti, ii. 19
Consular Tomb at Palazzuola, i. 82
Conti, family of,—their possessions at Segni, i. 242; their fortress at Monte Fortino, i. 268
Corchiano, ii. 54
Corcolo, i. 161
Corese, i. 180
Corfinium, ii. 179
Corioli, i. 95
Corneto, ii. 315—327
Cornufelle, Lake of, i. 116
Cosa, ii. 345
Cosmati, the family of,—the Gaetani tomb at Anagni by, i. 266;
mosaics at Subiaco by, i. 304; at Civita Castellana by, ii. 34
Crimera, the river, i. 133, 175
Crustumerium, i. 182
Cyclopean walls of—
    Alatri, i. 251—253
    Amelia, ii. 139
    Arpino, ii. 200
    Atina, ii. 203
    Cori, i. 228
    Cosa, ii. 345
    Ferentino, i. 256
    Norba, i. 231
    Palestrina, i. 280
    Pyrgi, ii. 313
    Segni, i. 243

D.

Dennis, his work on Etruria, i. 17
Digentia, the brook, i. 209
Diligence travelling, i. 34
Domenichino, his frescoes at Grotta Ferrata, i. 127
Doria Pamphili, family of, — their property at Valmontone, i. 269
Dragoncello, ii. 291

E.

Egeria, fountain of, near Nemi, i. 89
Emissarium of the Alban Lake, i. 69
    of the Lago Fucino, ii. 188
Empulum, i. 207
Eretum, i. 181
Expenses, of living, in the Roman castelli, i. 28

F.

Fajola, La, i. 87
Falacrino, ii. 161
Falacrinum, ii. 141
Falerium Novum, ii. 42
Falerium Vetus, ii. 36
Falleri, ii. 40—42
Fara, ii. 25
Farfa, ii. 21—31
Farnese, ii. 338
Farnese, Cardinal Odoardo, chapel of Grotta Ferrata built by, i. 127
Farnese, family of,—their palace at Caprarola, ii. 68

Ferentino, station of, i. 250 ; town of, i. 255—257
Ferentinum, ii. 105
Ferento, ii. 105
Feriæ Latinæ, i. 85
Feronia, the fountain of, ii. 250
Fescennium, ii. 55
Festa degli Artisti, i. 163
Fiano, ii. 54
Ficulea, i. 179
Fiora, the river, ii. 329
Fiume Conca, ii. 273
Fiume Rapido, ii. 207
Fiumicino, ii. 301
Fons Blandusiæ, i. 216
Fossanuova, ii. 257
Fosso de' due Fossi, i. 133, 144
   dell' Incastro, ii. 278
Frangipani, the, — their castle at Olevano, i. 291 ; their betrayal of Conradin at Astura, ii. 271
Frascati, i. 99—107
Fregellæ, ii. 301
Frosinone, ii. 21
Fucino, Lago di, ii. 186
Fumone, i. 254 ; ii. 7.

G.

Gaetani, family of,—property of, at Ninfa, i. 236 ; history and memorials of, at Anagni, i. 260, 266 ; palace of, at Cisterna, ii. 244 ; property of, at Sermoneta, ii. 246 ; property of, at Monte Circello, ii. 254 ; castle of, at Astura, ii. 272
Galera, i. 144
Galleria, di Sopra, Albano, i. 69
   di Sotto, Albano, i. 75
Gallese, ii. 54
Gallicano, i. 160
Gallo, Marchese del, castle of, i. 209
Gasperoni, his imprisonment at Civita Castellana, ii. 36
Gell, Sir William, his work on Roman Topography, i. 17
Genazzano, i. 283
Genzano, i. 89
Gonsalvi, death of Cardinal, i. 129
Gran Sasso d' Italia, ii. 163
Graviscæ, ii. 328
Grazioli, Duke of, i. 164
Greco, Stammatico, picture at Subiaco by, i. 313
Gregorovius, works of, i. 17
Grosseto, ii. 349

Grotta della Maga, ii. 250
   Ferrata, i. 123
   Marozza, i. 181
Guadagnolo, i. 291

H.

Hadrian, his villa near Palestrina, i. 277 ; his villa near Tivoli, i. 188
Handbooks, the best on the neighbourhood of Rome, i. 18
Hermitage of Pietro Murrone, ii. 173
Horace, farm of, i. 210—218

I.

Ibi, Sinibaldo, picture at Orvieto by, ii. 133
Il Toraccio, ii. 273
Incile, ii. 188
Infiorata, festival of the, i. 91
Interamna, ii. 140
Ischia, ii. 338
Isernia, ii. 179
Isola, ii. 202
Isola Farnese, i. 132
Isola Sacra, ii. 299
Isole Natanti, Lago dei, i 186

J.

Jenne, i. 316
Joanopolis, i. 39

L.

Labicum, i. 119
Lacordaire, the profession of, ii. 89
Lacus Sabatinus, i. 152
La Civita, i. 268
La Fallonica, ii. 351
La Maiella, ii. 163, 170
La Mercareccia, ii. 327
La Quercia, ii. 88
La Solfatara, ii. 280
La Storta, i. 132, 143
La Vaccareccia, i. 140
Lago di Albano, i. 67
   Bolsena, ii. 100
   Bracciano, i. 147
   Caldano, ii. 350
   Caprolace, ii. 273
   Castiglione, ii. 353
   Celano, ii. 186
   Cornufelle, i. 116

INDEX.

Lago di—*continued.*
    Fogliano, ii. 273
    Fucino, ii. 181, 186
    Gabii, i. 157
    La Posta, ii. 203
    Lago Morto, i. 146
    Mezzano, ii. 339
    Nemi, i. 88
    Paolo, ii. 256
    Pié di Lugo, ii. 143
    Regillus, i. 116
    Scanno, ii. 177
Lancellotti, family of,—their villa at Frascati, i. 105; their palace at Velletri, i. 221
Lante, family of,—their villa at Bagnaja, ii. 89
Lautulæ, pass of, ii. 253
Lavinium, ii. 281
Le Caldane, ii. 353
Le Casacce del Bacuco, ii. 105
Le Frattocchie, i. 53
Le Molette, the river, i. 185
Le Vene, ii. 153
Licenza, the, i. 209
    village of, i. 211
Ligorio, Pirro, the architect of the Villa d' Este, i. 203
Lionessa, ii. 160
Lippi, Filippo, tomb of, ii. 147
Liris, falls of the, ii. 202
Lo Schioppo, ii. 191
Lo Spagna, his frescoes at Todi, ii. 143; at Spoleto, ii. 147, 149, 150; at S. Giacomo, ii. 151; at Trevi, ii. 156
Lomentana, Ponte, i. 178
Loreto, ii. 241
Luco, ii. 189
Lucus Ferentinæ, i. 130
Lunghezza, i. 164

M.

Maccarese, ii. 301
Madonna del Tufo, shrine of, i. 82
Madonna di Buon Consiglio, shrine of, i. 283
Maglian Sabina, ii. 33
Magliano, ii. 347
Magliano, river, i. 185
Malaria, the, i. 26, 145
Mandela, i. 209
Marcian Aqueduct, near Tivoli, i. 206

Marcigliana Vecchia, the site of Crustumerium at, i. 182
Marco da Siena, frescoes at Monte Cassino by, ii. 229
Marino, i. 130
Marrana, river, i. 185
Marsica, the, ii. 182
Marta, the river, ii. 328
Martana, island of, ii. 100
Massa, ii. 356
Massimi, family castle at Arsoli, i. 320; dukes of Rignano, ii. 52
Matthias, Maria de, i. 267
Mazzaroppi, Marco, — frescoes at Monte Cassino by, ii. 228
Medullia, Latin city of, i. 178
Memmi, Luca, his picture at Orvieto, ii. 127
Mengs, Raphael, picture at Sulmona by, ii. 136
Mentana, i. 179
Mentorella, i. 292, 295
Mesa, ii. 248
Mignone, river, ii. 314
Minio, river, ii. 314
Miollis, General, his works at Tivoli, i. 195
Monica, S., her death at Ostia, i 45
Mons Lucretilis, i. 209
    Sacer, i. 178
Montalto, ii. 329
Monte Affliano, i. 190
    Algido, i. 118
    Argentaro, ii. 347
    di Canino, ii. 334
    Carpineto, i. 317
    Cassino, i. 208—230
    Catillo, i. 198, 203
    Circello, ii. 253
    Compatri, i. 118
    di Decima, ii. 291
    Due Torre, i. 95
    Fortino, i. 268
    Gennaro, i. 218
    Gentile, i. 179
    Giove, i. 95
    di Grano, i. 97
    Libretti, i. 209
    Luco, ii. 150
    Migliore, ii. 284
    Musino, i. 140
    Peschiavatore, i. 198
    Porzio, i. 117, 121
    Rotondo, i. 181
    Salviano, ii. 191
    Somma, ii. 145

Montefiascone, ii. 107—110
Monterozzi, the,—of Corneto, ii. 317
Montes Corniculani, i. 178, 186, 219
Montopoli, ii. 25
Morolo, i. 259
Musignano, ii. 334

N.

Nar, the river, ii. 136
Narni, ii. 136—139
Nemi, i. 88
Nepi, ii. 58, 59
Nepete, ii. 58
Nequinum, ii. 136
Nero, his death, i. 170—173 ; his residence at Subiaco, i. 294
Nero's Tomb, i. 131
Nettuno, ii. 268
Ninfa, i. 235—240
Nomentana, Ponte, Torre, i. 178
Nomentum, i. 180
Norba, i. 231
Norcia, in the Abruzzi, ii. 160
Norchia, ii. 95—104
Norma, i. 233
Novels, about Rome and its surroundings, i. 17

P.

Palace (Palazzo)—
  Barberini, at Palestrina, i. 275
  Bruschi, at Corneto, ii. 315
  of Castel Gandolfo, i. 73
  Cesarini, at Genzano, i. 90
  Cisterna, ii. 244
  Chigi, at Ariccia, i. 63
    at Viterbo, ii. 85
  Doria, at Valmontone, i. 219
  of Musignano, ii. 334
  of Theodoric (ruined), at Terracina, ii. 253
  Vincentini, at Rieti, ii. 160
  Vitelleschi, at Corneto, ii. 315
Palazzuola, i. 82
Palestrina, i. 269—281
Paliano, i. 288
Palo, ii. 302
Palombara, i. 178
Pan di Neve, i. 84
Pandataria, island of, i. 227
Panetella di S. Nicolo, i. 150
Papal Palace, Anagni, i. 260
    Castel Gandolfo, i. 72

Papal Palace, Orvieto, ii. 120
    Subiaco, i. 317
    Viterbo, ii. 77
Papignia, i. 97 ; ii. 141
Papigno, ii. 158
Parco dei Barberini, i. 122
    Chigi, i. 64
    Colonna, i. 131
Passerano, i. 206
Patrica, i. 259
Pedum, i. 160
Pelasgic Remains, i. 22
Pentima, i. 179
Pescina, ii. 190
Petrella, ii. 162
Pie de Lugo, ii. 143
Pifferari, the exile from Rome of the, i. 14
Pino, rivulet, i. 133
Piombino, ii. 350
Piperno, ii. 257
Pitigliano, ii. 339
Plautii, tomb of the, i. 187
Poggio Catino, ii. 25
    Mirteto, ii. 25
    Reale, i. 136
Polo, i. 218
Pompeo, ii. 25
Ponte dell' Abbadia, ii. 330
    dell' Acquoria, i. 200
    S. Antonio, i. 281
    alla Catena, i. 230
    dell Isola, i. 134
    Lucano, i. 187
    Mammolo, i. 184
    Nomentana, i. 178
    Nona, i. 155
    Salara, i. 168
    Sodo, i. 134
Pontecorvo, ii. 241
Pontine Marshes, ii. 247—250
Ponza, island of, i. 226
Popoli, ii. 170
Populonia, ii. 351
Porcigliano, ii. 287
Portella, frontier gateway of, ii. 253
Porto, ii. 296—299
Porto d'Anzio, ii. 263—267
    d'Ercole, ii. 347
    Falese, ii. 350
    di Paolo, ii 256
    di Troja, ii. 350
Posi, i. 259
Pozzo di Santulla, ii. 13
Pratica, ii. 281
Prato Rotondo, i. 169

INDEX. 331

Precious Blood, the Order of the, i. 267
Privernum, ii. 257
Punicum, Roman station of, ii. 313
Puntone del Castrato, ii. 313
Pyrgi, ii. 313

Q.

Querquetula, i. 161
Quintiliolo, i. 198

R.

Rapinium, Roman station of, ii. 314
Regillus, Lake of, i. 116
Rieti, ii. 158
Rignano, ii. 52
Rio Torto, ii. 279
Ripoli, i. 190
Rocca di Cavi, i. 291
    Circea, ii. 254
    Giovane, i. 209
    Gorga, i. 259
    Janula, ii. 208
    Massima, i. 226
    di Mezzo, ii. 181
    di Papa, i. 82
    Priora, i. 118
Ronciglione, ii. 64
Rosa S., di Viterbo, ii. 83
Rospigliosi, family of,—their property at Colonna, i. 119; at Zagarola, their title, i. 161
Roviano, i. 320
Ruspoli, family of,—their property at Cervetri, their title, ii. 304
Russelæ, ii. 349
Rustica, i. 163

S.

Sacro Speco, monastery of the, i. 306
Salt Mines, near Ostia, i. 41
S. Agostino, tower of, ii. 314
    Angelo in Cappoccia, i. 178, 186, 219
    Appetite, ii. 181
    Bartolomeo, i. 127
    Benedetto, ii. 190
    Clementino, ii. 329
    Cosimato, i. 320
    Domenico Abáte, ii. 194
    Elia, ii. 56
    Felice, ii. 253
    Felice, island of, i. 226
    Germano, ii. 206
    Giacomo, ii. 151
    Giorgio, the family of,—at Bieda, ii. 99
    Giovanni, Lago di, i. 186
    Giulianello, i. 226
    Maria in Forcassi, ii. 95
    Maria della villa, i. 277
    Marinella, ii. 313
    Oreste, ii. 44
    Pietro, i. 280
    Procula, ii. 279
    Severa, ii. 312
    Vito, i. 290
    Vittorino, ii. 161
Saturnia, ii. 341
Saturnian Cities, the five, i. 259
Savelli, castle of the, i. 99; their fortress at Palombara, i. 178
Scalza, Ippolito,—his works at Orvieto, ii. 125, 132
Scaptia, i. 161
Schizzanello, ii. 284
Scholastica, Convent of, at Subiaco, i. 301—305; grave of, at Monte Cassino, ii. 229
Sciarra, family of, their castle at Roviano, i. 320
Scrofano, i. 141
Scurgola, i. 259; ii. 184
Segni, i. 241—247
Sermoneta, ii. 245—247
Setia, ii. 256
Sette Basse, i. 97
    Vene, i. 142
Sezza, ii 256
Sforza-Cesarini, family of,—gardens and villa of, at Genzano, i. 90; possessions of, at Segni, i. 242
Signorelli, Luca, his works at Orvieto, ii. 127—137.
Silva Laurentina, the, ii. 275
Simbriviæ Aquæ, i. 294
Simone, church at Vicovaro built by, i. 205; his death, i. 207
Solfatara, the, near Ardea, ii. 280; near Tivoli, i. 181
Sonnino, ii. 260, 261
Sora, ii. 192
Soracte, ii. 42—52
Sorano, ii. 339
Soriano, ii. 54
Sovana, ii. 339
Spaccato, i. 190
Spina Cristi, the, i. 250

Spoleto, ii. 145—151
Stagno, the, of Ostia, i. 41, 47
Storta, rivulet, i. 133
Strada del Diavolo, i. 53
Stretti di S. Luigi, ii. 178
Strozzi, the,—their property at Lunghezza, i. 164
Subiaco, i. 294—318
Sugareto, the, ii. 280
Sulmona, ii. 171—177
Superstitions of the Campagna, i. 30
Supino, i. 259
Sutri, ii. 59—64

T.

Tarquinii, ii. 315
Tartari, Lago dei, i. 186
Telamone, ii. 349
Temple of—
  Castor and Pollux, at Cori, i. 229
  the Clitumnus, ii. 153
  Equestrian Fortune, at Porto d' Anzio, ii. 262
  Esculapius, at Porto d' Anzio, ii. 264
  Fortune, at Palestrina, i. 271
  Hercules, at Tivoli, i. 200, 202
  Juno, at Civita Lavinia, i. 95
  Juno, at Gabii, i. 156
  Jupiter Latiaris, on the Alban Mount, i. 86
  Leucothea, at Pyrgi, ii. 313
  Minerva, at Cori, i. 229
  the Sibyl, at Tivoli, i. 194
  the Sun, on the Circean Mount, ii. 254
  Tiburtus, at Tivoli, i. 195
  Tosse, at Tivoli, i. 200
  Vacuna, at Rocca Giovane, i. 209
Temple Tombs at Norchia, ii. 103
Terni, ii. 140
Terracina, ii. 250—253
Testament, the, at Ferentino, i. 258
Teverone, the river, i. 185
Theatre—
  of Civita Lavinia, i. 95
  of Gabii, i. 157
  of Tusculum, i. 107
Tiber, the river described, ii. 288—290
Tibur, history of, i. 190—192
Timone, river, ii. 333
Todi, ii. 143
Toleria, i. 268
Tolfa, ii. 311
Tomb of—
  Aruns, i. 59
  the Buonapartes at Frascati, i. 105
  C. Mænius Bassus near Tivoli, i. 207
  Cardinal Altieri at Albano, i. 78
  Cardinal de Braye at Orvieto, ii. 133
  Charles Edward at Frascati, i. 99
  Consular, at Palazzuola, i. 82
  P. V. Marianus, i. 131
  Pompey, at Albano, i. 56
Torano, ii. 162
Torfea, ii. 25
Torlonia, family of,—at Frascati, i. 103; at Bracciano, i. 149; at Gabii, i. 151; at Musignano, ii. 334.
Torre (tower)—
  della Bella Marsilia, ii. 349
  Cervaro, i. 163
  Flavia, ii. 312
  Lupara, i. 179
  Nuova, ii. 97
  Paterno, ii. 284
  Salara, i. 169
  Sapienza, i. 155, 162
  degli Schiavi, i. 154
  Tre Teste, i. 155, 162
Toscanella, ii. 335—338
Trasacco, ii. 190
Trevignano, i. 152
Tribucci, ii. 26
Trisulti, ii. 15—19
Tuder, ii. 144
Turchina, hill of, ii. 317, 326
Tusculum, i. 107
Tutia, river, i. 185, 186

V.

Val del Paradiso, i. 219
Valentano, ii. 338
Vallericcia, i. 60
Valle Santa, i. 318
Valmontone, i. 268
Veii, i. 133—141
Velino, the river, ii. 140
Velletri, i. 220—225
Venafro, ii. 179
Veroli, ii. 10
Vespasian, the Emperor,—born at

INDEX.

Amiternum, ii. 161 ; died at Aquæ Cutiliæ, ii. 162
Vetralla, ii. 94
Vetulonia, ii. 348
Via Appia Nova, i. 52
   Appia Vecchia, i. 53
   Ardeatina, ii. 280
   Aurelia, ii. 313, 348
   Cassia, i. 181
   Collatina, i. 164
   Constantina, i. 201
   Ficulea, i. 179
   Flaminia, ii. 135
   Gabina, i. 154
   Labicana, i. 121
   Latina, i. 52
   Laurentina, ii. 285, 287
   Nomentana, 177, 181
   Prænestina, i. 154, 160
   Salara, i. 177, 181
   Severiana, i. 48
   Sublacensis, i. 318
   Valeria, ii. 186, 318 .
Vicarello, i. 159
Vicovaro, i. 207
Vignanello, ii. 54
Vignola, his work at Caprarola, ii. 69 ; at Bagnaja, ii. 89 ; at Rieti, ii. 159
Villa Adriana, i. 188—190
   Aldobrandini, at Frascati, i. 103
   Altieri, at Albano, i. 76
   Altieri, at Oriolo, i. 152
   of Attilius Regulus, i. 97
   Barberini, at Albano, i. 71
   Braschi, at Tivoli, i. 204
   of Cato the Younger, i. 117
   of Catullus, at Tivoli, i. 205
   of Cicero, at Frascati, i. 106
   Villa Doria, at Albano, i. 79
   D'Este, at Tivoli, i. 203
   Falconieri, at Frascati, i. 105
   of the Gens Cassia, at Tivoli, i. 206.
   Imperial, of the Sette Basse, i. 97
   Lante, at Bagnaja, ii. 89
   of Mæcenas, at Tivoli, i. 199
   Mondragone, at Frascati, i. 115
   of Nero, at Porto d'Anzio, ii. 264
   Pallavicini, at Frascati, i. 103
   of Phaon, i. 169
   Rufinella, at Frascati, i. 105
   Savorelli, at Sutri, ii. 63
   Sora, at Frascati, i. 114
   Taverna, at Frascati, i. 114
   Torlonia, at Frascati, i. 103
   of Vopiscus, at Tivoli, i. 197
Vitalian, S., his statue at Segni, i. 245
Viterbo, ii. 75—87
Viterbo, Lorenzo di, frescoes by, ii. 81
Vitorchiano, ii. 105
Volci, ii. 329—333

U.

Ufente, the river, ii. 249
Ulmanus, the, i. 185

Z.

Zagarola, i. 161
Zuccheri, the,—their works at Caprarola, ii. 71 ; at Bagnaja, ii. 90

By the same Author.

I.
CITIES OF NORTHERN AND CENTRAL ITALY.

Intended as a Companion to all those parts of Italy which lie between the Alps and the Districts described in "Days near Rome."

With numerous Illustrations.

Two Vols., Crown 8vo.

[*In the Press.*

II.
WALKS IN ROME.

Fourth Edition.   2 Vols.   Crown 8vo., 21s.

"The best handbook of the city and environs of Rome ever published.... Cannot be too much commended."—*Pall Mall Gazette.*

"This book supplies the peculiar sort of knowledge which the traveller in Rome evidently needs. He does not want a mere guide-book to mark the localities, or a mere compendious history to recall the most interesting associations. He wants a sympathetic and well-informed friend who has himself been over the places described, and has appreciated them with the same mingled sentiments of inquisitiveness, reverence, and inexplicable historical longing with which the traveller of taste must approach a city of such vast and heterogeneous attractions as Rome."—*Westminster Review.*

"This book is sure to be very useful. It is thoroughly practical, and is the best guide that yet has been offered."—*Daily News.*

"Mr Hare's book fills a real void, and gives to the tourist all the latest discoveries and the fullest information bearing on that most inexhaustible of subjects, the city of Rome. . . . . It is much fuller than 'Murray,' and any one who chooses may now know how Rome really looks in sun or shade."—*Spectator.*

"The real richness of Rome as well as its interest are known only to those who stay a long time there; but for such, or even for those whose visit is a brief one, we know no single work that can replace this of Mr Hare. We heartily recommend it to past and future visitors to Rome; they will find it a condensed library of information about the Eternal City."—*Atlantic Monthly.*

III.
WANDERINGS IN SPAIN.

With Illustrations.   Third Edition.   Crown 8vo., 10s. 6d.

"We recollect no book that so vividly recalls the country to those who have visited it, and we should recommend intending tourists to carry it with them as a companion of travel."—*Times.*

"Mr Hare's book is admirable. We are sure no one will regret making it the companion of a Spanish journey. It will bear reading repeatedly when one is moving among the scenes it describes—no small advantage when the travelling library is scanty."—*Saturday Review.*

"Here is the ideal book of travel in Spain; the book which exactly anticipates the requirements of everybody who is fortunate enough to be going to that enchanted land; the book which ably consoles those who are not so happy, by supplying the imagination from the daintiest and most delicious of its stores."—*Spectator.*

"Since the publication of 'Castilian Days,' by the American diplomat, Mr John Hay, no pleasanter or more readable sketches have fallen under our notice."—*Athenæum.*

DALDY, ISBISTER & CO., 56, LUDGATE HILL.

Uniform with "Walks in Rome."

WALKS IN FLORENCE.

By SUSAN AND JOANNA HORNER.

With Illustrations. Third Edition.

Two Vols., Crown 8vo., 21*s*.

TIMES.

"No one can read it without wishing to visit Florence, and no one ought to visit Florence without having read it."

BRITISH QUARTERLY REVIEW.

"It will make one who has never seen the historic city of Dante as familiar with it as though he had spent years there. To visitors it will hereafter be almost a *sine qua non* as a hand-book."

GRAPHIC.

"A pleasanter literary companion could scarcely be found. Teeming with the results of observation, reading, and a sympathetical critical taste, its value is beyond question."

SPECTATOR.

"We have in these two volumes a valuable acquisition."

NONCONFORMIST.

"The book will hereafter be a *sine qua non* for English and American visitors to Florence, whose numbers, we are fain to think, it will also tend very considerably to increase."

GUARDIAN.

"A work which, by the accuracy of its information, the exactness of its detail, and the refined taste conspicuous in every page, proves its authors to be worthy inheritors of the honoured name they bear. Henceforward it will be as indispensable to every intelligent visitor to the 'City of Flowers' as Mr Hare's is for 'The Eternal City.'"

DALDY, ISBISTER & CO., 56, LUDGATE HILL.

THROUGH NORMANDY.

By Mrs MACQUOID.

Author of "Patty," &c.

With 90 Illustrations by T. R. Macquoid.

Crown 8vo., 12s.

SATURDAY REVIEW.

"'Through Normandy' possesses the great charm of being written in a cheerful spirit. It leaves a bright and pleasant impression upon the mind; and while those who already know Normandy will recognize the truth of her descriptions, and sympathize with her in her enthusiasm, those who are yet in ignorance of its attractions may be stirred by Mrs Macquoid's advocacy to the amendment of their education."

ATHENÆUM.

"The illustrations are excellent, and the work is pleasant as well as accurate."

SCOTSMAN.

"It so unites all necessary information with descriptions of scenery, with fine-art criticism, and with appropriate historical sketches, that it becomes a literary treasure."

BRITISH QUARTERLY REVIEW.

"One of the few books which can be read as a piece of literature, whilst at the same time handy and serviceable in the knapsack."

RECORD.

"Few readers will fail to catch some of her enthusiasm for a land so intimately connected with the early history of our race."

TABLET.

"All will read with interest every chapter of Mrs Macquoid's delightful, well-arranged book."

DALDY, ISBISTER & CO., 56, LUDGATE HILL.